Hands-On Predictive Analytics with Python

Master the complete predictive analytics process, from problem definition to model deployment

Alvaro Fuentes

BIRMINGHAM - MUMBAI

Hands-On Predictive Analytics with Python

Commissioning Editor: Sunith Shetty
Acquisition Editor: Divya Poojari
Content Development Editor: Ishita Vora
Technical Editor: Sneha Hanchate
Copy Editor: Safis Editing
Project Coordinator: Namrata Swetta
Proofreader: Safis Editing
Indexer: Pratik Shirodkar
Graphics: Jisha Chirayil
Production Coordinator: Deepika Naik

First published: December 2018

Production reference: 1261218

Published by Packt Publishing Ltd.
Livery Place
35 Livery Street
Birmingham
B3 2PB, UK.

ISBN 978-1-78913-871-9

www.packtpub.com

`mapt.io`

Mapt is an online digital library that gives you full access to over 5,000 books and videos, as well as industry leading tools to help you plan your personal development and advance your career. For more information, please visit our website.

Why subscribe?

- Spend less time learning and more time coding with practical eBooks and videos from over 4,000 industry professionals

- Improve your learning with Skill Plans built especially for you

- Get a free eBook or video every month

- Mapt is fully searchable

- Copy and paste, print, and bookmark content

Packt.com

Did you know that Packt offers eBook versions of every book published, with PDF and ePub files available? You can upgrade to the eBook version at `www.packt.com` and as a print book customer, you are entitled to a discount on the eBook copy. Get in touch with us at `customercare@packtpub.com` for more details.

At `www.packt.com`, you can also read a collection of free technical articles, sign up for a range of free newsletters, and receive exclusive discounts and offers on Packt books and eBooks.

Contributors

About the author

Alvaro Fuentes is a data scientist with more than 12 years of experience in analytical roles. He holds an M.S. in applied mathematics and an M.S. in quantitative economics. He worked for many years in the Central Bank of Guatemala as an economic analyst, building models for economic and financial data. He founded Quant Company to provide consulting and training services in data science topics and has been a consultant for many projects in fields such as business, education, medicine, and mass media, among others.

He is a big Python fan and has been using it routinely for five years to analyze data, build models, produce reports, make predictions, and build interactive applications that transform data into intelligence.

About the reviewer

Doug Ortiz is an experienced enterprise cloud, big data, data analytics, and solutions architect who has architected, designed, developed, re-engineered, and integrated enterprise solutions. His other expertise is in Amazon Web Services, Azure, Google Cloud, business intelligence, Hadoop, Spark, NoSQL databases, and SharePoint, to name a few.

Huge thanks to my wonderful wife, Milla, as well as Maria, Nikolay, and our children, for all their support.

Packt is searching for authors like you

If you're interested in becoming an author for Packt, please visit authors.packtpub.com and apply today. We have worked with thousands of developers and tech professionals, just like you, to help them share their insight with the global tech community. You can make a general application, apply for a specific hot topic that we are recruiting an author for, or submit your own idea.

Table of Contents

Preface

Predictive analytics is one of the most important technologies of our time. Every day, companies in all industries and all types of institutions are using predictive techniques to solve a wide range of problems. Although many of the main ideas and techniques have been around for many decades, the use of predictive analytics has exploded recently due to the increased ability to capture and store **data**, which is the raw material from which we build predictive models. There are two other big factors that explain the increasing adoption of this technology: the first is the astonishing increase in computing power, and the second is the availability of many open source software projects that have given access to professionals outside academia to many of the most powerful predictive analytics techniques. The Python programming language and its ecosystem of analytical libraries, also known as Python's data science stack, is such a project and has democratized the use of advanced analytical techniques.

This is a book about predictive analytics, but rather than focusing exclusively on explaining in detail the algorithms and techniques, this book is more about the **process** of doing predictive analytics in the real world. The main goal of this book is to make you familiar with all the stages in the process of solving a business problem using predictive modeling and to show, with hands-on examples, how to use Python and its data analytics ecosystem to implement many of the main techniques and approaches used in real-world predictive analytics projects. We use two main projects in this book and walk you through the entire predictive analytics process: from business and problem understanding to model deployment, all through hands-on examples.

There are many techniques that can be used for predictive analytics: statistical models, time series analysis, and spatial statistics to mention a few; however, in this book, we focus on the most widely applicable and successful set of techniques: machine learning, specifically the branch of supervised learning.

In my view, a predictive model is only a means to an end. The goal of using predictive analytics is to **solve problems**; therefore, a good predictive model is not one that uses the latest and most fashionable techniques, nor is it the most complicated or the simplest one. A good predictive model one can be used to solve a real-world problem in a satisfactory way. My goal is that by the end of this book you will have the foundations that you need to start solving real-world problems using predictive analytics.

Who this book is for

This book is aimed at data scientists, data engineers, software engineers, and business analysts. Also, students and professionals who are constantly working with data in quantitative fields such as finance, economics, and business, among others, who would like to build models to make predictions will find this book useful. In general, this book is aimed at all professionals who would like to focus on the practical implementation of predictive analytics with Python.

What this book covers

Chapter 1, *The Predictive Analytics Process*, presents the foundational concepts of the field, explains at a high level the different stages in the predictive analytics process, and gives an overview of the libraries we will use in the book.

Chapter 2, *Problem Understanding and Data Preparation*, introduces the problems and datasets we will be using throughout the book and shows the basics of how to collect and prepare a dataset for modeling.

Chapter 3, *Dataset Understanding – Exploratory Data Analysis*, shows how to get important information from a dataset using visualizations and other numerical techniques.

Chapter 4, *Predicting Numerical Values with Machine Learning*, introduces the main ideas and concepts of machine learning and some of the most popular regression models.

Chapter 5, *Predicting Categories with Machine Learning*, introduces some of the most important classification machine learning models.

Chapter 6, *Introducing Neural Nets for Predictive Analytics*, shows how to build neural network models. These have become very popular because they are very powerful and are capable of producing highly accurate models.

Chapter 7, *Model Evaluation*, shows the main metrics and approaches you need to evaluate how good the predictions produced by a predictive model are.

Chapter 8, *Model Tuning and Improving Performance*, presents important techniques such as K-fold cross-validation that will improve the performance of our predictive model.

Chapter 9, *Implementing a Model with Dash*, shows how to build an interactive web application that will take input from the user and will use a trained predictive model to provide predictions.

To get the most out of this book

To get the most out of this book, these are the prerequisites:

- Fluency in Python programming
- Knowledge of basic statistical concepts

Knowledge of Python's data science stack is an advantage but is not essential. We will also be using Python 3.6 and many of the main analytical libraries. The easiest way to get them is by installing the Anaconda distribution. This is not required, but it will make your life easier. Go to `https://www.anaconda.com/download/` to learn more about this software.

Download the example code files

You can download the example code files for this book from your account at `www.packt.com`. If you purchased this book elsewhere, you can visit `www.packt.com/support` and register to have the files emailed directly to you.

You can download the code files by following these steps:

1. Log in or register at `www.packt.com`.
2. Select the **SUPPORT** tab.
3. Click on **Code Downloads & Errata**.
4. Enter the name of the book in the **Search** box and follow the onscreen instructions.

Once the file is downloaded, please make sure that you unzip or extract the folder using the latest version of:

- WinRAR/7-Zip for Windows
- Zipeg/iZip/UnRarX for Mac
- 7-Zip/PeaZip for Linux

The code bundle for the book is also hosted on GitHub at `https://github.com/PacktPublishing/Hands-On-Predictive-Analytics-with-Python`. In case there's an update to the code, it will be updated `https://github.com/PacktPublishing` on the existing GitHub repository.

We also have other code bundles from our rich catalog of books and videos available at `https://github.com/PacktPublishing/`. Check them out!

Download the color images

We also provide a PDF file that has color images of the screenshots/diagrams used in this book. You can download it here:
`http://www.packtpub.com/sites/default/files/downloads/9781789138719_ColorImages.pdf`.

Conventions used

There are a number of text conventions used throughout this book.

`CodeInText`: Indicates code words in text, database table names, folder names, filenames, file extensions, pathnames, dummy URLs, user input, and Twitter handles. Here is an example: "Mount the downloaded `WebStorm-10*.dmg` disk image file as another disk in your system."

A block of code is set as follows:

```
carat_values = np.arange(0.5, 5.5, 0.5)
preds = first_ml_model(carat_values)
pd.DataFrame({"Carat": carat_values, "Predicted price":preds})
```

When we wish to draw your attention to a particular part of a code block, the relevant lines or items are set in bold:

```
numerator = ((ccd['default']==1) & (ccd['male']==1)).sum()/N
denominator = Prob_B
Prob_A_given_B = numerator/denominator
print("P(A|B) = {:0.4f}".format(Prob_A_given_B))
```

Any command-line input or output is written as follows:

```
dim_features.corr()
```

Bold: Indicates a new term, an important word, or words that you see onscreen. For example, words in menus or dialog boxes appear in the text like this. Here is an example: "Select **System info** from the **Administration** panel."

 Warnings or important notes appear like this.

Tips and tricks appear like this.

Get in touch

Feedback from our readers is always welcome.

General feedback: If you have questions about any aspect of this book, mention the book title in the subject of your message and email us at customercare@packtpub.com.

Errata: Although we have taken every care to ensure the accuracy of our content, mistakes do happen. If you have found a mistake in this book, we would be grateful if you would report this to us. Please visit www.packt.com/submit-errata, selecting your book, clicking on the Errata Submission Form link, and entering the details.

Piracy: If you come across any illegal copies of our works in any form on the Internet, we would be grateful if you would provide us with the location address or website name. Please contact us at copyright@packt.com with a link to the material.

If you are interested in becoming an author: If there is a topic that you have expertise in and you are interested in either writing or contributing to a book, please visit authors.packtpub.com.

Reviews

Please leave a review. Once you have read and used this book, why not leave a review on the site that you purchased it from? Potential readers can then see and use your unbiased opinion to make purchase decisions, we at Packt can understand what you think about our products, and our authors can see your feedback on their book. Thank you!

For more information about Packt, please visit packt.com.

1
The Predictive Analytics Process

This will be the only conceptual chapter of the book; you may want to start coding and building predictive models from the start, but trust me, we need a common understanding of the fundamental concepts that we will use in the rest of the book. First, we will discuss in detail what predictive analytics is, then we will define some of the most important concepts of this exciting field. With those concepts as a foundation, we will go on to provide a quick overview of the stages in the predictive analytics process, and finally briefly talk about them, as we will devote entire chapters to each of them in the rest of the book.

The following topics will be covered in this chapter:

- What is predictive analytics?
- A review of important concepts of predictive analytics
- The predictive analytics process
- A quick tour of Python's data science stack

Technical requirements

Although this is mostly a conceptual chapter, you need at least the following software to follow the code snippets:

- Python 3.6 or higher
- Jupyter Notebook
- Recent versions of the following Python libraries: NumPy and matplotlib

I strongly recommend that you install Anaconda Distribution (go to `https://www.anaconda.com/`) so you have most of the software we will use in the rest of the book. If you are not familiar with Anaconda, we will talk about it later in the chapter, so please keep reading.

What is predictive analytics?

With the exponentially growing amounts of data the world has been observing, especially in the last decade, the number of related technologies and terms also started growing at a faster rate. Suddenly, people in industry, media, and academia started talking (sometimes maybe too much) about big data, data mining, analytics, machine learning, data science, data engineering, statistical learning, artificial intelligence, and many other related terms, and of course one of those terms is **predictive analytics**, the subject of this book.

There is still a lot of confusion about these terms and exactly what they mean, because they are relatively new. As there is some overlap between them, for our purposes, instead of attempting to define all these terms, I will give a working definition that we can keep in mind as we work through the content of this book. You can also use this definition to find out what predictive analytics is:

> *Predictive analytics is an applied field that uses a variety of quantitative methods that make use of data in order to make predictions*

Let's break down and analyze this definition:

- **Is an applied field**: There is no such thing as *Theoretical Predictive Analytics*; the field of predictive analytics is always used to solve problems and it is being applied in virtually every industry and domain: finance, telecommunications, advertising, insurance, healthcare, education, entertainment, banking, and so on. So keep in mind that you will be always using predictive analytics to solve problems within a particular domain, which is why having the context of the problem and *domain knowledge* is a key aspect of doing predictive analytics. We will discuss more about this in the next chapter.

- **Uses a variety of quantitative methods**: When doing predictive analytics, you will be a user of the techniques, theorems, best practices, empirical findings, and theoretical results of mathematical sciences such as computer science and statistics and other sub-fields of those disciplines, and of mathematics such as optimization, probability theory, linear algebra, artificial intelligence, machine learning, deep learning, algorithms, data structures, statistical inference, visualization, and Bayesian inference, among others. I would like to stress that you will be a user of these many sub-fields; they will give you the analytical tools you will use to solve problems and you won't be producing any theoretical results when doing predictive analytics, but your results and conclusions must be consistent with the established theoretical results. This means that you must be able to use the tools properly, and for that, you need the proper conceptual foundation: you need to feel comfortable with the basics of some of the mentioned fields to be able to do predictive analytics correctly and rigorously. In the following chapter, we will discuss many of these fundamental topics at a high and intuitive level and we will provide you with proper sources if you need to go deeper in any of these topics.

- **That makes use of data**: If quantitative methods are the tools of predictive analytics, then data is the raw material out of which you will (literally) build the models. A key aspect of predictive analytics is the use of data to extract useful information from it. Using data has been proven highly valuable for guiding decision-making: all over the world, organizations of all types are adopting a data-driven approach for making decisions at all levels; rather than relying on intuition or *gut feeling*, organizations rely increasingly on data. Predictive analytics is another application that uses data, in this case, to make predictions that can then be used to solve problems which can have a measurable impact.

Since the operations and manipulations that need to be done in predictive analytics (or any other type of advanced analytics) usually go well beyond what a spreadsheet allows us to do, to properly carry out predictive analytics we need a programming language. Python and R have become popular choices (although people do use different ones, such as Julia, for instance).

In addition, you may need to work directly with the data storage systems such as relational or non-relational databases or any of the big data storage solutions, which is why you may need to be familiar with things such as SQL and Hadoop; however, since what is done with those technologies is out of the scope for this book, we won't discuss them any further. We will start all the examples in the book assuming that we are given the data from a storage system and we won't be concerned with how the data was extracted. Starting from raw data, we will see some of the manipulations and transformations that are commonly done within the predictive analytics process. We will do everything using Python and related tools and we'll delve deeper into these manipulations in the coming sections and chapters.

- **To make predictions**: The last part of the definition seems straightforward, however, one clarification is needed here—in the context of predictive analytics, a *prediction* is an unknown event, not necessarily about the future as is understood in the colloquial sense. For instance, we can build a predictive model that is able to "predict", if a patient has the disease X using his clinical data. Now, when we gather the patient's data, the disease X *is already present or not*, so we are not "predicting" if the patient *will have the disease X in the future*; the model is giving an assessment (an educated guess) about the unknown event "the patient has disease X". Sometimes, of course, the prediction will actually be about the future, but keep in mind that won't be necessarily the case.

Let's take a look at some of the most important concepts in the field; we need a firm grasp of them before moving forward.

Reviewing important concepts of predictive analytics

In this section, we introduce and clarify the meaning of some of the terms we will be using throughout the book. Part of what is confusing for beginners in this field is sometimes the terminologies. There are many words for the same concept. One extreme example is *variable, feature, attribute, independent variable, predictor, regressor, covariate, explanatory variable, input,* and *factor*: they all may refer to the same thing! The reason for this (I must admit) shameful situation is that many practitioners of predictive analytics come from different fields (statistics, econometrics, computer science, operations research, and so on) and their community has its own way to name things, so when they come to predictive analytics they bring their vocabulary with them. But don't worry, you'll get used to it.

OK, now let's look at some of the fundamental concepts. Keep in mind that the terms won't be defined too formally, and you don't need to memorize them word by word (nobody will test you!). My intention is for us to have a common understanding of what we will be talking about. Since we have seen that data is the raw material of predictive analytics, let's define some key concepts:

- **Data**: Any record that is captured and stored and that is meaningful in some context.
- **Unit of observation**: The entity that is the subject of analysis. Although many a time it will be clear from the context, sometimes it can be tricky to define (especially when talking at a high level with non-technical people). Suppose that you are asked to analyze "sales data" for a set of stores in a supermarket chain. There can be many units of observation that can be defined for this (vaguely defined) task: stores, cash registers, transactions, days, and so on. Once you know what the unit of observation is (customers, houses, patients, cities, cells, rocks, stars, books, products, transactions, tweets, websites, and so on) you can start asking about their attributes.
- **Attribute**: A characteristic of a unit of analysis. If our unit of analysis is a patient, then examples of attributes of the patient could be age, height, weight, body mass index, cholesterol level, and so on.
- **Data point, sample, observation, and instance**: A single unit of observation with all its available attributes.
- **Dataset**: A collection of data points, usually in a table format; think of a relational database table or a spreadsheet.

For many problems, the data comes in an unstructured format, such as video, audio, a set of tweets, and blog posts. However, in predictive analytics, when we talk about a dataset, we often implicitly mean a structured dataset: a table or a set of mutually related tables. It is very likely that a big portion of your time at your job when doing predictive analytics is spent transforming unstructured raw data into a structured dataset.

From here, when we refer to a dataset, we will be talking about a single table; although in the real world a dataset may consist of multiple tables, when we do predictive modeling we do it with a single table. The typical table looks like this:

Customer id	Age	...	Preferential status	Location	Average monthly requests
123	56	...	FALSE	A	456
321	25	...	FALSE	B	65
...	...	...	...	...	...
654	38	...	TRUE	B	965

(Observations — rows; Attributes — columns)

In the former dataset, our unit of observation is a *customer*, the entity of interest. Every row is an observation or a data point and, as you can see, each data point has a number of attributes (**Customer ID**, **Age**, **Preferential status**, and so on). Now, let's talk about the vocabulary used for modeling in relation to a dataset: first, every column in our dataset is considered a *variable* in the mathematical sense: their values are subject to change; they can *vary* from one data point to another data point. One of the most important things to know about the variables in a dataset is their types, which can be the following:

- **Categorical variables**: Variables that can be accepted as values with only a finite number of categories such as gender, country, type of transaction, age group, marital status, movie genre, and so on. Within this type of variables there are two sub-types:
  - **Ordinal variables**: When the categories have some natural ordering: for instance, age groups (21–30, 31–40, 41–50, 51+) or shirt size (small, medium, large)
  - **Nominal variables**: Those categorical variables whose values have no meaningful order
- **Numerical variables**: Variables whose values can vary in some defined interval. There are two sub-types, although the distinction in most cases won't be as important:
  - **Continuous variables**: Those that in principle can take any value within an interval: the height of a person, stock prices, the mass of a star, and credit card balance are examples of continuous variables
  - **Integer variables**: Those that can take only values that are integer numbers: number of children, age (if measured in years), the number of rooms in a house, and so on

One of the columns in our dataset plays a very important role: the one that we are interested in predicting. We call this column *target, dependent variable, response, outcome,* and *output variable*: the quantity or event that is being predicted. It is usually denoted by **y** and it is one of the columns in the dataset. We will use the term **target** throughout the book.

Once the target is identified, the rest of the columns are candidates to become *features, attributes, independent variables, predictors, regressors, explanatory variables,* and *inputs*: the columns in our dataset that will be used to predict the target. We will use the terms **variables** and **feature** throughout the book.

Finally, we can give a definition of **Predictive Model**: a method that uses the features to predict the target. It can also be thought of like a mathematical function: a predictive model takes inputs, meaning the set of features, the target, and outputs the predictions for the values of the target. At a high level, one way to think about a predictive model is like this:

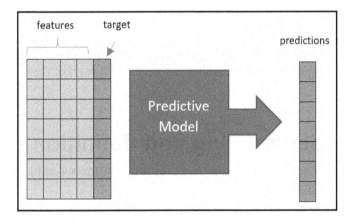

This diagram is limited (and some might say it is even wrong), but for now I think it will give you a general idea of what a predictive model is. We will, of course, delve deeper into the details of predictive models and we will build many of them in the following chapters.

Now that we have a clear understanding of what predictive analytics is, and some of the most important terminology we will be using in the book, it is time to take a look at how it is done in practice: the predictive analytics process.

The predictive analytics process

There is a common misunderstanding about predictive analytics: that it is all about models. In fact, that is actually just part of doing predictive analytics. Practitioners of the field have established certain standard phrases that different authors refer to by different names. However, the order of the stages is logical and the relationships between them are well understood. In fact, this book has been organized in the logical order of these stages. Here they are:

1. Problem understanding and definition
2. Data collection and preparation
3. Data understanding using **exploratory data analysis** (**EDA**)
4. Model building
5. Model evaluation
6. Communication and/or deployment

We will dig deeper into all of them in the following chapters. For now, let's provide a brief overview of what every stage is about. I like to think about each of these phases as having a defined goal.

Problem understanding and definition

Goal: Understand the problem and how the potential solution would look. Also, define the requirements for solving the problem.

This is the first stage in the process. This is a key stage because here we establish together with the stakeholders what the objectives of the predictive model are—which is the problem that needs to be solved and how the *solution* looks from the business perspective.

In this phase, you also establish explicitly the requirements for the project. The requirements should be in terms of *inputs*: what the data needed for producing the solution is, in what format it is needed, how much data is needed, and so on. You also discuss what the outputs of the analysis and predictive model will look like and how they provide solutions for the problems that are being discussed. We will discuss much more about this phase in the next chapter.

Data collection and preparation

Goal: Get a dataset that is ready for analysis.

This phase is where we take a look at the data that is available. Depending on the project, you will need to interact with the database administrators and ask them to provide you with the data. You may also need to rely on many different sources to get the data that is needed. Sometimes, the data may not exist yet and you may be part of the team that comes up with a plan to collect it. Remember, the goal of this phase is to have a dataset you will be using for building the predictive model.

In the process of getting the dataset, potential problems with the data may be identified, which is why this phase is, of course, very closely related with the previous one. While performing the tasks for getting the dataset ready, you will go back and forth between this and the former phase as you may realize that the available data is not enough to solve the proposed problem as was formulated in the business understanding phase, so you may need to go back to the stakeholders and discuss the situation and maybe reformulate the problem and solution.

While building the dataset, you may notice some problems with some of the features. Maybe one column has a lot of missing values or the values have not been properly encoded. Although in principle it would be great to deal with problems such as missing values and outliers in this phase, that is often not the case, which is why there isn't a hard boundary between this phase and the next phase: EDA.

Dataset understanding using EDA

Goal: Understand your dataset.

Once you have collected the dataset, it is time for you to start understanding it using **EDA** which is a combination of numerical and visualization techniques that allow us to understand different characteristics of our dataset, its variables, and the potential relationship between them. The limits between this phase and the previous and next ones are often blurry, so you may think that your dataset is ready for analysis, but when you start your analysis you may realize that you have got five months of historical data from one source and two months from another source, or, for instance, you may find that three features are redundant or that you may need to combine some features to create a new one. So, after a few trips back to the previews phase you may finally get your dataset ready for analysis.

Now it is time for you to start understanding your dataset by starting to answer questions like the following:

- What types of variables are there in the dataset?
- What do their distributions look like?
- Do we still have missing values?
- Are there redundant variables?
- What are the relationships between the features?
- Do we observe outliers?
- How do the different pairs of features correlate with each other?
- Do these correlations make sense?
- What is the relationship between the features and the target?

All the questions that you try to answer in this phase must be guided by the goal of the project: always keep in mind the problem you are trying to solve. Once you have a good understanding of the data, you will be ready for the next phase: model building.

Model building

Goal: Produce some predictive models that solve the problem.

Here is where you build many predictive models that you will then evaluate to pick the best one. You must choose the type of model that will be *trained* or *estimated*. The term *model training* is associated with machine learning and the term *estimation* is associated with statistics. The approach, type of model, and training/estimation process you will use must be absolutely determined by the problem you are trying to solve and the solution you are looking for.

How to build models with Python and its data science ecosystem is the subject of the majority of this book. We will take a look at different approaches: machine learning, deep learning, Bayesian statistics. After trying different approaches, types of models, and fine-tuning techniques, at the end of this phase you may end up with some models considered to be *finalists*, and from the most promising ones of which the candidate winner will emerge: the one that will produce the best solution.

Model evaluation

Goal: Choose the best model among a subset of the most promising ones and determine how good the model is in providing the solution.

Here is where you evaluate the subset of "finalists" to see how well they perform. Like every other stage in the process, the evaluation is determined by the problem to be solved. Usually, one or more main metrics will be used to evaluate how good the model performs. Depending on the project, other criteria may be considered when evaluating the model besides metrics, such as computational considerations, interpretability, user-friendliness, and methodology, among others. We will talk in depth about standard metrics and other considerations in `Chapter 7`, *Model Evaluation*. As with all the other stages, the criteria and metrics for model evaluation should be chosen considering the problem to be solved.

Please remember that the best model is not the fanciest, the most complex, the most mathematically impressive, the most computationally efficient, or the latest in the research literature: the best model is the one that solves the problem in the best possible way. So, any of the characteristics that we just talked about (fanciness, complexity, and so on) should not be considered when evaluating the model.

Communication and/or deployment

Goal: Use the predictive model and its results.

Finally, the model has been built, tested, and well evaluated: you did it! In the ideal situation, it solves the problem and its performance is great; now it is time to use it. How the model will be used depends on the project; sometimes the results and predictions will be the subject of a report and/or a presentation that will be delivered to key stakeholders, which is what we mean by communication—and, of course, good communication skills are very useful for this purpose.

Sometimes, the model will be incorporated as part of a software application: either web, desktop, mobile, or any other type of technology. In this case, you may need to interact closely with or even be part of the software development team that incorporates the model into the application. There is another possibility: the model itself may become a "data product". For example, a credit scoring application that uses customer data to calculate the chance of the customer defaulting on their credit card. We will produce one example of such data products in `Chapter 9`, *Implementing a Model with Dash*.

Although we have enumerated the stages in order, keep in mind that this is a highly iterative, non-linear process and you will be going back and forth between these stages; the frontiers between adjacent phases are blurry and there is always some overlap between them, so it is not important to place every task under some phase. For instance, when dealing with outliers, is it part of the *Data collection and preparation* phase or of the *Dataset understanding* phase? In practice, it doesn't matter, you can place it where you want; what matters is that it needs to be done!

Still, knowing the logical sequence of the stages is very useful when doing predictive analytics, as it helps with preparing and organizing the work, and it helps in setting the expectations for the duration of a project. The sequence of stages is logical in the sense that a previous stage is a prerequisite for the next: for example, you can't do model evaluation without having built a model, and after evaluation you may conclude that the model is not working properly so you go back to the *Model building* phase and come up with another one.

CRISP-DM and other approaches

Another popular framework for doing predictive analytics is the cross-industry standard process for data mining, most commonly known by its acronym, CRISP-DM, which is very similar to what we just described. This methodology is described in Wirth, R. & Hipp, J. (2000). In this methodology, the process is broken into six major phases, shown in the following diagram. The authors clarify that the sequence of the phases is not strict; although the arrows indicate the most frequent relationships between phases, those depend on the particularities of the project or the problem being solved. These are the phases of a predictive analytics project in this methodology:

1. Business understanding
2. Data understanding
3. Data preparation
4. Modeling
5. Evaluation
6. Deployment

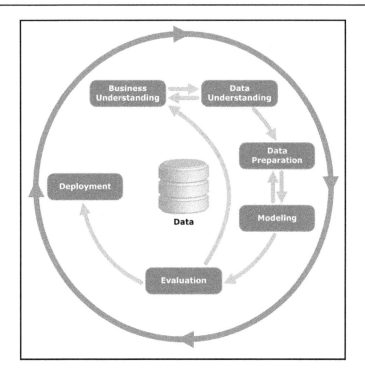

By Kenneth Jensen-Own work based on `ftp://public.dhe.ibm.com/ software/analytics/spss/documentation/modeler/18.0/en/ ModelerCRISPDM.pdf` (Figure 1), CC BY-SA 3.0, `https://commons. wikimedia.org/w/index.php?curid=24930610`.

There are other ways to look at this process; for example, R. Peng (2016) describes the process using the concept of *Epicycles of Data Analysis*. For him, the epicycles are the following:

1. Develop expectations
2. Collect data
3. Match expectations with the data
4. State a question
5. Exploratory data analysis
6. Model building
7. Interpretation
8. Communication

The word *epicycle* is used to communicate the fact that these stages are interconnected and that they form part of a bigger wheel that is the data analysis process.

A quick tour of Python's data science stack

In this section, I will introduce the main libraries in Python's data science stack. These will be our computational tools. Although proficiency in them is not a prerequisite for following the contents of this book, knowledge of them will certainly be useful. My goal is not to provide complete coverage of these tools, as there are many excellent resources and tutorials for that purpose; here, I just want to introduce some of the basic concepts about them and in the following chapters of the book we will see how to use these tools for doing predictive analytics. If you are already familiar with these tools you can, of course, skip this section.

Anaconda

Here's the description of Anaconda from the official site:

> *Anaconda is a package manager, an environment manager, a Python distribution, and a collection of over 1,000+ open source packages. It is free and easy to install, and it offers free community support.*

The analogy that I like to make is that Anaconda is like a toolbox: a ready-to-use collection of related tools for doing analytics and scientific computing with Python. You can certainly go ahead and get the individual tools one by one, but it is definitely more convenient to get the whole toolbox rather than getting them individually. Anaconda also takes care of package dependencies and other potential conflicts and pains of installing Python packages individually. Installing the main libraries (and dependencies) for predictive analytics will probably end up causing conflicts that are painful to deal with. It's difficult to keep packages from interacting with each other, and more difficult to keep them all updated. Anaconda makes getting and maintaining all these packages quick and easy.

It is not required, but I strongly recommend using Anaconda with this book, otherwise you will need to install all the libraries we will be using individually. The installation process of Anaconda is as easy as installing any other software on your computer, so if you don't have it already please go to `https://www.anaconda.com/download/` and look for the downloader for your operating system. Please use Python version 3.6, which is the latest version at the time of writing. Although many companies and systems are still using Python 2.7, the community has been making a great effort to transition to Python 3, so let's move forward with them.

One last thing about Anaconda—if you want to learn more about it, please refer to the documentation at `https://docs.anaconda.com/anaconda/`.

Jupyter

Since we will be working with code, we will need a tool to write it. In principle, you can use one of the many IDEs available for Python, however, Jupyter Notebooks have become the standard for analytics and data science professionals:

> *Its versatility and the possibility of complementing the code with text explanations, visualizations, and other elements have to make Jupyter Notebooks one of the favorites of the Analytics community.*

Jupyter comes with Anaconda; it is really easy to use. Following are the steps:

1. Just open the Anaconda prompt, navigate to the directory where you want to start the application (in my case it is in **Desktop | PredictiveAnalyticsWithPython**), and type `jupyter notebook` to start the application:

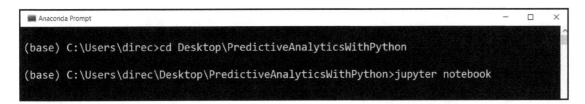

You will see something that looks like this:

2. Go to **New** | **Python 3**. A new browser window will open. Jupyter Notebook is a web application that consists of cells. There are two types of cells: **Markdown** and **Code** cells. In **Markdown**, you can write formatted text and insert images, links, and other elements. Code cells are the default type.

3. To change to markdown in the main menu, go to **Cell** | **Cell Type** | **Markdown**. When you are editing markdown cells, they look like this:

The largest

Hello this is just regular text.

The second largest heading

In the words of a great guy:

> Pardon my French

The smallest heading

1. First list item
   - First nested list item
     - Second nested list item

And the result would look like this:

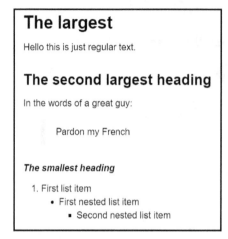

You can find a complete guide to markdown syntax here: `https://help.github.com/articles/basic-writing-and-formatting-syntax/`.

4. On the other hand, in code cells you can write and execute Python code, and the result of the execution will be displayed; to execute the code, the keyboard shortcut is *Ctrl + Enter*:

```
In [2]:  x = 7
         x ** 2

Out[2]:  49

In [1]:  for i in range(10):
             print(str(i) + ' squared is ' + str(i**2))

         0 squared is 0
         1 squared is 1
         2 squared is 4
         3 squared is 9
         4 squared is 16
         5 squared is 25
         6 squared is 36
         7 squared is 49
         8 squared is 64
         9 squared is 81
```

We will use Jupyter Notebooks in most of the examples of the book (sometimes we will use the regular Python shell for simplicity).

5. In the main Notebook menu, go to **Help** and there you can find a **User Interface Tour**, **Keyboard Shortcuts**, and other interesting resources. Please take a look at them if you are just getting familiar with Jupyter.

Finally, at the time of writing, the Jupyter Lab is the next project of the Jupyter community. It offers additional functionality; you can also try it if you want—the notebooks of this book will run there too.

NumPy

NumPy is the foundational library for the scientific computing library for the Python ecosystem; the main libraries in the ecosystem—pandas, matplotlib, SciPy, and scikit-learn—are based on NumPy.

 For more information, please refer to `http://numpy.org`.

As it is a foundational library, it is important to know at least the basics of NumPy. Let's have a mini tutorial on NumPy.

A mini NumPy tutorial

Here are a couple of little motivating examples about why we need *vectorization* when doing any kind of scientific computing. You will see what we mean by vectorization in the following example.

Let's perform a couple of simple calculations with Python. We have two examples:

- First, let's say we have some distances and times and we would like to calculate the `speeds`:

```
distances = [10, 15, 17, 26]
times = [0.3, 0.47, 0.55, 1.20]
# Calculate speeds with Python
speeds = []
for i in range(4):
    speeds.append(distances[i]/times[i])

speeds
```

Here we have the speeds:

```
[33.333333333333336,
 31.914893617021278,
 30.909090909090907,
 21.666666666666668]
```

An alternative to accomplish the same in Python methodology would be the following:

```
# An alternative
speeds = [d/t for d,t in zip(distances, times)]
```

- For our second motivating example, let's say we have a list of product quantities and their respective prices and that we would like to calculate the total of the purchase. The code in Python would look something like this:

```
product_quantities = [13, 5, 6, 10, 11]
prices = [1.2, 6.5, 1.0, 4.8, 5.0]
total = sum([q*p for q,p in zip(product_quantities, prices)])
total
```

This will give a `total` of `157.1`.

The point of these examples is that, for this type of calculation, we need to perform operations element by element and in Python (and most programming languages) we do it by using for loops or list comprehensions (which are just convenient ways of writing for loops). Vectorization is a style of computer programming where operations are applied to arrays of individual elements; in other words, a vectorized operation is the application of the operation, element by element, without explicitly doing it with `for` loops.

Now let's take a look at the NumPy approach to doing the former operations:

1. First, let's import the library:

```
import numpy as np
```

2. Now let's do the `speeds` calculation. As you can see, this is very easy and natural: just add the mathematical definition of speed:

```
# calculating speeds
distances = np.array([10, 15, 17, 26])
times = np.array([0.3, 0.47, 0.55, 1.20])
speeds = distances / times
speeds
```

This is what the output looks like:

```
array([ 33.33333333,  31.91489362,  30.90909091,  21.66666667])
```

Now, the purchase calculation. Again, the code for running this calculation is much easier and more natural:

```
#Calculating the total of a purchase
product_quantities = np.array([13, 5, 6, 10, 11])
prices = np.array([1.2, 6.5, 1.0, 4.8, 5.0])
total = (product_quantities*prices).sum()
total
```

After running this calculation, you will see that we get the same `total`: `157.1`.

Now let's talk about some of the basics of array creation, main attributes, and operations. This is of course by no means a complete introduction, but it will be enough for you to have a basic understanding of how NumPy arrays work.

As we saw before, we can create arrays from lists like so:

```
# arrays from lists
distances = [10, 15, 17, 26, 20]
times = [0.3, 0.47, 0.55, 1.20, 1.0]
distances = np.array(distances)
times = np.array(times)
```

If we pass a list of lists to `np.array()`, it will create a two-dimensional array. If passed a list of lists of lists (three nested lists), it will create a three-dimensional array, and so on and so forth:

```
A = np.array([[1, 2], [3, 4]])
```

This is how A looks:

```
array([[1, 2], [3, 4]])
```

Take a look at some of the array's main attributes. Let's create some arrays containing randomly generated numbers:

```
np.random.seed(0) # seed for reproducibility
x1 = np.random.randint(low=0, high=9, size=12) # 1D array
x2 = np.random.randint(low=0, high=9, size=(3, 4)) # 2D array
x3 = np.random.randint(low=0, high=9, size=(3, 4, 5)) # 3D array
print(x1, '\n')
print(x2, '\n')
print(x3, '\n')
```

Here are our arrays:

```
[5 0 3 3 7 3 5 2 4 7 6 8]

[[8 1 6 7]
 [7 8 1 5]
 [8 4 3 0]]

[[[3 5 0 2 3]
  [8 1 3 3 3]
  [7 0 1 0 4]
  [7 3 2 7 2]]

 [[0 0 4 5 5]
  [6 8 4 1 4]
  [8 1 1 7 3]
  [6 7 2 0 3]]

 [[5 4 4 6 4]
  [4 3 4 4 8]
  [4 3 7 5 5]
  [0 1 5 3 0]]]
```

Important array attributes are the following:

- `ndarray.ndim`: The number of axes (dimensions) of the array.
- `ndarray.shape`: The dimensions of the array. This tuple of integers indicates the size of the array in each dimension.
- `ndarray.size`: The total number of elements of the array. This is equal to the product of the elements of shape.
- `ndarray.dtype`: An object describing the type of the elements in the array. One can create or specify dtype's using standard Python types. Also, NumPy provides types of its own. `numpy.int32`, `numpy.int16`, and `numpy.float64` are some examples:

```
print("x3 ndim: ", x3.ndim)
print("x3 shape:", x3.shape)
print("x3 size: ", x3.size)
print("x3 size: ", x3.dtype)
```

The output is as follows:

```
x3 ndim:   3
x3 shape:  (3, 4, 5)
x3 size:   60
x3 size:   int32
```

One-dimensional arrays can be indexed, sliced, and iterated over, just like lists or other Python sequences:

```
>>> x1
array([5, 0, 3, 3, 7, 3, 5, 2, 4, 7, 6, 8])
>>> x1[5] # element with index 5
3
>>> x1[2:5] # slice from of elements in indexes 2,3 and 4
array([3, 3, 7])
>>> x1[-1] # the last element of the array
8
```

Multi-dimensional arrays have one index per axis. These indices are given in a tuple separated by commas:

```
one_to_twenty = np.arange(1,21) # integers from 1 to 20
>>> my_matrix = one_to_twenty.reshape(5,4) # transform to a 5-row by 4-
column matrix
>>> my_matrix
array([[ 1, 2, 3, 4],
[ 5, 6, 7, 8],
[ 9, 10, 11, 12],
[13, 14, 15, 16],
[17, 18, 19, 20]])
>>> my_matrix[2,3] # element in row 3, column 4 (remember Python is
zeroindexed)
12
>>> my_matrix[:, 1] # each row in the second column of my_matrix
array([ 2, 6, 10, 14, 18])
>>> my_matrix[0:2,-1] # first and second row of the last column
array([4, 8])
>>> my_matrix[0,0] = -1 # setting the first element to -1
>>> my_matrix
```

The output of the preceding code is as follows:

```
array([[-1, 2, 3, 4],
[ 5, 6, 7, 8],
[ 9, 10, 11, 12],
[13, 14, 15, 16],
[17, 18, 19, 20]])
```

Finally, let's perform some mathematical operations on the former matrix, just to have some examples of how vectorization works:

```
>>> one_to_twenty = np.arange(1,21) # integers from 1 to 20
>>> my_matrix = one_to_twenty.reshape(5,4) # transform to a 5-row by 4-
column matrix
```

```
>>> # the following operations are done to every element of the matrix
>>> my_matrix + 5 # addition
array([[ 6,  7,  8,  9],
 [10, 11, 12, 13],
 [14, 15, 16, 17],
 [18, 19, 20, 21],
 [22, 23, 24, 25]])
>>> my_matrix / 2 # division
array([[ 0.5, 1. , 1.5, 2. ],
 [ 2.5, 3. , 3.5, 4. ],
 [ 4.5, 5. , 5.5, 6. ],
 [ 6.5, 7. , 7.5, 8. ],
 [ 8.5, 9. , 9.5, 10. ]])
>>> my_matrix ** 2 # exponentiation
array([[ 1,  4,  9, 16],
 [ 25, 36, 49, 64],
 [ 81, 100, 121, 144],
 [169, 196, 225, 256],
 [289, 324, 361, 400]], dtype=int32)
>>> 2**my_matrix # powers of 2
array([[ 2,  4,  8, 16],
 [ 32, 64, 128, 256],
 [ 512, 1024, 2048, 4096],
 [ 8192, 16384, 32768, 65536],
 [ 131072, 262144, 524288, 1048576]], dtype=int32)
>>> np.sin(my_matrix) # mathematical functions like sin
array([[ 0.84147098, 0.90929743, 0.14112001, -0.7568025 ],
       [-0.95892427, -0.2794155 , 0.6569866 , 0.98935825],
       [ 0.41211849, -0.54402111, -0.99999021, -0.53657292],
       [ 0.42016704, 0.99060736, 0.65028784, -0.28790332],
       [-0.96139749, -0.75098725, 0.14987721, 0.91294525]])
```

Finally, let's take a look at some useful methods commonly used in data analysis:

```
>>> # some useful methods for analytics
>>> my_matrix.sum()
210
>>> my_matrix.max() ## maximum
20
>>> my_matrix.min() ## minimum
1
>>> my_matrix.mean() ## arithmetic mean
10.5
>>> my_matrix.std() ## standard deviation
5.766281297335398
```

I don't want to reinvent the wheel here; there are many excellent resources on the basics of NumPy.

If you go through the official quick start tutorial, available at `https://docs.scipy.org/doc/numpy/user/quickstart.html`, you will have more than enough background to follow the materials in the book. If you want to go deeper, please also take a look at the references.

SciPy

SciPy is a collection of sub-packages for many specialized scientific computing tasks.

For more detailed description, please refer to `https://docs.scipy.org`.

The sub-packages available in SciPy are summarized in the following table:

Sub-package	Description
cluster	This contains many routines and functions for clustering and more such related operations.
constants	These are mathematical constants used in physics, astronomy, engineering, and other fields.
fftpack	Fast Fourier Transform routines and functions.
integrate	Mainly tools for numerical integration and solvers of ordinary differential equations.
interpolate	Interpolation tools and smoothing splines functions.
io	Input and output functions to read/save objects from/to different formats.
linalg	Main linear algebra operations, which are the core NumPy.
ndimage	Image processing tools, works with objects of *n* dimensions.
optimize	Contains many of the most common optimization and root-finding routines and functions.
sparse	Complements the linear algebra routines by providing tools for sparse matrices.
special	Special functions used in physics, astronomy, engineering, and other fields.
stats	Statistical distributions and functions for descriptive and inferential statistics.

Source: docs.scipy.org

We will introduce some functions and sub-packages of SciPy as we need them in the next chapters.

pandas

Pandas was fundamentally created for working with two types of data structures. For one-dimensional data, we have the Series. The most common use of Pandas is the two-dimensional structure, called the DataFrame; think of it as an SQL table or as an Excel spreadsheet.

Although there are other data structures, with these two we can cover more than 90% of the use cases in predictive analytics. In fact, most of the time (and in all the examples of the book) we will work with DataFrames. We will introduce the basic functionality of pandas in the next chapter, not explicitly, but *by doing*.

 If you are totally new to the library, I would recommend the 10 minutes to pandas tutorial (available at `https://pandas.pydata.org/pandas-docs/stable/10min.html`).

Matplotlib

This is the main library for producing 2D visualizations and is one of the oldest scientific computing tools in the Python ecosystem. Although there is an increasing number of libraries for visualization for Python, Matplotlib is still widely used and actually incorporated into the pandas functionality; in addition, other more specialized visualization projects such as Seaborn are based on Matplotlib.

 For additional information, please refer to `https://matplotlib.org/`.

In this book, we will use base matplotlib only when needed, because we will prefer to use higher-level libraries, especially Seaborn and pandas (which includes great functions for plotting). However, since both of these libraries are built on top of matplotlib, we need to be familiar with some of the basic terminology and concepts of matplotlib because frequently we will need to make modifications to the objects and plots produced by those higher-level libraries. Now let's introduce some of the basics we need to know about this library so we can get started visualizing data. Let's import the library as is customary when working in analytics:

```
import matplotlib.pyplot as plt
%matplotlib inline # This is necessary for showing the figures in the
notebook
```

First, we have two important objects—**figures subplots** (also known as axes). The diagram is the top-level container for all plot elements and is the container of subplots. One diagram can have many subplots and each subplot belongs to a single diagram. The following code produces a diagram (which is not seen) with a single empty subplot. Each subplot has many elements such as a *y*-axis, *x*-axis, and a title:

```
fig, ax = plt.subplots()
ax.plot();
```

This looks like the following:

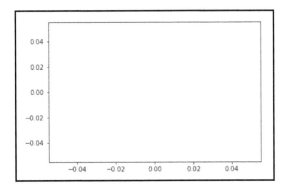

A diagram with four subplots would be produced by the following code:

```
fig, axes = plt.subplots(ncols=2, nrows=2)
fig.show();
```

The output is shown in the following screenshot:

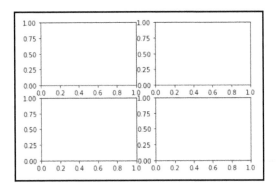

One important thing to know about matplotlib is that it can be confusing for the beginner because there are two ways (interfaces) of using it—**Pyplot** and the **Object Oriented Interface (OOI)**. I prefer to use the OOI because it makes explicit the object you are working with. The formerly produced `axes` object is a NumPy array containing the four subplots. Let's plot some random numbers just to show you how we can refer to each of the subplots. The following plots may look different when you run the code. Since we produced random numbers, we can control that by setting a random seed, which we will do later in the book:

```python
fig, axes = plt.subplots(ncols=2, nrows=2)
axes[0,0].set_title('upper left')
axes[0,0].plot(np.arange(10), np.random.randint(0,10,10))

axes[0,1].set_title('upper right')
axes[0,1].plot(np.arange(10), np.random.randint(0,10,10))

axes[1,0].set_title('lower left')
axes[1,0].plot(np.arange(10), np.random.randint(0,10,10))

axes[1,1].set_title('lower right')
axes[1,1].plot(np.arange(10), np.random.randint(0,10,10))
fig.tight_layout(); ## this is for getting nice spacing between the
subplots
```

The output is as follows:

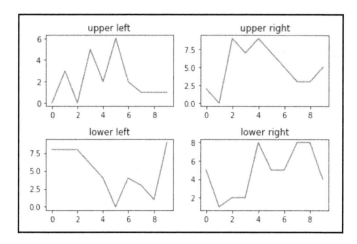

Since the axes object is a NumPy array, we refer to each of the subplots using the NumPy indexation, then we use methods such as .set_title() or .plot() on each subplot to modify it as we would like. There are many of those methods and most of them are used to modify elements of a subplot. For example, the following is almost the same code as before, but written in a way that is a bit more compact and we have modified the *y*-axis's tick marks.

The other API, pyplot, is the one you will find in most of the online examples, .including in the documentation. This is the code to reproduce the above plots using pyplot:

```
titles = ['upper left', 'upper right', 'lower left', 'lower right']
fig, axes = plt.subplots(ncols=2, nrows=2)
for title, ax in zip(titles, axes.flatten()):
    ax.set_title(title)
    ax.plot(np.arange(10), np.random.randint(0,10,10))
    ax.set_yticks([0,5,10])
fig.tight_layout();
```

The output is as follows:

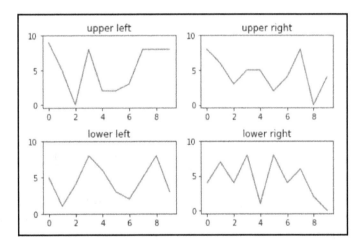

 On the other hand, as we see from the documentation pyplot (https://matplotlib.org/users/pyplot_tutorial.html).

The following code is a minimal example of pyplot:

```
plt.plot([1,2,3,4])
plt.title('Minimal pyplot example')
plt.ylabel('some numbers')
```

The following screenshot shows the output:

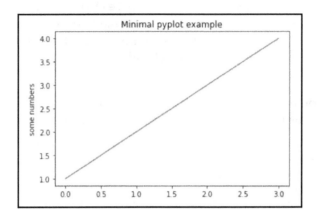

We won't use pyplot (except for a couple of times) in the book and it will be clear from the context what we do with those functions.

Seaborn

This is a high-level visualization library that specializes in producing statistical plots commonly used in data analysis. The advantage of using Seaborn is that with very few lines of code it can produce highly complex multi-variable visualizations, which are, by the way, very pretty and professional-looking.

The Seaborn library helps us in creating attractive and informative statistical graphics in Python. It is built on top of matplotlib, with a tight PyData stack integration. It supports NumPy and pandas data structures and statistical routines from SciPy and statsmodels.

 Some of the features that Seaborn offers are built-in themes for styling matplotlib graphics tools for choosing color palettes to make beautiful plots that reveal patterns in your data, functions for visualizing univariate and bivariate distributions or for comparing them between subsets of data, tools that fit and visualize linear regression models for different kinds of independent and dependent variables, functions that visualize matrices of data and use clustering algorithms to discover structure in those matrices, a function to plot statistical time series data with flexible estimation and representation of uncertainty around the estimate, and high-level abstractions for structuring grids of plots that let you easily build complex visualizations

Seaborn aims to make visualization a central part of exploring and understanding data. The plotting functions operate on DataFrames and arrays containing a complete dataset, which is why it is easier to work with Seaborn when doing data analysis.

We will use Seaborn through the book; we will introduce a lot of useful visualizations, especially in `Chapter 3`, *Dataset Understanding – Exploratory Data Analysis*.

Scikit-learn

This is the main library for traditional machine learning in the Python ecosystem. It offers a consistent and simple API not only to build Machine Learning models but for doing many related tasks such as data pre-processing, transformations, and hyperparameter tuning. It is built on top of NumPy, SciPy, and matplotlib (another reason to know the basics of these libraries) and it is one of the community's favorite tools for doing predictive analytics. We will learn more about this library in `Chapter 5`, *Predicting Categories with Machine Learning*, and `Chapter 6`, *Introducing Neural Nets for Predictive Analytics*.

TensorFlow and Keras

TensorFlow is Google's specialized library for deep learning. Open sourced in November 2015, it has become the main library for Deep Learning for both research and production applications in many industries.

TensorFlow includes many advanced computing capabilities and is based on a dataflow programming paradigm. TensorFlow programs work by first building a computational graph and then running the computations described in the graph within specialized objects called "sessions", which are in charge of placing the computations onto devices such as CPUs or GPUs. This computing paradigm is not as straightforward to use and understand (especially for beginners), which is why we won't use TensorFlow directly in our examples. We will use TensorFlow as a "backend" for our computations in `Chapter 6`, *Introducing Neural Nets for Predictive Analytics*.

Instead of using TensorFlow directly, we will use Keras to build Deep Learning models. Keras is a great, user-friendly library that serves as a "frontend" for TensorFlow (or other Deep Learning libraries such as Theano). The main goal of Keras is to be "Deep Learning for humans"; in my opinion, Keras fulfills this goal because it makes the development of deep learning models easy and intuitive.

Keras will be our tool of choice in `Chapter 6`, *Introducing Neural Nets for Predictive Analytics*, where we will learn about its basic functionality.

Dash

Dash is a Python framework for building web applications quickly and easily without knowing Javascript, CSS, HTML, server-side programming, or related technologies that belong to the web development world.

Summary

In this chapter, we have established the conceptual foundations upon which we will build our understanding and practice of predictive analytics. We defined predictive analytics as *an applied field that uses a variety of quantitative methods that make use of data in order to make predictions*. We also discussed at a high level each of the stages in the predictive analytics process. In addition, we presented the main tools of Python's data science stack that we will use during the book. We will learn more about these libraries as we use them for doing predictive analytics.

Keep in mind that this will be the only conceptual chapter in the book; from the following chapter, everything will be **hands-on**, as promised in the title!

Further reading

- Chin, L., Dutta, Tanmay (2016). *NumPy Essentials*. Packt Publishing.
- Fuentes, A. (2017). *Become a Python Data Analyst*. Packt Publishing
- VanderPlas, J. (2016). *Python Data Science Handbook: Essential Tools for Working with Data*, O'Reilly Media.
- Wirth, R., Hipp, J. (2000). CRISP-DM: Towards a standard process model for data mining. In Proceedings of the 4th international conference on the practical applications of knowledge discovery and data mining.
- Yim, A., Chung, C., Yu. A. (2018) *Matplotlib for Python Developers*. Packt Publishing.

Problem Understanding and Data Preparation

In the last chapter, we learned about the predictive analytics process; we also learned about some of the fundamental definitions and the main libraries in the Python data ecosystem. In this chapter, we will start getting our hands on a couple of datasets and delve deeper into the first and second phases of the predictive analytics process: *Problem understanding and definition* and *Data collection and preparation*.

In the first part of this chapter, we talk about some of the most important considerations when defining and understanding the problem: having enough context and domain knowledge about the problem, and defining what is being predicted and the data that we have to work with. This phase also includes proposing a solution; we talk about some of the main topics to consider.

We put this idea into practice in the second part of the chapter where we introduce two datasets (which will be used in the rest of the book), along with some hypothetical business problems. Using these datasets, we not only talk about *Problem understanding and definition*, but we also talk about *Data collection and preparation* and we introduce some practical topics concerning these stages, such as dealing with missing values, encoding categorical features, the problem of collinearity, low variance features, and finally we give a brief introduction to feature engineering.

These are the main points of this chapter:

- Understanding the business problem and proposing a solution
- Introducing the diamond prices dataset and the practical project associated with it
- Introducing the credit card default dataset and the practical project associated with it

Technical requirements

- Python 3.6 or higher
- Jupyter Notebook
- Recent versions of the following Python libraries: NumPy, pandas, and matplotlib

Understanding the business problem and proposing a solution

In this section, we talk about problem understanding and definition, and other aspects related to the activity of defining the problem that will be solved using predictive analytics. Of course, the specifics of this stage depend entirely on the project, so we will provide only very generic guidance about this. However, when discussing the practical examples, we will touch on some of the important considerations when understanding the problem in a predictive analytics project.

Context is everything

What we call *Problem understanding and definition* is the first stage in the process, and as we mentioned in the last chapter, this is a key stage because here is where we establish, together with the stakeholders, what the goals of the predictive analytics project are:

- What is the problem that needs to be solved?
- How does the solution look from a business perspective?

So, your first task in any predictive analytics project is to understand the *business* or *subject* the problem comes from. As we mentioned back in `Chapter 1`, *The Predictive Analytics Process*, you will always be doing predictive analytics within a specific domain and it is obvious that the more you understand that domain, the better you will be able to understand its problems and propose good solutions.

In fact, domain knowledge is maybe the one thing that will make you very valuable and that will give you a great advantage over other analytics professionals; other people may have better software skills, write code in 12 programming languages, or be able to write a proof of Lévy's continuity theorem (by the way, none of those things will be important to the business people you will interact with in 99% of predictive analytics projects); however, if you understand the vocabulary used in the industry, the problems the organization is dealing with, and how the potential solution will bring value to the business, then you will be much more valuable than other professionals, with massive bonus points if you can state the impact of your solution in measurable terms such as money, hours saved, costumers retained, and so on.

Even if you are not an expert in the industry you are working for (as has been the case for me many times), you need to have enough context about the problem: context is everything to be able to understand the problem and propose a solution that delivers value. The task of translating a business need into an analytical problem is a key part of the predictive analytics process; most of the time it won't be so easy because you will encounter vague and general statements such as, "We need to give tools to the customer service representatives to avoid the churn of our clients," "We want to know what the effects of competition on our business are," or, "Why is the default rate going up in our credit card segment?" So, to understand how to use predictive analytics to deliver satisfactory answers to those questions, you need to know something about the interactions of the customer service representatives with the customers, the dynamics of competition in the industry, and how the "default rate" is defined.

Define what is going to be predicted

When working in predictive analytics, sometimes the stakeholder will have a general idea about what they want to predict: for example, churners, buyers, prices of houses, fraudulent transactions, and so on. In other cases, as we discussed before, you will get vague statements such as, "How can we know which product to offer to a customer who wants to leave the company?" In either case, in the *Problem definition and understanding* stage, it is your job to clarify and make the requirements explicit in terms of the outputs of the model: What do the outputs look like? In other words, what is being predicted, and what is the target that will solve the business problem?

For example, suppose we are asked to build a model for predicting the churn of clients in a telecommunications company; the target, in this case, could be a categorical variable, with two categories: "churners" (clients who will leave the company) versus "non-churners" (clients that will stay). However, based on your domain knowledge, you know that in fact there are two types of churners: "voluntary churners" and "involuntary churners." So, which target is better? The first one with two categories (churners versus non-churners) or the second one with three (voluntary churners, involuntary churners, and non-churners)? That answer of course, depends on the business goals for the model, and it will be your task to recommend or decide which target is better.

Make explicit the data that will be required

Once the output of the model has been defined, you should make explicit which data will be required to solve the problem and produce the predictions you intend: which data sources you need to be able to access, in what format the data is needed, how much data is needed, and so on. Of course, you may have a list of requirements of what is needed, but in predictive analytics (as in life) most of the time you don't get what you want or even what you need, you get what the circumstances allow you to have; in fact, in most cases you won't have any decision over the data that is available to work with, as the data is already there and you will have to work with what is available, period. For example, you may want 12 months of customer data to produce a credit card default model; however, the guys in charge of the data may tell you, "We only have 6 months of historical data."

At this stage, you must also discuss with the key stakeholders what is the data that they think is relevant from a business perspective. It is very important that these discussions are as clear as possible, as you don't want to work hard developing a model for credit card defaults based on historical payment data, only to find out that they wanted to include the demographic characteristics of the customer.

Think about access to the data

This is another key aspect that must be carefully thought out and explicitly stated in the requirements: How are you are going to get the dataset? Maybe you already have access to the company database, or maybe you need to get permission to access it. Another possibility is that you will ask the people in charge (database administrators or data engineers) to provide you with the data you need; in that case, you need to be really clear in your communication about what you actually need, so make sure you understand the data's particularities.

Here are some of the considerations to keep in mind when asking for a dataset:

- The format in which you expect the dataset
- If given in a table format, the type of each of the dataset columns
- How the missing values will be encoded
- In which encoding the files will be provided
- In the case of historical data, how much time will be needed

Proposing a solution

After you have understood the problem, learned about the data you have available, and have made sure you can actually get access to the data, it is time for you to propose a solution. Here is where you plan what you will do to deliver the solution and what it will look like. Of course this will be just an initial plan; you will realize that you will end up changing the plan and you will find many situations that you did not consider initially. However, it is always useful to have a general route to reach your destination in mind.

Since we haven't yet talked about the methodology of model building, how to evaluate it, and the different ways there are to deliver the results, here we will talk very generically about these topics.

Define your methodology

It may be a good idea to state ahead of time the methodology you plan to use. The degree to which you will specify it will depend on the technical level of the people you are having the discussion with. You may describe your plan's methodology at a high level with statements like "a classification model will be trained…," or maybe you are required to be more specific: "Method XYZ will be used to scale the features… then an SVM with a linear kernel will be trained…"; make sure that you explain the reasons you have for proposing your methodology.

A word of advice: Don't use this as an opportunity to brag about your technical knowledge; you may come across as pedantic or as someone who doesn't know how to communicate with stakeholders. Keep in mind that technical details are often not important for most of the nontechnical business people; they want the solution and they do not care about your fancy methodologies or how advanced and complicated your deep **convolutional neural network** (**CNN**) is. Keep in mind one of the golden rules of human communication: Know your audience, and if they understand and require technical details, then provide them; otherwise, keep the discussion at a high level.

Of course, it will be impossible to anticipate every detail of the procedure you will actually follow when producing the model. The proposed methodology, rather than a complete plan, will be just a sort of initial guide for what you will do, and when you get your hands on the data you may decide to proceed in a different way.

Define key metrics of model performance

It is important to anticipate how you will measure the performance of the model. Start thinking about the metric or metrics you plan to use to measure the performance of the model, and most importantly why these metrics are relevant for the problem at hand. We will talk in depth about model evaluation and the different metrics in Chapter 7, *Model Evaluation*.

A word of advice: Don't promise anything about the performance of your model; don't say things like, "I am confident we can get above 95% accuracy," because you do not know ahead of time how good the model will be.

Define the deliverables of the project

In this context, when we talk about deliverables we refer not only to the outputs of the model, but also the deliverables for the project. Think about the following aspects:

- How will the model outputs be used? This can be in many ways: through a dedicated application, via an API, as a module of an existing application, and so on.
- Besides the predictions of the model, what other outputs are needed?
- Are you going to be required to write a report about the results of your model and analysis?
- Will you be required to deliver a presentation?

This is, of course, part of the communication/deployment phase and we will talk about other considerations that we must keep in mind when thinking about the deliverables of the project in the last chapter of the book.

To make what we talked about in this section more concrete, it is time for us to start getting our hands dirty. In the following two sections, we will introduce two of the datasets we will use in the book, along with some hypothetical business problems we are asked to solve. These examples (as well as others in the book) will, of course, be simplified versions of the problems you will encounter in reality, but the essence of doing predictive analytics will be preserved.

Practical project – diamond prices

In this section, we introduce the diamond prices dataset. Let's start implementing the predictive analytics process we discussed in the first chapter. We begin with the stage we just discussed in the last section, *Problem understanding and definition*.

Diamond prices – problem understanding and definition

A new company, **Intelligent Diamond Reseller** (**IDR**), wants to get into the business of reselling diamonds. They want to innovate in the business, so they will use predictive modeling to estimate how much the market will pay for diamonds. Of course, to sell diamonds in the market, first they have to buy them from the producers; this is where predictive modeling becomes useful. Let's say people at IDR know ahead of time that they will be able to sell a specific diamond in the market for USD 5,000. With that information, they know how much to pay when buying this diamond. If someone tries to sell that diamond to them for USD 2,750, then that would be a very good deal; likewise, it would be a bad deal to pay USD 6,000 for such a diamond. So, as you can see, for IDR it would be very important to be able to predict the price the market will pay for diamonds accurately.

They have been able to get a dataset (this is actually real-world data) containing the prices and key characteristics of about 54,000 diamonds; here we have the metadata about the dataset:

- **Number of attributes**: 10

Feature information: A DataFrame with 53,940 rows and 10 variables:

- `price`: Price in US dollars
- `carat`: Weight of the diamond
- `cut`: Quality of the cut (fair, good, very good, premium, ideal)
- `color`: Diamond color, from J (worst) to D (best)
- `clarity`: A measurement of how clear the diamond is (I1 (worst), SI2, SI1, VS2, VS1, VVS2, VVS1, IF (best))
- `x`: Length in mm
- `y`: Width in mm

- z: Depth in mm
- depth: Total depth percentage = *z / mean(x, y) = 2 * z / (x + y)*
- table: Width of the top of the diamond relative to the widest point

This is how this dataset looks:

	carat	cut	color	clarity	depth	table	price	x	y	z
0	0.23	Ideal	E	SI2	61.5	55.0	326	3.95	3.98	2.43
1	0.21	Premium	E	SI1	59.8	61.0	326	3.89	3.84	2.31
2	0.23	Good	E	VS1	56.9	65.0	327	4.05	4.07	2.31
3	0.29	Premium	I	VS2	62.4	58.0	334	4.20	4.23	2.63
4	0.31	Good	J	SI2	63.3	58.0	335	4.34	4.35	2.75

Getting more context

According to the website https://www.diamonds.pro, the most important factor in the price of the diamond is the *carat* or *weight* of the diamond. Along with the carat, other very important characteristics that play an important role in the price of diamonds are color, clarity, and cut. This is good news, since it seems that we have all these features contained in our dataset.

Another key characteristic about diamonds is the certification process, and there is no information about certification in the dataset, which is potentially problematic since our research shows that people will be willing to pay much less for a diamond that is not certified. This is one of the key questions that you will have to ask the IDR people. After talking with them, they inform you that they will only deal with certified diamonds and that the dataset you will work with is about certified diamonds.

This is an example of the limitations that must be considered in any predictive model. In this case, since only certified diamonds will be used for model building and training, it would be incorrect to use this model to predict the price of diamonds that are not certified. We will discuss model limitations much more in the modeling chapters.

Diamond prices – proposing a solution at a high level

Now, we have a general understanding of the problem, what IDR would like to accomplish, and we know something about the dataset and the context of the problem. Let's formalize the problem using the terminology we defined in `Chapter 1`, *The Predictive Analytics Process*: our *unit of observation* is the diamond, the dataset we have consists of 10 *attributes*, and each diamond is a *data point*. Let's make explicit the goal we would like to accomplish and the deliverables.

Goal

After discussions with the top management from IDR, you state the general goals of the project. They are listed as follows:

- To use the features contained in the dataset (all columns except for the price)
- To build a predictive model that predicts the price of diamonds, as accurately as possible, based on those features
- To predict the prices of diamonds offered to IDR by the producers, so IDR can decide how much to pay for those diamonds

These goals will guide all of our actions and the development of the project.

Methodology

For the problem we have defined, the *target* is the price of the diamond, and our *features* will be the nine remaining columns in our dataset: `carat`, `cut`, `color`, `clarity`, `x`, `y`, `z`, `depth`, and `table`.

Since we are talking about prices, the type of variable we want to predict is a continuous variable; it can take (in principle) any numeric value within a range. (Of course, we are talking about a practical definition of continuity, not a strictly mathematical definition.) Since we are predicting a continuous variable, we are trying to solve a **regression problem**; in predictive analytics, when the target is a numerical variable, we are within a category of problems known as **regression tasks**.

This is a whole category of problems and we will talk about them in Chapter 4, *Predicting Numerical Values with Machine Learning*. Perhaps you are already familiar with the term **linear regression**, which is very popular in statistics; however, these terms should not be confused, as the latter refers to a specific statistical technique and the former to a whole category of machine learning problems.

For now, it will be enough to say that the methodology will consist mainly of the following: *building a regression model with the price of the diamond as a target*.

Metrics for the model

How are we going to evaluate how good our model is? To answer this question, in predictive analytics we usually use *metrics*. Since we are dealing with a regression problem, and there are many standardized metrics that are routinely used for these problems, we will usually use one or some of these metrics and evaluate our model. We must choose a metric that is appropriate for our problem, but sometimes none of the standard metrics will be useful, so it may be that we need to build our own personalized metric or metrics.

The logic behind almost all of the standard metrics is very straightforward:

- If the predictions are close to the actual (real) values then that is considered good
- Conversely, if the prediction is far away from the real value then that is not good

The mathematical formulas that define all of the metrics are based on this principle.

For now, let's just say that the metrics for model evaluation will be chosen in such a way that *the model will try to minimize the difference between the predicted and the actual prices; in other words, we will try to build a model that is as accurate as possible*.

Deliverables for the project

The people from IDR have stated that they would like a software tool where they can input the different features of the diamond and based on that, the tool gives back a prediction for the price of the diamond. That is their only concern; they care only about the price of the diamond. You agree with their request and you propose that the solution will be a simple web application that will contain a form where they will be able to input the features of a diamond, and the application will give a prediction of the price based on the model that will be built using the available dataset.

We will see how to build such an application in Chapter 9, *Implementing a Model with Dash*.

Diamond prices – data collection and preparation

Great! The project, together with your proposed solution, has been approved and now it is time for the second phase in the predictive analytics process: data collection and preparation. Finally, it's time for us to get our hands dirty!

As mentioned in the first chapter, the data collection process is entirely dependent on the project. Sometimes you will need to get the data yourself using some **extract, transform, load** (**ETL**) technologies, sometimes you will need access to some internal database, or you may get access to external data via services such as Bloomberg or Quandl, from public APIs, and so on. The point is that this process is so unique to any predictive analytics project that we won't be able to say too much about it. In the rest of the chapter, we will introduce some of the recurrent topics you will find in this phase: missing values, outliers, feature transformations, and so on.

Now, back to our example, consider the following scenarios:

1. We already have a dataset provided to us, so the data has been collected, but now we need to prepare it.
2. As we stated in `Chapter 1`, *The Predictive Analytics Process*, the goal of this stage is to *get a dataset that is ready for analysis.*
3. Fortunately for us, the dataset is already cleaned and almost ready for analysis, unlike most projects in the real world, where a good portion of your time will be spent cleaning and preparing the dataset.
4. In our case (intentionally), very little data preparation needs to be done for this project; similarly to the data collection process, data cleaning is very much unique to each project.

 Data cleaning often takes a lot of time and effort. There is no standard way to proceed, since this process is unique to every dataset. It includes identifying corrupt, incomplete, useless, or incorrect data and replacing or removing such pieces of data from the dataset. Almost always, a programming language such as Python is used for this process because of its many libraries, as well as for its capability at handling regular expressions.

5. Most of the time, after cleaning the data, you will arrive at a dataset that looks like the one we have; let's show the code for loading the dataset:

```
# loading important libraries
import numpy as np
import pandas as pd
import matplotlib.pyplot as plt
import os

# Loading the data
DATA_DIR = '../data'
FILE_NAME = 'diamonds.csv'
data_path = os.path.join(DATA_DIR, FILE_NAME)
diamonds = pd.read_csv(data_path)
diamonds.shape
```

6. After running the preceding code, we found that our dataset has 53940 rows and 10 columns:

```
(53940, 10)
```

7. Now, it is time for us to check if the dataset is ready for analysis; let's begin by checking the summary statistics of the numerical variables of the dataset:

```
diamonds.describe()
```

8. This is what we get:

	carat	depth	table	price	x	y	z
count	53940.000000	53940.000000	53940.000000	53940.000000	53940.000000	53940.000000	53940.000000
mean	0.797940	61.749405	57.457184	3932.799722	5.731157	5.734526	3.538734
std	0.474011	1.432621	2.234491	3989.439738	1.121761	1.142135	0.705699
min	0.200000	43.000000	43.000000	326.000000	0.000000	0.000000	0.000000
25%	0.400000	61.000000	56.000000	950.000000	4.710000	4.720000	2.910000
50%	0.700000	61.800000	57.000000	2401.000000	5.700000	5.710000	3.530000
75%	1.040000	62.500000	59.000000	5324.250000	6.540000	6.540000	4.040000
max	5.010000	79.000000	95.000000	18823.000000	10.740000	58.900000	31.800000

This output is very convenient for quickly checking for strange values in the numerical variables; for instance, given the definitions of all of them, we would not expect to find negative values, and indeed, based on the minima (min row) all values are non-negative, which is good.

Let's begin our analysis with the *carat* column. The maximum value for the `carat` column seems to be a little too high; why would 5.01 be considered high? Well, considering the 75th percentile, which is close to 1.0, and the standard deviation (0.47), the maximum value is more than eight standard deviations from the 75th percentile, which is definitely a big difference.

This diamond with a carat of 5.01 is a candidate for consideration as an *outlier*: a value that is so distant from the typical range of variability of the values that it may indicate an error in the measurement or recording of the data.

Even if the outlier is a legitimate value, it may be so rare that it may be appropriate to exclude it from the analysis, since we are *almost always* interested in the generality of what we are analyzing. For example, in a study of the income of the general population of the USA, would you include Jeff Bezos in your sample? Probably not. Now, we won't be doing anything at this moment about the rare heavy diamond, let's just make a mental note about the current scenario:

- Let's continue with the next columns, depth, and table; since by definition these two quantities are percentages, all values should be between 0 and 100, which is the case, so everything looks OK with those columns.
- Now, let's take a look at the descriptive statistics for the *price* column; remember this one is our target.
- The cheapest diamond we observe is one with a price of USD 326, the mean price is almost USD 4,000, and the most expensive diamond has a price of USD 18,823; could this price be an outlier?
- Let's quickly evaluate how far, in terms of standard deviations, this price is from the 75th percentile: (18,823 - 5,324.25) / 3,989.4 = 3.38 standard deviations.
- So, although it is indeed very expensive, given the high variability observed in the prices (a standard deviation of 3,989.4), I would not consider the maximum as an outlier.

Dealing with missing values

Now, let's take a look at the variables regarding the dimension of the diamonds: x, y, and z.

The first thing we notice is that the minimum values for these features are zero. From what these variables represent, we know this can't be possible (otherwise, we would be talking about two-dimensional diamonds).

Let's examine the values of x that are equal to zero:

```
diamonds.loc[diamonds['x']==0]
```

The output is shown in the following screenshot:

	carat	cut	color	clarity	depth	table	price	x	y	z
11182	1.07	Ideal	F	SI2	61.6	56.0	4954	0.0	6.62	0.0
11963	1.00	Very Good	H	VS2	63.3	53.0	5139	0.0	0.00	0.0
15951	1.14	Fair	G	VS1	57.5	67.0	6381	0.0	0.00	0.0
24520	1.56	Ideal	G	VS2	62.2	54.0	12800	0.0	0.00	0.0
26243	1.20	Premium	D	VVS1	62.1	59.0	15686	0.0	0.00	0.0
27429	2.25	Premium	H	SI2	62.8	59.0	18034	0.0	0.00	0.0
49556	0.71	Good	F	SI2	64.1	60.0	2130	0.0	0.00	0.0
49557	0.71	Good	F	SI2	64.1	60.0	2130	0.0	0.00	0.0

Interesting... some of the diamonds with the value of zero in x also have zeros in the other dimensions. Although the actual value is zero, it makes more sense to consider these as *missing values,* since in this context, zero is not an admissible value. There are many techniques for dealing with missing values, ranging from the simplest way, which is removing the whole row in the dataset, to very complex *imputation* algorithms that try to guess the best values to substitute for the missing ones.

Popular techniques for imputation include using other features for predicting the values that are missing, or to use algorithms such as K-nearest neighbors to perform the imputation; once we know how to build basic predictive models, you will understand how to use some of these techniques for dealing with missing values.

Since we are just getting started, we will keep it simple and do the following: excluding the first row (we will get back to that one in a second), we will remove the remaining seven data points. Of course, we are losing some information, but remember we have 53,940 data points so losing seven is actually not a big deal, so let's keep the rows where x or y are greater than zero:

```
diamonds = diamonds.loc[(diamonds['x']>0) | (diamonds['y']>0)]
```

Now, let's examine the only row left where we have x with a value of zero; since we know that the index for that row is 11182, let's use it to get the pandas series of the corresponding data point:

```
diamonds.loc[11182]
```

The output is shown in the following screenshot:

```
carat       1.07
cut        Ideal
color          F
clarity      SI2
depth       61.6
table         56
price       4954
x              0
y           6.62
z              0
Name: 11182, dtype: object
```

Now, let's use another simple method of imputation for the missing value in x. Since this seems like a diamond that is not very far from the average price (or average carat), let's replace the remaining missing value with the median of x:

```
diamonds.loc[11182, 'x'] = diamonds['x'].median()
```

Why the median? Because the median, being the number at the middle of the distribution of a continuous variable, is a good indicator of the *typical* value of a variable; besides (unlike the arithmetic mean), it is not affected by outliers. Now, as you can see by running the following code, there are no more rows in which x has a value of zero:

```
diamonds.loc[diamonds['x']==0].shape
```

We get the following output:

```
(0, 10)
```

Now, let's repeat the same process with y:

```
diamonds.loc[diamonds['y']==0]
```

We again get an empty data frame, indicating no more zero (missing) values for y. Finally, take a look at the rows where z equals zero:

	carat	cut	color	clarity	depth	table	price	x	y	z
11182	1.07	Ideal	F	SI2	61.6	56.0	4954	5.7	6.62	0.0

This is just one sample so there is no problem with imputing this value with the median of z:

```
diamonds.loc[11182, 'z'] = diamonds['z'].median()
```

Finally, if we go back to the table containing the descriptive statistics for the numerical features, you will notice really extreme maximum values for both y and z. It would be very hard to find a (normal) diamond of more than 3 centimeters (30 mm) in size in any of the dimensions, so if you observe such values, we can be sure that those are errors in measurement. Since there are only three, the safest option is to remove them from our analysis:

```
diamonds.loc[(diamonds['y'] > 30) | (diamonds['z'] > 30)]
```

We get the following output:

	carat	cut	color	clarity	depth	table	price	x	y	z
24067	2.00	Premium	H	SI2	58.9	57.0	12210	8.09	58.90	8.06
48410	0.51	Very Good	E	VS1	61.8	54.7	1970	5.12	5.15	31.80
49189	0.51	Ideal	E	VS1	61.8	55.0	2075	5.15	31.80	5.12

Now, let's remove those three data points from our dataset by negating the condition we use to get them:

```
diamonds = diamonds.loc[~((diamonds['y'] > 30) | (diamonds['z'] > 30))]
```

Great! We are done with our data preparation of the numerical variables of this dataset. Of course, in reality, it will take a lot more effort and time on your part to have a clean dataset to work with; this was just a mini-example. In addition, we still have to address the three categorical variables in our dataset: cut, clarity, and color. We will get back to them after introducing our next practical project.

Practical project – credit card default

This is our second practical project, in which we will solve a *classification* problem. As we did with the diamonds dataset, let's begin the predictive analytics process for this new project by understanding and defining the problem.

Credit card default – problem understanding and definition

TFI is the Taiwanese Financial Institution and it offers credit cards. It has been detecting an increase in defaults among its customers; a *default* is defined as a customer missing a payment for a single month. This situation is negatively affecting the revenue of the company and they know they can do something about it if they could anticipate which credit card holders are going to default on their next payment. You are asked to build a predictive model to help the institution with this problem. They hand you the data about customers that is available; they have two types of data about each customer: profile data and historical data about payments, (by the way, this is another real-world dataset from a Taiwanese financial institution). Here, we have the metadata about the dataset:

- SEX: Gender (1 = male; 2 = female).
- EDUCATION: Education (1 = graduate school; 2 = university; 3 = high school; 4 = others).
- MARRIAGE: Marital status (1 = married; 2 = single; 3 = others).
- AGE: Age (year).
- LIMIT_BAL: Amount of given credit (New Taiwan dollar); it includes both the individual consumer credit and his/her family (supplementary) credit.
- PAY_1 – PAY_6: History of past payment. We tracked the past monthly payment records (from April to September 2005) as follows: 0 = the repayment status in September 2005; 1 = repayment status in August 2005; . . .; 6 = repayment status in April 2005. The measurement scale for the repayment status is as follows: -1 = pay duly; 1 = payment delay for 1 month; 2 = payment delay for 2 months; . . .; 8 = payment delay for 8 months; 9 = payment delay for 9 months and above.
- BILL_AMT1-BILL_AMT6: Amount of bill statement (New Taiwan dollar). X12 = amount of bill statement in September 2005; X13 = amount of bill statement in August 2005; . . .; X17 = amount of bill statement in April 2005.
- PAY_AMT1-PAY_AMT6: Amount of previous payment (New Taiwan dollar).
- Default payment next month.

Credit card default – proposing a solution

Now we understand the problem they would like to solve, let's put everything in more explicit and technical terms: the *unit of observation* is the customer, the dataset we have consists of 24 attributes, and each customer is considered a data point.

Goal

The goal of the project is to use the features contained in the dataset (all columns except for *default payment next month*) to build a predictive model that predicts which customers will default on their next credit card payment, based on both types of features: personal information and history of payments. This model will be used by the team at TFI to take action with potential defaulters and minimize the losses due to defaults.

This is the goal that will guide all of our actions and the development of the project.

Methodology

We know that we would like to predict who will default on their credit card payment next month. For this project, there are only two possibilities: the customer either *pays* or *defaults*. Since our target variable can only have two possible values or categories, we know it is a categorical variable: it can only take a fixed number of categories, two in this case. Since we are predicting a categorical variable, we are dealing with a **classification problem**. In predictive analytics, when the target is a categorical variable we are in a category of tasks known as **classification tasks**. This is a whole category of problems, in fact, that is the most common type of problem you will find when doing predictive analytics in practice.

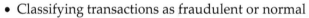

Common applications include the following:

- Classifying transactions as fraudulent or normal
- Classifying emails in one of many categories such as spam, promotions, social, and inbox
- Identifying customers that will leave the company (churners)
- Classifying the level of risk of a patient getting to an emergency room (low, mid, high)
- Classifying the type of cancer in a tissue
- Many, many other problems

Since the target of the problem we are dealing with has only two categories (pay and default), we call this type of problem a *binary classification* problem; when we have more than two categories, then we have a *multiclass* or *multinomial* classification problem.

This methodology consists mainly of *building a binary classification model with the default payment next month as a target, using the profile of the customer and the history of payment as features.*

Metrics for the model

As before, we have to ask this very important question: How are we going to evaluate how good our predictive model is? To answer this, we need to use the appropriate metrics. As with regression problems, there are many standardized and commonly used metrics for classification problems.

Intuitively, a good model makes good predictions; those customers that will pay next month should be identified by the model as those who "will pay" and the customers that will default should be identified as those that "will default." Of course, in real-world problems, no model will make perfect predictions, so we can expect the model will make mistakes. What kinds of mistakes? Since we are dealing with a binary classification problem, there are only two types of mistakes the model can make:

- Predict that a customer will *pay* when in fact he will default
- Predict that a customer will *default* when in fact he will pay

These two types of mistakes must be taken into consideration when deciding how to evaluate our model. Let's just say the following about model evaluation: *the model will be evaluated using metrics that will take into consideration the two types of errors that the model can make; in addition, the evaluation methodology will be aligned with the strategy the company will follow to minimize the consequences of credit card defaults.*

Deliverables of the project

The management from TFI have stated that for them it is important not only to predict which customers will default, but they would like to know *why* there are defaulting.

In other words, what are the features that are most associated with default. They would like to get a report with a detailed analysis of the situation so they can have a better understanding of the problem and have information to do something about it; in other words, they are asking for *actionable insights*. So, we won't only be delivering a predictive model, but also an important understanding of the credit card default problem.

Credit card default – data collection and preparation

Now, we understand the problem, it's time to get our hands on the data!

1. Let's begin by loading some useful libraries:

   ```
   import numpy as np
   import pandas as pd
   import os
   ```

2. Now, let's load the dataset:

   ```
   DATA_DIR = '../data'
   FILE_NAME = 'credit_card_default.csv'
   data_path = os.path.join(DATA_DIR, FILE_NAME)
   ccd = pd.read_csv(data_path, index_col="ID") # we are using the
   ID of the customer as index column
   ccd.head()
   ```

3. Using the `head` method on the data frame, we get this as a partial look at the dataset:

ID	LIMIT_BAL	SEX	EDUCATION	MARRIAGE	AGE	PAY_0	PAY_2	PAY_3	PAY_4	PAY_5	...	BILL_AMT4	BILL_AMT5	BILL_AMT6
1	20000	2	2	1	24	2	2	-1	-1	-2	...	0	0	0
2	120000	2	2	2	26	-1	2	0	0	0	...	3272	3455	3261
3	90000	2	2	2	34	0	0	0	0	0	...	14331	14948	15549
4	50000	2	2	1	37	0	0	0	0	0	...	28314	28959	29547
5	50000	1	2	1	57	-1	0	-1	0	0	...	20940	19146	19131

4. Using the `ccd.shape` method, we find out that there are `30000` observations and `24` features:

   ```
   (30000, 24)
   ```

The dataset actually has 25 columns, but we are using the ID column as an *index* for the rows of our DataFrame. According to pandas documentation `https://pandas.pydata.org/pandas-docs/stable/indexing.html`, the axis labeling information in pandas objects serves many purposes:

- It identifies data (by providing metadata) using indicators that are known and important for analysis, visualization, and an interactive console display
- It enables automatic and explicit data alignment
- It allows for the intuitive getting and setting of subsets of the dataset

5. When working with pandas, if you have a column in your dataset that can be considered as a unique identifier of the data points, it is usually a good practice to use it as an index.

In pandas parlance, Axis 0 corresponds to the rows and Axis 1 corresponds to the columns of a DataFrame. This terminology can be confusing but you will find it throughout the documentation, so you'd better get used to it. I will keep referring to the rows and columns of a DataFrame using the familiar terms... well... rows and columns.

6. Since we will be referring to the columns of the DataFrame multiple times in our analysis, it would be more convenient to have the columns in lowercase:

```
ccd.rename(columns=lambda x: x.lower(), inplace=True)
```

7. This line of code applies the lambda function `x.lower()` to the columns of the DataFrame. The `inplace=True` argument makes this change permanent.

This is an example of some of the pandas methods where you can either make a change without modifying the object (`inplace=False`) or modify the object like we did, using `inplace=True`.

Credit card default – numerical features

Let's take a look at the numerical features in our dataset:

1. Let's create some lists containing the names of groups of features; we may find this useful later:

```
bill_amt_features = ['bill_amt'+ str(i) for i in range(1,7)]
pay_amt_features = ['pay_amt'+ str(i) for i in range(1,7)]
numerical_features = ['limit_bal','age'] + bill_amt_features +
pay_amt_features
```

2. Now, let's see the statistical summary of the columns to see whether everything looks OK:

```
ccd[['limit_bal','age']].describe()
```

3. The output is shown as follows:

	limit_bal	age
count	30000.000000	30000.000000
mean	167484.322667	35.485500
std	129747.661567	9.217904
min	10000.000000	21.000000
25%	50000.000000	28.000000
50%	140000.000000	34.000000
75%	240000.000000	41.000000
max	1000000.000000	79.000000

Starting with the limit balance column, we see values ranging from 10,000 to 1 million, with a mean of about 167,000; this is what we expect: a few big accounts and most of the values rather close to the average. In the age column, we also see values in the range of what we expect: from 21 to 79 years. Now, the bill amount features:

```
ccd[bill_amt_features].describe().round()
```

The output is shown in the following screenshot:

	bill_amt1	bill_amt2	bill_amt3	bill_amt4	bill_amt5	bill_amt6
count	30000.0	30000.0	30000.0	30000.0	30000.0	30000.0
mean	51223.0	49179.0	47013.0	43263.0	40311.0	38872.0
std	73636.0	71174.0	69349.0	64333.0	60797.0	59554.0
min	-165580.0	-69777.0	-157264.0	-170000.0	-81334.0	-339603.0
25%	3559.0	2985.0	2666.0	2327.0	1763.0	1256.0
50%	22382.0	21200.0	20088.0	19052.0	18104.0	17071.0
75%	67091.0	64006.0	60165.0	54506.0	50190.0	49198.0
max	964511.0	983931.0	1664089.0	891586.0	927171.0	961664.0

These are the features indicating the bill amount in the last 6 months. We see that in every case, the minimum value is a negative value. This is the way the financial institution tells the customer that they have a credit or a positive balance in their favor, so it is OK to see negative values in these features. So far, these values look fine, nothing strange. Now, let's examine the pay amount features:

```
ccd[pay_amt_features].describe().round()
```

The output is as follows:

	pay_amt1	pay_amt2	pay_amt3	pay_amt4	pay_amt5	pay_amt6
count	30000.0	30000.0	30000.0	30000.0	30000.0	30000.0
mean	5664.0	5921.0	5226.0	4826.0	4799.0	5216.0
std	16563.0	23041.0	17607.0	15666.0	15278.0	17777.0
min	0.0	0.0	0.0	0.0	0.0	0.0
25%	1000.0	833.0	390.0	296.0	252.0	118.0
50%	2100.0	2009.0	1800.0	1500.0	1500.0	1500.0
75%	5006.0	5000.0	4505.0	4013.0	4032.0	4000.0
max	873552.0	1684259.0	896040.0	621000.0	426529.0	528666.0

These features correspond with the history of payments the customer has made. As we expect, the minimum value in every case is zero; those correspond with the customers that did not make any payment. The means of these features are significantly lower than the means of the bill amount, indicating that, on average, customers pay much less than they are billed. Again, we see most values are relatively low and we have very huge maximums; however, this is an expected distribution of values for these types of monetary features.

So far, our quick inspection has not revealed anything wrong with these features, and we have gained some understanding about them. Now, let's examine the categorical features in this dataset.

Encoding categorical features

By quickly inspecting the first rows of the dataset, we realize that we have only numeric values in our DataFrame. However, from the dataset description, we know that many features are in fact categorical; the numbers there are just *encodings* or different ways to represent the information.

You should be careful when using numbers to represent categories; the main problem with this approach is that many models (all scikit-learn models, in the case of Python) will consider these numbers as representing *values* of a numerical variable. For instance, many models will treat the number 2 in the sex column as being actually a number 2, not a female customer. Likewise, the 1s in that column will be considered and treated as a number 1, which would imply that in the sex column, female customers have "two times the quantity" of males, which of course does not make sense at all. Now from the information point of the view, any encoding will do the job: `-1` = `male, 2=female; 0.25=male,` `52.3=female; -2.36=male, -6.33=female;` this is since any of those will preserve the information contained in the column of the dataset. However, from a modeling perspective, any of those will be terrible choices, and there is one encoding format that is better than others for many reasons, especially its mathematical properties: it is called *one-hot encoding*, which represents one categorical variable with a set of columns of 0s and 1s.

The easiest case is when the categorical variable has only two possible values, as is the case for the `sex` column. We have two options that are equivalent; the first option would be to create a new column called `male` and assign the value of `1` when the observation is `male` and `0` when it is not male, since there is only one other option that would be indicative of `female`; the second option would be the opposite: assign the value of `1` to females and `0` to males, and call that new column `female`. The two options are equivalent from a modeling perspective, so either of them is fine.

1. Let's go for the first one:

```
ccd['male'] = (ccd['sex'] == 1).astype('int')
```

2. Here, we have the first 10 values of the newly created `male` column:

```
ID
1       0
2       0
3       0
4       0
5       1
6       1
7       1
8       0
9       0
10      1
Name: male, dtype: int32
```

3. In other contexts (such as econometrics), these types of variables are known as **dummy variables** or **binary variables**. We will prefer the term **indicator variables** (or **indicator features**), because the 1 indicates the presence of the attribute, in this case, the attribute of a customer of being male, and 0 to the absence of this attribute.

These types of variables are mathematically and computationally very convenient for many types of models, as we will see in the following chapters. One of the properties that I would like to show you now is that the mean of an indicator variable is the proportion of the samples that have the respective attribute:

```
ccd['male'].mean()
```

We get 0.3962666, which corresponds to the proportion of males in our dataset.

OK, now we know how to encode the values of the binary categorical variable (it has only two categories). Now, let's see how to use one-hot encoding with a categorical variable that has more than two categories, for example, the `education` feature. According to the dataset description, it has four different categories:

- 1 = `grad_school`
- 2 = `university`
- 3 = `high_school`
- 4 = `others`

Let's check the distribution of values:

```
ccd['education'].value_counts(sort=False)
```

The output is as follows:

```
0        14
1     10585
2     14030
3      4917
4       123
5       280
6        51
Name: education, dtype: int64
```

This is strange… we were supposed to get only numbers from 1 to 4, but we got 0, 5, and 6. We do not know what these numbers represent, so it is time to use our judgment: Are these missing values? Maybe they belong to the other category. Since there are relatively few values, just for the sake of this example, let's pretend that the values 0, 5, and 6 are actually 4s, meaning that they refer to "other" levels of education. With that in mind, let's create the one-hot encoding for the education feature. We will create one indicator variable for just the first three categories "graduate school," "university," and "high school":

```
ccd['grad_school'] = (ccd['education'] == 1).astype('int')
ccd['university'] = (ccd['education'] == 2).astype('int')
ccd['high_school'] = (ccd['education'] == 3).astype('int')
```

I know what you are thinking: "Wait. Didn't we have four categories in our education feature? Why are we creating only three indicator variables?" Good question! The answer is that we implicitly already have the information about the others category when the three variables are simultaneously equal to zero; this implies that for those data points the corresponding education level is other. We can verify this by filtering the rows of the DataFrame and then looking at the education column:

```
ccd.loc[(ccd['grad_school']==0) & (ccd['university']==0) &
(ccd['high_school']==0)]['education']
```

Some of the values of the series we get are as follows:

```
ID
48      5
70      5
359     4
386     5
449     4
503     6
505     6
1074    6
1266    5
1283    5
1367    4
1370    5
1491    4
1832    6
```

Which are the values we agreed correspond to the education category other? So as you can see, the information about the customers with the other level of education is implicitly contained in the indicator variables we created. Likewise, for the `sex` variable, a feature with two categories, we do not need to produce one indicator feature for male and another for female; one is enough to preserve the information. In fact, for many models, it will cause problems if you include redundant features, or in other words, if there are some features in the dataset that show *collinearity*; this occurs when you can know the value of one feature perfectly from a linear combination of other features.

For example:

- If we had the *female* column defined as *1* when the customer is `female` and 0 when it is not, it is easy to see that:

$$female + male = 1 \Rightarrow female = 1 - male$$

- Likewise, for the education *feature*, since every customer belongs to one (and only one) category of education, for our indicator variables we would have that:

$$grad\_school + university + high\_school + other = 1$$

- Therefore, we derive:

$$other = 1 - grad\_school - university - high\_school$$

The last equation says that you can obtain the value of the other column from the columns representing the other three categories. This is an example of collinearity and must always be avoided; otherwise, your models will almost surely present errors.

 When using one-hot encoding for a categorical feature with *K* categories, then you need only *K-1* indicator features to represent the same information. If you include the *K* indicator features, you will have collinearity in your dataset, which will cause problems and errors when building predictive models. Any of the *K-1* categories may be used; the information will be equivalent. The excluded category is known as the **base category** because it is the category that serves are a reference or default value when all indicator features are zero; this will be clearer later when we use these encoding schemes for model building.

Low variance features

Let's continue with the next categorical variable, marriage:

1. Let's calculate the total counts and the proportions for the different categories:

```
ccd['marriage'].value_counts(sort=False)
```

2. We get the following output:

```
1       13713
2       15964
3         323
Name: marriage, dtype: int64
```

3. We see that we have three categories: 1 = married; 2 = single; 3 = other.

Since we have three categories, according to what we said before, we would need two indicator variables, and we can basically use any two of the three categories and the results would be equivalent. Let's use other and single:

```
ccd['single'] = (ccd['marriage'] == 2).astype('int')
ccd['marital_other'] = (ccd['marriage'] == 3).astype('int')
print("Proportion of singles: ", ccd['single'].mean())
print("Proportion of other marital status: ", ccd['marital_other'].mean())
# Proportion of singles: 0.5321333333333333
# Proportion of other marital status: 0.010766666666666667
```

As we see, the percentage of customers with the `other` marital status is around 1%, which means that nearly 99% of the values in that indicator variable are just zeros; in other words, that variable can be considered to have *almost* a constant value.

Such types of features usually don't provide useful information to any model. Those features are known as *low variance features,* because their values almost never vary (and therefore their variance is near to zero) and it is better not to include them in any model since they won't have any predictive value due to their lack of variability.

 If you detect a feature (numerical or binary) that has a variance that is very near to zero, it would be better to exclude it from the dataset as it won't provide any useful information to the model.

Near collinearity

Now, again I know what you are thinking: "What if we use *married* and *single* to create the indicator variables; those two features surely have a lot of variation?":

1. OK, let's produce the `married` column:

```
ccd['married'] = (ccd['marriage'] == 1).astype('int')
```

2. We have created the new `married` column; by themselves, these two columns seem to be perfectly fine. However, when we consider them together, it is almost always `true` that in this dataset, a customer that is not `married` is `single`. This implies that equality *almost always* holds:

$$married + single = 1 \Rightarrow married = 1 - single$$

3. This implies that *almost always* you can know the value of the `single` variable from the value of the `married` variable; thus, we are in a situation of *near collinearity,* which is also something to avoid. You can verify this by running the following line, which is just the implementation of the former equation:

```
(ccd['married'] == (1 - ccd['single'])).mean()
```

4. You will get 0.9823, which is the proportion of observations in which the former equality holds; in other words, these two features contain the same information for nearly 99% of observations.

This is just another version of the same problem of low variance in a feature that we had before. Remember that all one-hot encodings are equivalent, so it is logical that we have the same problem when using a different encoding. What should we do then? In this case, the most appropriate action would be to use only *one* indicator value to encode the information of the original `marriage` feature. We would, of course, lose the information about the 323 customers that have another marital status; however, we will avoid the problem of including a low variance feature or the equivalent problem of having two features that have the same information for almost 99% of the data points.

One-hot encoding with pandas

Because one-hot encoding is such a common operation in analytics, pandas provide a function to get the corresponding new features representing the categorical variable. Remember that we still have this issue pending with our diamonds dataset? Let's go back to that dataset for a moment and use the pandas functionality to get the one-hot encoding for three categorical variables in that dataset (`cut`, `clarity`, and `color`):

1. Let's see how the `pd.get_dummies` function works:

    ```
    pd.get_dummies(diamonds['cut'], prefix='cut')
    ```

2. Here, we have the first few rows:

	cut_Fair	cut_Good	cut_Ideal	cut_Premium	cut_Very Good
0	0	0	1	0	0
1	0	0	0	1	0
2	0	1	0	0	0
3	0	0	0	1	0
4	0	1	0	0	0
5	0	0	0	0	1
6	0	0	0	0	1

3. As you can see, this generates a new DataFrame containing five indicator columns, corresponding to the five categories in the *cut* feature.
4. However, as we said before, for modeling we don't need one indicator variable for each category; for a categorical feature with *K* categories, we need only *K-1* indicator variables.

5. In the case of five categories, we need only four indicator variables to preserve the information (and avoid collinearity). That is why the `pd.get_dummies` function has another Boolean argument, `drop_first=True`, which drops the first category:

```
pd.get_dummies(diamonds['cut'], prefix='cut', drop_first=True)
```

6. Here, we have the first few rows:

	cut_Good	cut_Ideal	cut_Premium	cut_Very Good
0	0	1	0	0
1	0	0	1	0
2	1	0	0	0
3	0	0	1	0
4	1	0	0	0
5	0	0	0	1
6	0	0	0	1

7. This is exactly what we need for modeling purposes; the first category (*Fair* in this case) will become the base category.

8. Now, let's create the one-hot encoding version of the three categorical features in this dataset, and add them to the DataFrame we have been working on:

```
diamonds = pd.concat([diamonds, pd.get_dummies(diamonds['cut'],
prefix='cut', drop_first=True)], axis=1)
diamonds = pd.concat([diamonds,
pd.get_dummies(diamonds['color'], prefix='color',
drop_first=True)], axis=1)
diamonds = pd.concat([diamonds,
pd.get_dummies(diamonds['clarity'], prefix='clarity',
drop_first=True)], axis=1)
```

9. Since the `pd.get_dummies` function generates another DataFrame, we need to concatenate (or add) the columns to our original DataFrame.

Here, we use the `pd.concat` function, indicating with the `axis=1` argument that we want to concatenate the columns of the two DataFrames given in the list (which is the first argument of `pd.concat`).

A brief introduction to feature engineering

Feature engineering is the process of using raw data to create features that will be used for predictive modeling. Using, transforming, and combining existing features to define new features are also considered to be feature engineering. Depending on the data and the problem you are working with, it could be a key activity in the predictive analytics process; it can make or break your model. There are many standard techniques for performing feature engineering. We will explain and use some of them in later sections; however, in most contexts this activity is based on common sense, intuition, and mainly **domain knowledge**, and it can be considered more of an art.

There is a debate over which transformations of features are considered feature engineering; for instance, transforming our monetary features (limit balance, pay amount, and so on) from dollars to thousands of dollars is a transformation that most practitioners won't call feature engineering. For us, the exact definition is not important, what is important is how we come up with new features that will help us to solve our problem in the best possible way.

Let's introduce feature engineering with a simple example: there will be times where you will find features that in principle are well-defined, but in practice, you have to make decisions on how to use them best, according to common sense and domain knowledge. For example, take a look at the `pay_1` feature; this represents the repayment status last month. According to the dataset description, we have the following corresponding values: -1 = pay duly; 1 = payment delay for 1 month; 2 = payment delay for 2 months; . . .; 8 = payment delay for 8 months; and 9 = payment delay for 9 months and above. Now, let's take a look at the distribution of values in the dataset:

```
ccd['pay_1'].value_counts().sort_index()
```

Here, we can see the counts of each of the unique values:

```
-2      2759
-1      5686
 0     14737
 1      3688
 2      2667
 3       322
 4        76
 5        26
 6        11
 7         9
 8        19
Name: pay_1, dtype: int64
```

For the positive integer values, the number corresponds to the number of months the customer has been delayed in their payments. However, we see values such as -2 and 0, and from the description we do not know what these values represent. As you can see, 0 is the value with the largest number of observations. Let's pretend that we go back to the people who provided the data and ask them about these values, and they tell us that in fact, for all pay variables: "-2, -1, and 0 correspond to the people who were not delayed in their payments that month." OK, that makes sense. However, should we consider these features as categorical or numerical features? There are many ways in which we could work with these features, but for now let's consider the following two options:

- Simply transform the -1 and -2 to 0 (because these people are not delayed, that is, delayed by zero months) and use the features with the values they have, considering them as numerical variables. This transformation is not feature engineering; here, we are just cleaning the data.
- Transform them to categorical features with only two categories, pay and delayed, which would make sense because as we can see, very few people have been delayed for more than 2 months. This option would be an example of feature engineering.

From the model performance perspective, there is no way to know beforehand which option is best, so let's first clean the pay features and then produce the new features as features indicating delayed status for the respective month; in other words, the delayed_i feature will indicate whether the customer was delayed in his payment i months ago:

```
# fixing the pay_i features
pay_features= ['pay_' + str(i) for i in range(1,7)]
for x in pay_features:
    ccd.loc[ccd[x] <= 0, x] = 0

# producing delayed features
delayed_features = ['delayed_' + str(i) for i in range(1,7)]
for pay, delayed in zip(pay_features, delayed_features):
    ccd[delayed] = (ccd[pay] > 0).astype(int)
```

Now that the new columns have been produced, we can, for example, calculate the proportion of customers that have been delayed in their payments for every month out of the past 6:

```
ccd[delayed_features].mean()
```

The following screenshot shows the output:

```
delayed_1    0.227267
delayed_2    0.147933
delayed_3    0.140433
delayed_4    0.117000
delayed_5    0.098933
delayed_6    0.102633
dtype: float64
```

The results show that, in fact, the proportion of customers delayed in their payments has been growing, especially in the last month.

Let's provide another example of feature engineering: our common sense tells us that the number of months that a customer has been delayed in the last 6 months may be an indication of defaulting next month. This seems like a sensible hypothesis; however, we actually don't know if that would be the case until we examine the data more carefully. Let's create this new feature:

```
ccd['months_delayed'] = ccd[delayed_features].sum(axis=1)
```

When performing different aggregation operations (mean, sum, max, min, and so on) in a pandas DataFrame, the operation can be done in three ways: by row, by column, or in the whole DataFrame. Most of the time, you will want to calculate an aggregation in either the rows or the columns. By specifying the axis **along which** the operation will be performed, you can control this behavior. Since, in this case, for every row we want **the sum of all columns**, we use axis=1. On the other hand, if for every column we want the sum of all rows, then we would use axis=0. This notation can be confusing, but with enough practice, you will learn how to use it.

Of course, these new features will introduce collinearity into our dataset, so we should not use it for modeling together with the delayed features; however, this new feature may help us to understand which factors are behind the defaults.

Summary

In this chapter, we have covered two stages in the predictive analytics process: *Problem understanding and definition* and *Data collection and preparation*. We learned about important considerations for understanding the problem and proposing the solution; we also introduced the concepts of regression tasks and classification tasks. We got our hands dirty with a couple of datasets that we will continue within the following chapters, and in going through the second phase, *Data collection and preparation*, with these datasets, we introduce important concepts such as one-hot encoding, outliers, missing values, collinearity, and feature engineering. In addition, we got to practice how to use pandas for loading, exploring, transforming, and preparing a dataset to continue with the next stages of the predictive analytics process.

In the next chapter, we will study the goals of predictive analysis and also some of the important techniques of exploratory data analysis.

Further reading

- Berry, M. J., & Linoff, G. (1997). *Data mining techniques: for marketing, sales, and customer support.* John Wiley & Sons, Inc.
- To know more about the basics of diamond prices, visit `https://www.diamonds.pro/education/diamond-prices/`.

3
Dataset Understanding – Exploratory Data Analysis

In this chapter, we introduce and explain the main techniques of **exploratory data analysis** (**EDA**). We start by explaining the general goal of this stage of the predictive analytics process, and discuss how we accomplish this.

A natural and common way to classify EDA techniques is by the number of variables involved in the analysis—one, two, or more than two. Hence, this chapter has sections on univariate, bivariate, and multivariate analysis. Within the univariate and bivariate types of analysis, we have different numerical and graphical techniques that depend on the type of feature we are working with.

In this chapter, we use the diamond prices dataset to introduce and illustrate the main techniques of univariate and bivariate EDA. We will provide examples of how to produce the main visualizations used in analytics, and describe how to interpret them. We will be visualizing and interpreting relationships between variables using scatter plots, boxplots, and other visualizations.

In the final section, we use the credit card default dataset to provide some examples of multivariate EDA, and to show how to produce complex plots with a few lines of code using Seaborn.

We won't provide statistical definitions in this chapter, as those have been repeated in countless statistics books and classes. Here, we will focus more on interpretation and provide examples of how to use these concepts. The goal of this chapter is to explain the basics of using EDA techniques to answer questions about a dataset.

The following topics will be covered in this chapter:

- What EDA is
- How it can be used to understand a dataset
- Univariate EDA
- Bivariate EDA
- An introduction to graphical multivariate EDA

Technical requirements

- Python 3.6 or higher
- Jupyter Notebook
- Recent versions of the following Python libraries: NumPy, pandas, matplotlib, and Seaborn

What is EDA?

As we stated in Chapter 1, *The Predictive Analytics Process*, EDA is a combination of numerical and visualization techniques that allow us to understand different characteristics of a dataset, its features, and the potential relationships between them.

Keep in mind the goal of this phase: to understand your dataset. The goal is not to produce summary statistics, pretty visualizations, or complex multivariate analysis. These are simple activities that accomplish the ultimate goal of data understanding.

Also, please don't confuse calculation with understanding. Anyone can calculate the standard deviation of a numerical feature; it can be done (for example) with the std() pandas Series method. Your job here is to use that number to understand your features and your dataset better.

Another example—after reading the definitions of symmetric and skewed distribution, anyone can differentiate between one or the other. The point is not to identify whether a feature has a symmetric or skewed distribution, but to use that knowledge to say something about the data— to interpret those facts in the context of the business problem you are trying to solve.

OK—now we know what we are trying to do with EDA. But what does EDA look like in practice? The first thing to know is that it is pretty messy. You will find yourself trying a lot of useless things, confusing yourself, getting the wrong ideas, finding contradictory information, correcting yourself, finding interesting or surprising facts, going back to the previous phase to get more data or to engineer some features... it is very complicated to explain, and only with practice will you realize what I mean.

However, even though this is a messy stage, the messiness comes from the details and the particularities of the dataset. When looking at the big picture, the process goes more or less something like this:

1. When the dataset is more or less ready for analysis, start applying the standard techniques to get a basic understanding of the features.
2. You will begin to form a hypothesis about some aspects of the dataset (from the context of the problem).
3. Apply EDA techniques to begin confirming/rejecting your hypothesis and preconceived ideas.
4. You will start to understand the dataset. New questions will come to mind.
5. Apply EDA techniques to try answering these new questions. You will gain more understanding, and further new questions will pop into your head.
6. Repeat *Step 4* and *Step 5* a few times.
7. Stop when you feel comfortable with the understanding you've got, and you think that you can move on to the modeling stage.

When do you know you are done? Well, it can be very hard to tell—but you can ask yourself the following questions and see whether you can answer them, based on your analysis:

- What types of variables are there in the dataset?
- What do their distributions look like?
- Do you have missing values?
- Are there redundant features?
- What are the relationships between the main features?
- Do you observe outliers?
- How do the different pairs of features correlate with one other? Do these correlations make sense?
- What is the relationship between the features and the target?
- Have you confirmed or rejected your hypothesis?
- What do you know now that will inform the modeling strategy?

In the process of answering these and other questions, you will find yourself eliminating features, engineering new ones, merging categories of categorical features, performing transformations on features, collecting more data, and doing many other things. As we have discussed previously, the predictive analytics process is not a linear process, and even after you think you are finished and can move on to modeling, you will still find yourself returning to this stage.

There are two types of complementary EDA techniques:

- Numerical calculations
- Visualizations

We say these are complementary because you can often gain a better understanding by using numerical and graphical techniques simultaneously. Different techniques help us identify some characteristics of the features while ignoring others—hence, it is better to use them in a complementary way to gain a better understanding of the dataset.

The techniques we will see in this chapter are commonly used by analytics practitioners. However, there are many different correct approaches for accomplishing a particular goal—some will be better than others, some will be equally as good, and in some cases, the choice will be a matter of personal taste.

As with all complex subjects, there is a huge deal of creativity involved. In fact, EDA can be considered to be something of an art. You may even end up inventing some new technique or innovative approach for understanding your dataset, or for communicating an insightful idea.

Univariate EDA

As the name implies, univariate EDA is EDA applied to a single feature (variable). Carrying out univariate EDA on all the features of your dataset is always the first step, and it is almost a mandatory activity. The goal here is to understand each of the features individually, their characteristics in terms of typical values, variation, distribution, and so on.

Let's use our diamond prices dataset. As always, the first step is to import the libraries that we'll use in this notebook, as follows:

```
import numpy as np
import pandas as pd
import matplotlib.pyplot as plt
import seaborn as sns
```

```
import os
%matplotlib inline
```

Now, let's load our raw diamond prices dataset. Since this is a new chapter, we will perform all the transformations we did in the previous chapter so that we can work with the transformed dataset, as follows:

```
DATA_DIR = '../data'
FILE_NAME = 'diamonds.csv'
data_path = os.path.join(DATA_DIR, FILE_NAME)
diamonds = pd.read_csv(data_path)
## Preparation done from Chapter 2
diamonds = diamonds.loc[(diamonds['x']>0) | (diamonds['y']>0)]
diamonds.loc[11182, 'x'] = diamonds['x'].median()
diamonds.loc[11182, 'z'] = diamonds['z'].median()
diamonds = diamonds.loc[~((diamonds['y'] > 30) | (diamonds['z'] > 30))]
diamonds = pd.concat([diamonds, pd.get_dummies(diamonds['cut'],
prefix='cut', drop_first=True)], axis=1)
diamonds = pd.concat([diamonds, pd.get_dummies(diamonds['color'],
prefix='color', drop_first=True)], axis=1)
diamonds = pd.concat([diamonds, pd.get_dummies(diamonds['clarity'],
prefix='clarity', drop_first=True)], axis=1)
```

The first thing you need to do is to differentiate between the types of features we have: numerical and categorical. This is because different techniques apply to each type.

We already know our dataset, so we can create two lists containing the names of the features, as follows:

```
numerical_features = ['price', 'carat', 'depth', 'table', 'x', 'y', 'z']
categorical_features = ['cut', 'color', 'clarity']
```

Univariate EDA for numerical features

In `Chapter 2`, *Problem Understanding and Data Preparation*, we produced descriptive statistics for the numerical features when preparing this dataset. We used them to identify possible problems with some of the values, and used the mean, the standard deviation, and some of the percentiles to determine whether some of the observed large values could be considered outliers.

Here, we will try to extract more information from these descriptive statistics and gain more understanding of each of our features.

For the numerical EDA, we will calculate the most commonly used descriptive statistics. In fact, they are so common that the pandas `describe()` Series method provides us with their calculations: count, mean, standard deviation, minimum, 25th, 50th, and 75th percentiles, and maximum. These numbers will intermediately help us identify some important quantitative characteristics of our numerical features.

I am sure you have a basic understanding (or at least an inkling) of the definition of these descriptive statistics. You can find their definition in any introductory statistics book, or by doing a quick internet search; therefore, instead of repeating what countless books and classes have said before, I would like to show you how to use these statistics to get useful information and get a better understanding of our dataset.

Let's use our target feature, diamond price, as an example of how to use these techniques. However, before doing the calculations and interpretation, let's talk about the default plot used to get a graphical representation of a continuous variable, the histogram.

This plot that shows the distribution of the values of a numerical variable by plotting a series of non-overlapping, contiguous bars: the values of the variable on the *x*-axis, and the frequency of observations on the *y*-axis. Thus, this graph tells us which ranges of values are more and less frequent.

I realize this explanation is a little confusing. Perhaps it is a good idea to explain the way the computer builds a histogram. First it divides the entire range of values into a series of intervals of equal length (these intervals are called bins). Then, for each bin, it counts how many values of the variable belong to that interval, and the height of the bar is set to that count.

OK, since we will calculate the same descriptive statistics on all of our numerical features and for all of them, we will use a histogram to visualize their distribution. It would be convenient to write a little function to make this process more efficient, as follows:

```python
def desc_num_feature(feature_name, bins=30, edgecolor='k', **kwargs):
    fig, ax = plt.subplots(figsize=(8,4))
    diamonds[feature_name].hist(bins=bins, edgecolor=edgecolor, ax=ax,
**kwargs)
    ax.set_title(feature_name, size=15)
    plt.figtext(1,0.15, diamonds[feature_name].describe().round(2),
size=17)
```

As you can see, we are using the pandas `hist()` method to produce the histogram. Incidentally, pandas has wonderful visualization capabilities to produce matplotlib-based visualizations in a straightforward fashion. It is basically a high-level interface for matplotlib, and, because of this convenience, we will use it as much as we can.

Now, we are ready to produce the descriptive statistics and histogram of the price feature, as follows:

```
desc_num_feature('price')
```

The output is as follows:

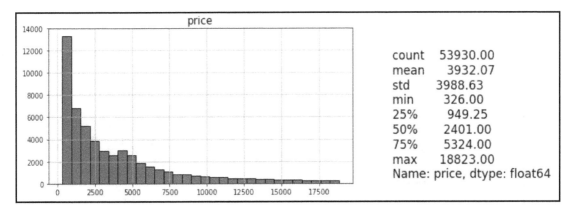

We created our histogram with 30 bins, so the size of each bin is rough:

$$bin\_size \approx \frac{18823 - 326}{30} \approx 615$$

The first bar goes from about 300 to about 300 + 615 = 915, and the graph shows that there are around 13,200 diamonds in that first range of values. As we can see, that is the range of values with the highest number of observations. Another characteristic that we can intermediately see from the histogram is that as prices increase, we tend to see fewer diamonds: expensive diamonds are rarer.

We also have a visual representation of the large range of prices. The right tail of the distribution (the right side of the histogram that starts around $17,500) stretches to almost $19,000, which is a lot of money for a diamond. This is what we call a skewed right distribution, because the tail is to the right.

The following diagram presents some of the most common distribution shapes you will find when producing histograms:

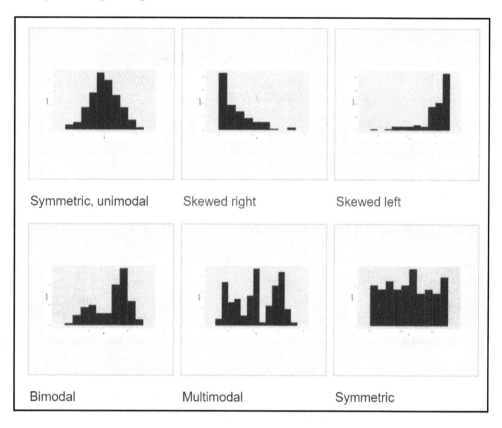

From: https://en.wikipedia.org/wiki/Histogram

Let's interpret the descriptive statistics:

- count: We have 53,930 diamonds in our dataset.

- `mean`: As we know, arithmetic mean is calculated by adding all the diamond prices and then dividing by the number of diamonds we have (53,930). We found a mean of $3,932—how do we interpret this? (Close your eyes and give it a try before reading on). If your answer was along the lines of *the average diamond costs $3,932*, you are just confusing the term *mean* with *average* rather than explaining anything. Don't worry, we all make this mistake. In the case of the typical statistics textbook example, where the histogram almost always has a nice bell-shaped and symmetric look, the interpretation of the mean is easy: it is a representative value, the center of the distribution, or the value around which we are expected to find most of the observations. In the case of a roughly symmetrical, bell-shaped distribution (such as the one in the upper left in the previous diagram), you can think of the mean as giving us a good idea of a typical value. However, this is real-world data, not a textbook example, so how do we interpret this number? In our case, the interpretation is actually not very straightforward because of the distribution of our feature. Firstly, the mean is affected by the expensive diamonds, so saying that a typical diamond has a price of almost $4,000 is misleading. Secondly, from the histogram we can see that the mean is not the center of the distribution—there *is* no center of the distribution (at least in an intuitive sense). So, based on the histogram, I would say that there is no such thing as a typical diamond price.
- `std` (standard deviation): This is a measure of the spread or variability of our feature, defined in relation to the mean. It is always useful to read and interpret it, using the mean as a reference. In our case, a useful interpretation is that, on average, the typical deviation from the mean we see in the diamond prices is of about $4,000, In other words, the typical distance in the price of a diamond from the mean price is about $4,000. What do you think of this? Is it high or low? I would say that in this context it is definitely a large number, which indicates a lot of variability in the prices of diamonds. This high standard deviation is consistent with our previous observation: because of the large variability in prices, there is no such thing as a typical diamond price.

- `25%`, `50%`, and `75%` (25th, 50th, and 75th percentiles): The interpretation of these numbers is straightforward and very useful. 25% of the prices are between $326 and $949.25. Think about this for a second: a quarter of the diamond prices in our sample (around 13,500) are in that small interval of 326.00 to 949.25—so, although the mean price of a diamond is almost $4,000, it would not be at all unusual to find a diamond below $1,000. The next number is the 50th percentile, otherwise known as the median. This is the number at the middle of the distribution—half the prices are below $2,401, and the other half are above that value. This is useful information—although we have concluded that there is no typical price for a diamond, we now know that half the diamonds in our sample have a price between $326 and $2,401. Finally, the 75% percentile tells us that three-quarters of the prices are below $5,324, and the top quarter is above that price. One more thing about the percentiles: half the diamond prices (the middle half) are located between the 25th and the 75th percentile. That is, excluding the bottom 25% and top 25%, the middle half of prices are between $949.25 and $5,324. In other words, if you want to avoid purchasing either very cheap or very expensive diamonds, you can expect to pay (rounding the numbers) between $950 and $5,300.

Let's make our observations explicit:

- As prices increase, we observe fewer diamonds in our sample.
- There is high variability in diamond prices; in fact, prices range from $326 to $18,823.
- This high variability of the prices is reflected in a standard deviation of $4,000.
- Because of the high variability of prices and the long tail of the distribution, there is no such thing as a typical diamond price.
- About 25% of the prices are below $950 (approximately).
- For a diamond that is not too cheap no too expensive, the price range is between $950 and $5,300.
- Half the diamond prices are below $2,401.
- The distribution of prices is right-skewed. As we'll see, this will have implications for modeling, so we'll keep it in mind.

Great! Now we know a great deal about our target feature. We definitely have extracted useful information about it. I hope this example has helped you interpret the descriptive statistics and the histogram; remember that the goal is to get useful information.

Since this takes a lot of practice, now it is your turn to analyze and get to know the rest of the numerical features in our dataset. You can run the following code to get all the descriptive statistics plus the histogram for each of the numerical features:

```
for x in numerical_features:
    desc_num_feature(x)
```

The output of the code is not shown since it would be too long, but you can take a look at it in the corresponding Jupyter Notebook for this chapter. Interpret the numbers in the context of the problem and have a look at the histograms. Describe what you see, and what useful information you can get from them.

We have said that it is always a good idea to carry out univariate EDA on all your features. But, what if your dataset has hundreds or even thousands of features? In that case, doing analysis for each individual variable becomes impractical. However, I always like to produce at least a histogram (using a `for` loop) for the numerical variables, and quickly scan the plots for irregularities, or for weird or unexpected distribution shapes. In addition, it is not hard to produce descriptive statistics on a large set of numerical features, and quickly scan the numbers to at least get a general sense of the distributions of the different features. Remember that you can take advantage of the power of Python for automating some of these tasks.

Univariate EDA for categorical features

For categorical features, EDA is actually easier, as features have a limited number of categories. The first thing we would like to know is the number that we have in every category. It is almost always useful to express this as a percentage or proportion of the total count.

On the other hand, just as the histogram is the default visualization for a numerical feature, the barplot is the default way to visualize the distribution of a categorical feature. pandas makes this very easy. Since we have only three categorical features, we won't create a function like the one we created for numerical features.

Let's take a look at the cut feature:

```
feature = categorical_features[0]
count = diamonds[feature].value_counts()
percent = 100*diamonds[feature].value_counts(normalize=True)
df = pd.DataFrame({'count':count, 'percent':percent.round(1)})
print(df)
count.plot(kind='bar', title=feature);
```

The output is as follows:

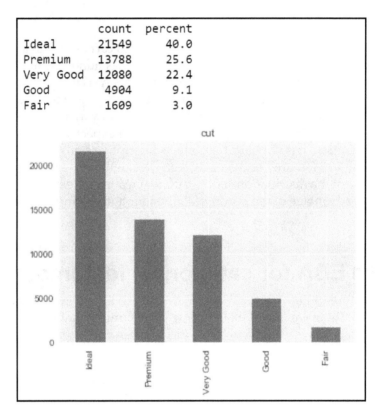

Now, let's replicate this code for color:

```
feature = categorical_features[1]
count = diamonds[feature].value_counts()
percent = 100*diamonds[feature].value_counts(normalize=True)
df = pd.DataFrame({'count':count, 'percent':percent.round(1)})
print(df)
count.plot(kind='bar', title=feature);
```

The output is as follows:

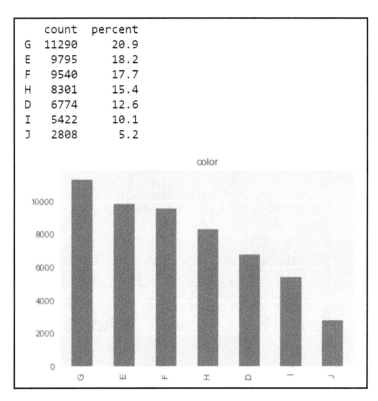

```
     count  percent
G    11290     20.9
E     9795     18.2
F     9540     17.7
H     8301     15.4
D     6774     12.6
I     5422     10.1
J     2808      5.2
```

Finally, let's do it for the clarity feature:

```python
feature = categorical_features[2]
count = diamonds[feature].value_counts()
percent = 100*diamonds[feature].value_counts(normalize=True)
df = pd.DataFrame({'count':count, 'percent':percent.round(1)})
print(df)
count.plot(kind='bar', title=feature);
```

The output of the code is as follows:

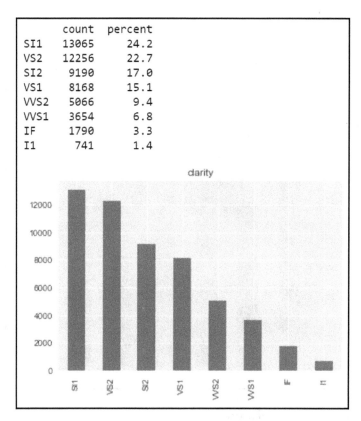

```
        count  percent
SI1     13065     24.2
VS2     12256     22.7
SI2      9190     17.0
VS1      8168     15.1
VVS2     5066      9.4
VVS1     3654      6.8
IF       1790      3.3
I1        741      1.4
```

There is not too much to explain here—the tables and barplots are very clear. We now have a clear picture of which categories of diamonds are more and less common for each cut, color, and clarity. We are gaining more understanding about our dataset.

 Note that when calculating the counts with `value_counts()`, pandas automatically sorts the series in descending order. To change this behavior, you can use the parameter `sort=False`. To sort in ascending order, use `ascending=True`.

Bivariate EDA

Now that we understand our features individually, it is time to start exploring whether there are any relationships between them. Bivariate EDA techniques are used to explore pairs of variables, and start understanding how they relate to each other.

How many pair relationships will we have? For a dataset of k features, we will have $\frac{k(k-1)}{2}$ distinct pairs. In our original dataset we have 10 features, so we will have $\frac{10 \times 9}{2} = 45$ pairs of variables to analyze. This is a very small dataset, (in terms of the number of features)—but as you can see, the formula is basically a quadratic term, so for a large dataset, the number of pairs goes up quickly.

Of course, you don't actually have to analyze every possible pair; only choose those that are interesting or which will answer a particular question you may have about the dataset. In addition, pandas and Seaborn will make our task a bit less daunting, as they can produce a large number of subplots with few lines (or even one line) of code.

To explore the relationships between pairs of features, first, we need to know which types of features we have. Given our broad categorization of numerical and categorical features, there are three possibilities for comparison:

- Two numerical features
- Two categorical features
- One numerical feature and one categorical feature

For each case, there are standard visualizations and numerical calculations that are used by practitioners—but that doesn't mean that you can't be creative and invent your own, or that these standard techniques will be sufficient to give you good information about the relationships you are exploring.

Let's take a look at each of the three situations in detail.

Two numerical features

To analyze the possible relationship between two numerical features, we have two fundamental standard tools: the scatter plot for visualization, and the Pearson correlation coefficient as a numerical calculation.

Scatter plots

The standard visualization is the popular, very important, and super-useful scatter plot. This is simply obtained by plotting pairs of points, each having the value of one variable determining the position on the x-axis, and the value of the other variable determining the position on the y-axis.

Scatter plots are good for showing the relationship between the variables. If there is a relationship, we can look for the following characteristics:

- **Overall pattern**: Generally, we will spot a pattern forming: it can be a linear pattern, a curvy pattern, an exponential pattern, or a more complicated one.
- **Strength/Noise**: This refers to how clearly we see the pattern, or how closely the points follow this pattern. We will also observe noise in the form of the amount of deviation or dispersion in the points from around the overall pattern. Stronger patterns show less noise, and vice versa.
- **Direction**: If there is a relationship between the features, we would notice a general direction. which can be either positive or negative, as follows:
  - **Positive**: This means that both variables move in the same direction. When one variable increases, the other also tends to increase, and vice versa. In this case, the pattern goes upward.
  - **Negative**: This means that both variables move in the opposite direction—so when one increases, the other tends to decrease, and vice versa. In this case, the overall pattern goes downward.

  In complicated cases, the relationship may be positive for some ranges and negative for others.

Let's look at an example, and use pandas to produce the scatter plot for `carat` and `price`:

```
diamonds.plot.scatter(x='carat', y='price', s=0.6);
```

The output is shown in the following screenshot:

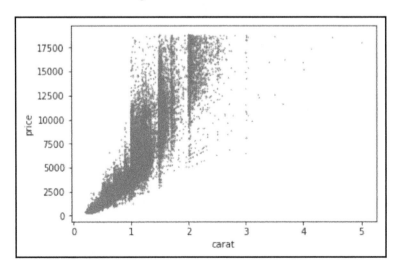

How would you read that scatter plot? Well, there is definitely a pattern here:

- **Overall pattern**: We see a nonlinear relationship—perhaps the overall pattern is a quadratic or an exponential curve.
- **Strength/Noise**: Although the pattern is clear, there is definitely a lot of noise in the relationship. Although we may imagine a curve passing through the center of the points, there is a lot of deviation from that general pattern.
- **Direction**: As the carat increases, we see that the prices also increase, therefore we observe a positive relationship.

The conclusion from this scatter plot? Carat will definitely help us in predicting the price of the diamond, but we have detected a nonlinear relationship, which will be an important consideration when modeling.

As we know from the context (back in `Chapter 1`, *The Predictive Analytics Process*), carat is perhaps the most important characteristic when determining the price of a diamond. Now we have confirmed this hypothesis with data, and have gained more knowledge about the relationship between carat and price.

What if there is no pattern? If there is no relationship between the features, the scatter plot will look like a cloud of dots: pure noise, no definite pattern. According to the typical statistics textbook, you should see something like this:

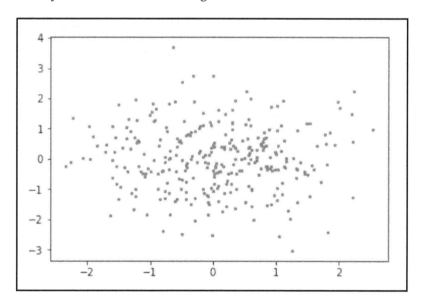

However, in the real world a lack of relationship can take many forms. For instance, take a look at the scatter plot of table and price:

```
diamonds.plot.scatter(x='table', y='price', s=0.6);
```

The output is as follows:

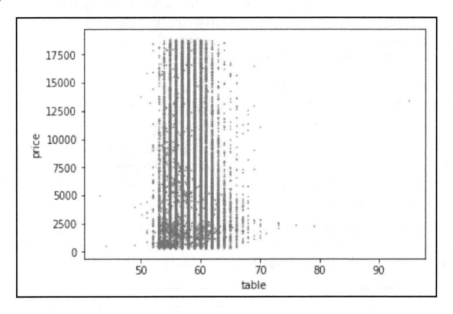

Do you see a pattern? If you do, please let me know, because I don't...! Now, we'll zoom in on the range that has most of the values, as follows:

```
diamonds.plot.scatter(x='table', y='price', s=0.6, xlim=(50,70));
```

The output is as follows:

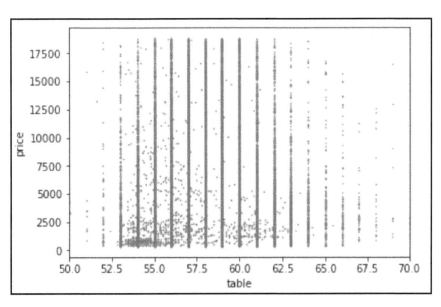

It's still pretty hard to see any clear relationship between table and price.

Finally, it is time to be a bit more efficient. Let's use the powerful visualization library Seaborn to produce what is known as a scatter plot matrix, which is a way to visualize many numerical features at the same time. The visualization should be self-explanatory:

```
sns.pairplot(diamonds[numerical_features], plot_kws={"s": 2});
```

The output is as follows, this is just a smaller, low-resolution image of the output, you can view the full image by running the code in the notebook:

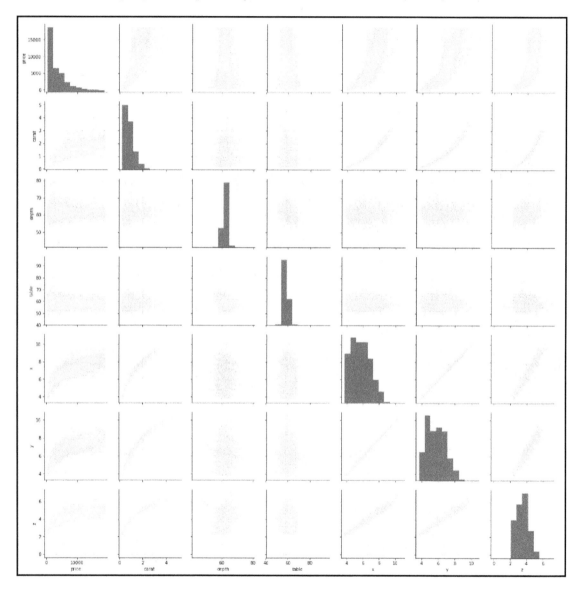

Wow! This is a beautiful, informative and powerful visualization, produced with a single line of code!

Seaborn also allows us to customize the diagonal of this matrix. For example, by setting the parameter `diag_kind='kde'` instead of the histogram, we can visualize the *density plot* (see `https://en.wikipedia.org/wiki/Density_estimation`), which is basically an approximation of the underlying probability distribution of the feature. Let's take a look:

```
sns.pairplot(diamonds[numerical_features], plot_kws={"s": 2},
diag_kind='kde');
```

The output is as follows, this is just a smaller, low-resolution image of the output, you can view the full image by running the code in the notebook:

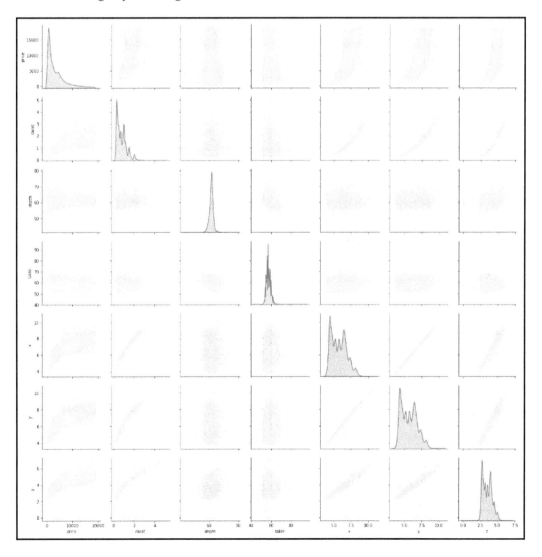

As an exercise, please take a look at the pair relationships, especially between the features and price, and gain more understanding about the dataset.

The Pearson correlation coefficient

The standard tool for comparing two numerical features is the Pearson correlation coefficient, commonly known simply as *the correlation coefficient* (there are many other correlation coefficients, but this one is by far the most popular). This is a numerical indication of the strength of the linear association between two numerical features.

I will repeat the keywords again: linear association. If the relationship between the features is nonlinear, then this correlation coefficient could be misleading, which is why it is always a good idea to take a look at both the scatter plot and the correlation coefficient.

Knowing the key characteristics of this coefficient will help us with the interpretation:

- Its value is always in the interval [-1, +1].
- Its value indicates the strength of the linear relationship between the features: values close to -1 indicate a strong negative relationship between them, while values close to +1 indicate a strong positive relationship. Values close to 0 are indicative of no linear relationship between the features.
- A value of exactly 0 indicates the absence of any linear relationship. Values of exactly -1 or +1 indicate a perfect linear relationship between the variables; negative for -1 and positive for +1.

This image taken from the Wikipedia page on this topic is very useful and illustrative:

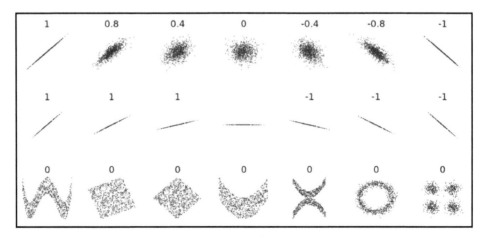

From: https://en.wikipedia.org/wiki/File:Correlation_examples2.svg

If there is no linear association between the features, then the correlation coefficient should be really close to zero. However, even if the coefficient is close to zero, this does not imply that there is no association between the features; there may be still a nonlinear relationship. This is why scatterplots should always be used along with the correlation coefficient.

Pandas makes it very easy to calculate the correlation coefficient. Just as we can calculate a scatter plot matrix for pair relationships, we can calculate a correlation matrix to take a look at all the pair correlations at once, as follows:

```
diamonds[numerical_features].corr()
```

The following screenshot shows the output:

	price	carat	depth	table	x	y	z
price	1.000000	0.921603	-0.010595	0.127157	0.887216	0.888810	0.877430
carat	0.921603	1.000000	0.028317	0.181650	0.977761	0.976844	0.970905
depth	-0.010595	0.028317	1.000000	-0.295722	-0.025020	-0.028151	0.097057
table	0.127157	0.181650	-0.295722	1.000000	0.196129	0.189964	0.155012
x	0.887216	0.977761	-0.025020	0.196129	1.000000	0.998652	0.985904
y	0.888810	0.976844	-0.028151	0.189964	0.998652	1.000000	0.985538
z	0.877430	0.970905	0.097057	0.155012	0.985904	0.985538	1.000000

Let's start with the top row, where we see the correlations between price and the other features. The correlation with carat is very high; although from the scatter plot we know there is a nonlinear relationship, this high correlation coefficient gives us additional evidence of the strength of the association between them.

For depth, the number is really close to zero, confirming the conclusion from the scatter plot: there is no relationship between depth and price. For the table, there is a positive but very small correlation of 0.127, which tells us that knowing a table is not very informative if you want to know how expensive the diamond is.

For the variables related to dimension, x, y, and z, the correlation is very strong and similar, around 0.88. We know from the scatter plot matrix that there is again a nonlinear relationship, but these numbers provide us with additional evidence of the importance of those features in determining price: bigger diamonds in any dimension are very likely to be more expensive.

If you continue examining the other pair correlation coefficients, what should catch your attention is the very high positive association between the features related with dimension, and carat. Let's calculate a scatter plot matrix and a correlation matrix for these four features.

However, before doing that, let's exclude from the analysis those annoying z values that are equal to zero (as we said back in Chapter 2, *Problem Understanding and Data Preparation*, we will deal with those later):

```
dim_features = diamonds[['carat','x','y','z']]
sns.pairplot(dim_features,plot_kws={"s": 3});
```

The output is as follows:

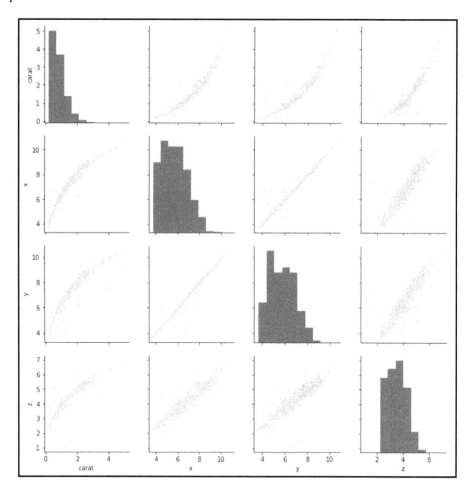

To the correlation matrix for the features we can run the following command:

```
dim_features.corr()
```

This would be the output:

	carat	x	y	z
carat	1.000000	0.977778	0.976860	0.976478
x	0.977778	1.000000	0.998657	0.991077
y	0.976860	0.998657	1.000000	0.990730
z	0.976478	0.991077	0.990730	1.000000

Firstly, all correlations are extremely high. Secondly, the scatter plots between x, y, and z look clearly linear. What would be the interpretation for this?

Basically, the three features contain almost the same information; in other words, they are not independent. Knowing the value of one immediately tells us a great deal about the values of the other features. We are again in the situation we encounter in Chapter 2, *Problem Understanding and Data Preparation*: near-collinearity, confirmed by the coefficients really close to one.

On the other hand, the relationship with carat looks like a quadratic, very strong association, which of course makes sense: bigger diamonds will weigh more. These dependencies between these four features may be problematic for some models—we must do something about it later.

As you can see, we keep discovering facts about our dataset that will be useful in the modeling phase.

Two categorical features

To explore the possible relationship between two categorical features, we also have two standard tools: barplots for visualization, and cross tables or contingency tables for numerical calculations.

There are some variations on these basic tools, and we should use the variation that fits our goal of understanding.

Cross tables

The cross table is just a table consisting of rows and columns, where we can see the counts of the observations for every combination of the categories of two categorical features. We can use the `crosstab` function from pandas, as follows:

```
pd.crosstab(diamonds['cut'], diamonds['color'])
```

The output of the code is shown in the following screenshot:

color	D	E	F	G	H	I	J
cut							
Fair	163	224	312	313	303	175	119
Good	662	933	907	871	702	522	307
Ideal	2834	3902	3826	4883	3115	2093	896
Premium	1602	2337	2331	2924	2358	1428	808
Very Good	1513	2399	2164	2299	1823	1204	678

There isn't too much to explain here—we can clearly see the counts, but, honestly, it is hard to detect if there is any relationship between these features.

Let's try something else. First let's calculate the `margins`, or totals for the columns and the rows, as follows:

```
ct = pd.crosstab(diamonds['cut'], diamonds['color'], margins=True,
margins_name='Total')
ct
```

The output is as follows:

color	D	E	F	G	H	I	J	Total
cut								
Fair	163	224	312	313	303	175	119	1609
Good	662	933	907	871	702	522	307	4904
Ideal	2834	3902	3826	4883	3115	2093	896	21549
Premium	1602	2337	2331	2924	2358	1428	808	13788
Very Good	1513	2399	2164	2299	1823	1204	678	12080
Total	6774	9795	9540	11290	8301	5422	2808	53930

Now, let's divide each column by the `Total` column, to see whether the proportion of diamonds of different colors vary across the different cuts. If the proportions stay roughly the same, then we can infer that there is no association between these features. This means that knowing that (for example) a diamond has a fair cut does not give us information about the possible color of the diamond, beyond the overall proportion observed in the sample (last row).

Let's perform the calculation to make this more clear:

```
100*ct.div(ct['Total'], axis=0).round(3)
```

The output is as follows:

color	D	E	F	G	H	I	J	Total
cut								
Fair	10.1	13.9	19.4	19.5	18.8	10.9	7.4	100.0
Good	13.5	19.0	18.5	17.8	14.3	10.6	6.3	100.0
Ideal	13.2	18.1	17.8	22.7	14.5	9.7	4.2	100.0
Premium	11.6	16.9	16.9	21.2	17.1	10.4	5.9	100.0
Very Good	12.5	19.9	17.9	19.0	15.1	10.0	5.6	100.0
Total	12.6	18.2	17.7	20.9	15.4	10.1	5.2	100.0

I multiplied by 100 only to make the numbers easier to read as percentages. The bottom row indicates that the overall proportion of diamonds of different colors is independent of their cut. This is also called the *marginal frequency* of colors: 12.6% are color D, 18.2% are color E, and so on.

These marginal frequencies give us a base to compare the frequencies observed for each category of cut. When we analyze the proportions within the different cuts, do we see any large deviation from this marginal frequency?

We will, of course, observe some natural variation, but we do not see any considerable deviation from the marginal frequency, which again tells us that knowing that a diamond is, for example, "Ideal" does not give us any information about its color.

The same thing happens with all other cut categories, which implies that there is little or no association between these two categorical features.

Now, it is your turn to explore the associations between cut and clarity, and between clarity and color.

 There are other numerical and more formal statistical procedures and tests to determine the relationships between two categorical features; however, those are out of the scope of this book. Take a look at the *Further reading* section of this chapter for more information.

Barplots for two categorical variables

Sometimes it might be useful to visualize the counts or proportions of two categorical features using barplots. As with the cross tables, there are some variations, and we should use the one that it is useful for us.

Let's see how to produce the main variations using pandas. This is the basic grouped-bars chart, which is useful for seeing the actual counts:

```
basic_ct = pd.crosstab(diamonds['cut'], diamonds['color'])
basic_ct.plot(kind='bar');
```

The output of the code is as follows:

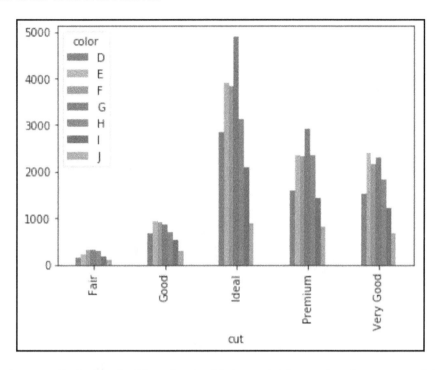

The following is called a stacked barplot, and it is useful for seeing the counts of the cut features, along with compositions of the different colors:

```
basic_ct.plot(kind='bar', stacked=True);
```

The output of the screenshot is as follows:

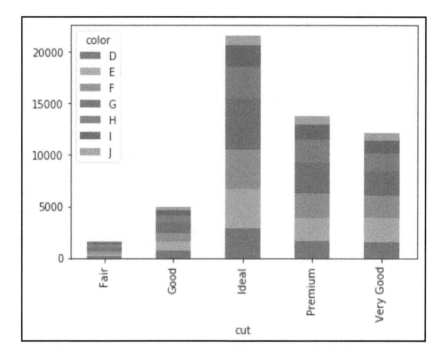

Perhaps, in this case, that one is not very useful, mainly because there are too many categories of color. However, on other occasions, you may find it useful.

Finally let's take a look at the normalized barplot, which is useful for comparing the proportions of colors across cuts, ignoring the number of diamonds in every cut category:

```
ct.div(ct['Total'], axis=0).iloc[:,:-1].plot(kind='bar', stacked=True);
```

The output is as follows:

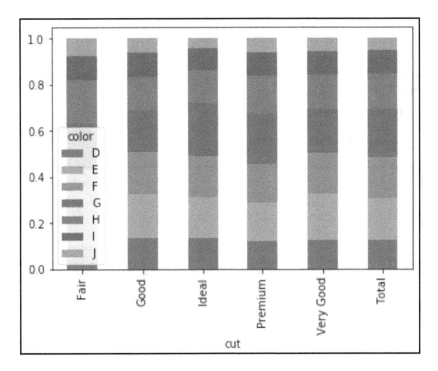

As we can see, every bar looks more or less the same, indicating that within each category of cut the proportion of color types is about the same. This confirms our previous conclusion about the association between these two features.

Now, it's your turn to create the appropriate visualizations for the other two pairs of categorical features: cut and clarity, and clarity and color.

One numerical feature and one categorical feature

This is the third possibility for bivariate relationships. Again, we have some standard widely used tools: the boxplot for visualization, and comparing means/medians for an initial exploration of the effect of the categories in the average values of a numerical feature.

Firstly, let's remember what a boxplot is. Although its basic construction can vary between different software tools, it is usually constructed as:

- The graph starts at the minimum value (bottom horizontal line).
- Then, the box starts at the 25th percentile. The horizontal line inside the box corresponds to the median (50th percentile), and the top of the box corresponds to the 75th percentile.
- Finally, it ends at the maximum value.

A typical boxplot will look like the following:

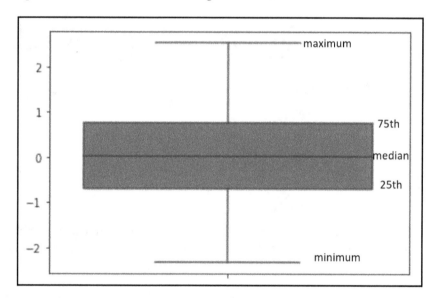

Most implementations of the boxplot will include a variation that will allow us to visualize potential outliers. The height of the box is known as the **interquartile range** (**IQR**), and it is a measure of the spread of the data. If there are values above $75th + 1.5 \times IQR$, then in this variation the top horizontal line will end there (not at the maximum value), and observations that exceed that value will be plotted as points above that top line.

The same will happen if there are values below $25th - 1.5 \times IQR$; in that case, those observations will be plotted below the bottom horizontal line.

It will look something like the following:

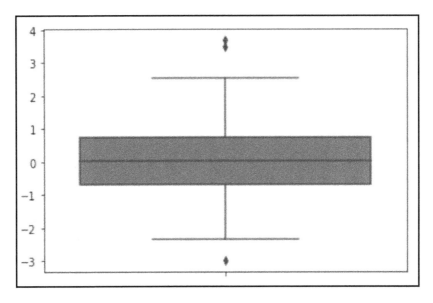

 Keep in mind that those values identified by the boxplot as outliers are just *candidates* for outliers. In fact, the concept of an outlier is not well defined—it depends on context and the distribution of the variable.

Although boxplots are also used for univariate analysis, they are much more useful for bivariate analysis because they offer a simplified way to compare distributions between different categories.

Let's begin by exploring if there is any association between `cut` and `price`:

```
sns.boxplot(x='cut', y='price', data=diamonds);
```

The output of the code is as follows:

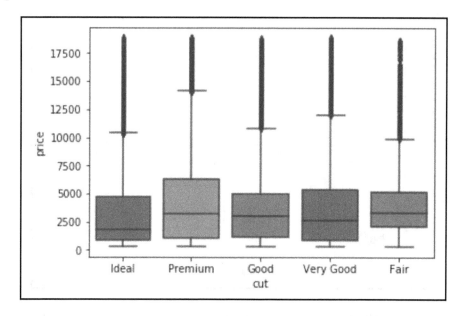

The boxplots look more or less similar. As the height of the box is a measure of spread, we can see that there is more variation in price within the **Premium** category. The boxplots identify many outliers in all categories, but this is essentially due to the distribution of prices, which we discussed previously.

Let's focus only on those diamonds costing less than $10,000:

```
sns.boxplot(x='cut', y='price',
data=diamonds.loc[diamonds['price']<10000]);
```

Try describing what you see before reading on:

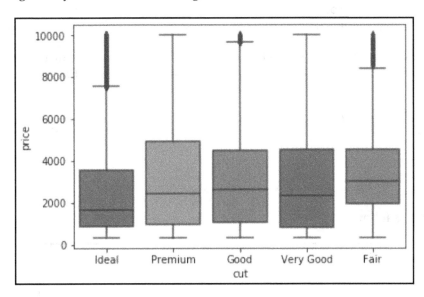

I see two things very clearly: firstly, the price distributions for **Premium, Good** and **Very Good** cuts are very similar.

Secondly, the largest differences are in the distribution of prices corresponding to the **Fair** and **Ideal** cut categories. For diamonds with an **Ideal** cut, more than half cost less than $2,000, whereas, for the **Fair** cut category, only about 25% of the diamonds cost less than $2,000. We can conclude that there is definitely a relationship between different cuts and the distribution of prices.

Now, let's perform some numerical calculations. As we know that the prices are extremely skewed, instead of comparing the means for the different categories, let's compare the medians, as follows:

```
diamonds.groupby('cut')['price'].agg(np.median).sort_values()
```

The output is shown in the following screenshot:

```
cut
Ideal           1810
Very Good       2648
Good            3054
Premium         3183
Fair            3282
Name: price, dtype: int64
```

Indeed, the medians are very different, especially for diamonds with **Ideal** and **Fair** cuts. Of course, you can compare other statistics for different groups. The `groupby` method of the pandas DataFrame, combined with the `agg` method, is extremely flexible and powerful.

As a final example, to see how to use these methods, let's calculate the median price for each category of clarity, and then use the order of the medians to plot a more informative boxplot:

```
medians_by_clarity =
diamonds.groupby('clarity')['price'].agg(np.median).sort_values()
print(medians_by_clarity)
sns.boxplot(x='clarity', y='price',
data=diamonds.loc[diamonds['price']<10000],
            order=medians_by_clarity.index);
```

The output is as follows:

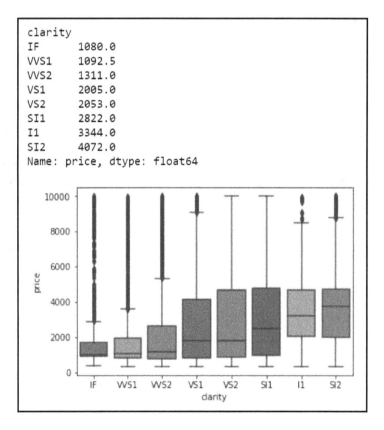

We observe a clear relationship between clarity and price. Keep practicing with the other features, and try to explain what you see.

Introduction to graphical multivariate EDA

As you may have guessed, multivariate EDA involves more than two variables. Here is where you will definitely get creative. A great deal of practice and effort is needed, to use the visualization and numerical techniques we've talked about so far in novel and interesting ways.

Common multivariate EDA techniques include:

- Coloring a scatter plot by categorical feature
- Using another categorical variable in the boxplots
- Conditional or lattice plots: dividing the analysis by different categories
- Parallel plots
- Heatmaps
- Principal component analysis and related plots

There are, of course, many others that we don't have the space to cover here. We will just provide a few examples of multivariate EDA to get you started.

For this section, we will go back to our credit card default dataset. Let's begin by importing the necessary libraries:

```
import numpy as np
import pandas as pd
import matplotlib.pyplot as plt
import seaborn as sns
import os
%matplotlib inline
```

Now, let's run all the transformations we applied back in Chapter 2, *Problem Understanding and Data Preparation*, to this dataset, as follows:

```
DATA_DIR = '../data'
FILE_NAME = 'credit_card_default.csv'
data_path = os.path.join(DATA_DIR, FILE_NAME)
ccd = pd.read_csv(data_path, index_col="ID")
ccd.rename(columns=lambda x: x.lower(), inplace=True)
ccd.rename(columns={'default payment next month':'default'}, inplace=True)

bill_amt_features = ['bill_amt'+ str(i) for i in range(1,7)]
```

```
pay_amt_features = ['pay_amt'+ str(i) for i in range(1,7)]
numerical_features = ['limit_bal','age'] + bill_amt_features +
pay_amt_features
delayed_features = ['delayed_' + str(i) for i in range(1,7)]

ccd['male'] = (ccd['sex'] == 1).astype('int')
ccd['grad_school'] = (ccd['education'] == 1).astype('int')
ccd['university'] = (ccd['education'] == 2).astype('int')
ccd['high_school'] = (ccd['education'] == 3).astype('int')
ccd['married'] = (ccd['marriage'] == 1).astype('int')

pay_features= ['pay_' + str(i) for i in range(1,7)]
for x in pay_features:
    ccd.loc[ccd[x] <= 0, x] = 0
delayed_features = ['delayed_' + str(i) for i in range(1,7)]
for pay, delayed in zip(pay_features, delayed_features):
    ccd[delayed] = (ccd[pay] > 0).astype(int)
ccd['months_delayed'] = ccd[delayed_features].sum(axis=1)
```

Finally, as we only want to create a few demonstration plots to prevent things from becoming too cluttered, let's work with a random sample of our original dataset, as follows:

```
sample_eda = ccd.sample(n=1000)
```

OK, we're ready. Our target, in this case, is a categorical feature—this is perfect for exploring whether relationships between the predictors are affected by the target feature.

One common technique is to visualize scatter plots with the points colored by category, as follows:

```
sns.scatterplot(x='bill_amt1', y='bill_amt2', hue='default',
data=sample_eda);
```

The output is shown in the following screenshot:

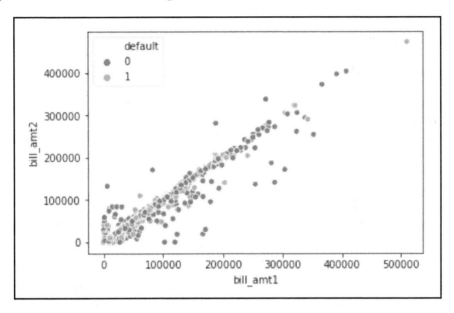

Another common approach is to use more than one categorical variable in a boxplot:

```
sns.boxplot(x='male', y='limit_bal', hue='default', data=sample_eda);
```

The output is shown as follows:

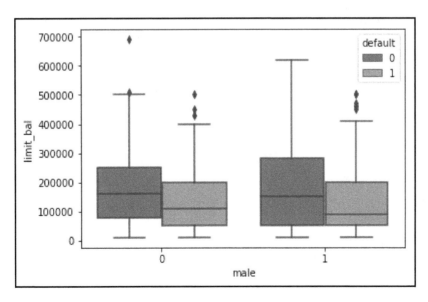

Note that in both cases we used the `hue` parameter in the Seaborn function to indicate the subgroups.

On the other hand, conditional plots are often used to produce complex visualizations. For these types of visualizations, Seaborn is an outstanding tool. For example, it provides the `FacetGrid` class (see `https://seaborn.pydata.org/tutorial/axis_grids.html`):

> *The* `FacetGrid` *class can be useful while visualizing the distribution of a variable or the relationship between multiple variables separately within the subsets of your dataset. A* `FacetGrid` *can be drawn mainly with up to three dimensions:* `row`, `col`, *and* `hue`. *The first two have a clear correspondence with the resulting array of axes; think of the* `hue` *variable as the third dimension along a depth axis, where different levels are mapped with different colors.*
> *The class can be used by initializing a* `FacetGrid` *object with a DataFrame and the names of the variables that will form the* `row`, `column`, *or* `hue` *dimensions of the grid. These variables should be categorical or distinct, and then the data at each level of the variable will be used for a facet along that axis.*

The following code will first create a `FacetGrid` instance, where the columns correspond to the `months_delayed` feature, the rows correspond to the `male` feature, and the points are colored according to the `default` category:

```
# create the FacetGrid instance
p = sns.FacetGrid(sample_eda, col="months_delayed", row='male',
hue='default')
# choose the graph to display in each subplot
p.map(plt.scatter, 'bill_amt1', 'bill_amt2')
p.add_legend();
```

Let's say that we are interested in examining the relationship between `bill_amt1` and `bill_amt2`, but we would like to see whether it changes with the features `male` and `months_delayed`. In addition, we would like to differentiate by `default` status.

Using a `FacetGrid` class, we could use these five features in a single visualization:

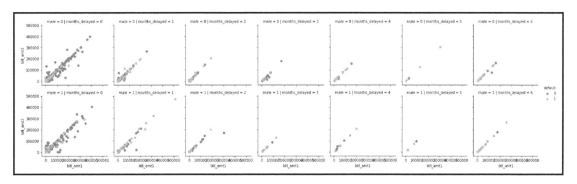

Although this visualization may or may not be useful, the point here is just to show you that we can produce very complex visualizations with just a few lines of code.

As a final example, let's say that we want to compare the distributions of `limit_bal` (limit balance) for people who defaulted and people who paid, separating the analysis by education level and gender. We could use a `FacetGrid` for this—but for, now instead of mapping a scatter plot, let's map a density plot to compare the distributions:

```
edu_levels123 = sample_eda.loc[sample_eda['education'].isin([1,2,3])]
p = sns.FacetGrid(edu_levels123, row='male', col='education',
hue='default')
p.map(sns.distplot, "limit_bal", hist=False);
```

The output is as follows:

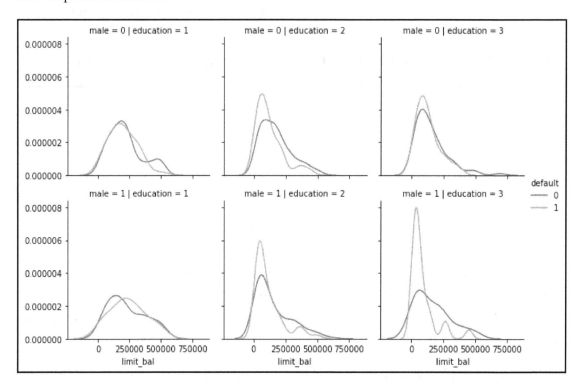

We see the comparison of the combination of `education` and gender, and the contrast between the distributions of `limit_bal` according to `default`.

As you may notice from the examples given in this chapter, Seaborn is truly great! I encourage you to take a look at the official tutorial for this library at `https://seaborn.pydata.org/tutorial.html`.

Summary

In this chapter, we learned some of the most basic and useful techniques for performing EDA. We provided many examples of how to produce visualizations and numerical calculations, and how to interpret them.

We learned about the main techniques for univariate and bivariate analysis, including histograms, bar plots, scatter plots, and boxplots. We also provided some examples of complex multivariate visualizations with Seaborn.

Please bear in mind that the reason for applying all these techniques is to understand the dataset, which will give us a better picture of the relationship between the business problem and the data. It also provides us with valuable information for the next stage of the process: predictive modeling, that will be the subject of our next chapter

Further reading

- Wasserman, L (2013) *All of Statistics: A concise course in statistical inference*, Springer Science & Business Media.
- Yim, A, Chung, C, and Yu, A (2018) *Matplotlib for Python Developers*, Packt Publishing.

4
Predicting Numerical Values with Machine Learning

Let's review what we have done so far: the business problem has been formulated, the data has been acquired and prepared, and we have a good understanding of the features and their possible relationships after applying **exploratory data analysis** (**EDA**). Now, it is finally time to build our first predictive models!

However, before building models for predictions, we should understand some of the basic foundational concepts of the field that we'll use in this book: **machine learning** (**ML**). We begin by providing a brief overview of what ML is and what the main ML techniques are. This is, of course, not a book on ML; it's just a tool, so we won't get into the theoretical or technical details that you would find in a typical ML book. Those books usually dedicate one chapter for each family of models. In addition, ML is a vast field and in this book we are mainly interested in a particular sub-branch: supervised learning. After introducing some of the basic concepts, we will train our first ML model, which will be really awful in terms of predictive performance, but it will help us to clarify most of the theoretical concepts we will discuss in the book.

After becoming familiar with the basic concepts, we talk about some of the practical considerations before model building; we provide a brief introduction to scikit-learn, and how to use it for data splitting and other important preprocessing tasks that are recommended before model building. After the pre-processing has been done, we will discuss some of the classical models for regression tasks. We will provide a high-level explanation of how these models work, and we will build three models for predicting diamond prices. Finally, in the last section, we will perform a correct evaluation of our models and take a look at some of the predictions.

These are the main things we will be doing in this chapter:

- Getting an introduction to ML
- Understanding what ML and its main branches are
- Presenting some practical considerations before modeling
- Introducing some of the most basic and popular regression models: multiple linear regression, lasso regression, and KNN
- Learn the concepts of training and testing errors

Technical requirements

- Python 3.6 or higher
- Jupyter Notebooks
- Recent versions of the following Python libraries: NumPy, pandas, matplotlib, Seaborn, and scikit-learn

Introduction to ML

Machine learning is a term that has seen an explosion in popularity, and that is mainly because it works. It has produced very good results when applied to many scientific and industrial problems, and is present, in one form or another, in many technological products and services people use daily. If you interact with the internet, use apps on your smartphone, check your email, or do any telecommunications or banking transactions, then you have definitely interacted with an ML model. This is not a book about ML; we will focus on giving the very basic concepts necessary to use ML as a tool for doing predictive analytics, we won't delve deeper into this exciting field, and there will be many important things that we will leave out. However, because of the huge rise in interest in the subject, there are many excellent resources covering everything from deeply theoretical aspects to applications of ML in very specific fields; check out the *Further reading* section for some of those resources.

Let's begin by giving some definitions:

- **ML**: ML can be defined as a sub-field of computer science and an approach to artificial intelligence that studies the methods for using data to give computer systems the ability to learn, to perform a task without being explicitly programmed. In the context of predictive analytics, the task that we would like to perform is to make predictions. Typically, ML is divided into three large sub-fields; this division is based on whether there is a learning *signal* available to the learning system. Although this division is not universal, it will be useful for us:
    - **Supervised learning**: This is the case when the computer system has some inputs and associated outputs, and the task that the system has to learn is how to use the inputs to produce the outputs. To use supervised learning, we need the data to come as a set of pairs *(inputs, output)*. This is the type of ML we will use in the book because this is exactly what we want to do: we have some diamond features (inputs) and their associated outputs (prices), and the task we want to perform is to learn how to use those features to predict the prices. We have historical data and personal information about credit card customers (inputs) and their associated outputs (default or no default), and we would like to learn how to use customer data to predict whether they will default on their payment next month.
    - **Unsupervised learning**: In this case, there is no *signal* to guide the learning of the system. These types of tasks frequently focus on learning some type of structure in the data, or in other words discovering hidden patterns in the data. Some of the tasks and applications of unsupervised learning include clustering, dimensionality reduction, retrieval, recommendation systems, generative models, and many others. Although some of these techniques could be used as part of a predictive analytics solution, we won't cover unsupervised learning in this book.
    - **Reinforcement learning**: In this type of task, learning happens as a consequence of a computer system, in this context called an *agent*, interacting with an environment. The feedback or signal that the system gets from the environment is frequently given in the form of rewards and punishments. Applications of this branch of ML include self-driving cars, robotics, trading algorithms, and much more. Reinforcement learning can also be used for predictive analytics, but we won't cover that topic in this book.

When doing predictive analytics, you can use the ML model as a **black box**—a thing that receives inputs (features) and somehow produces predictions. You could open the black box and really understand how the model produces predictions; however, the theory behind the ML models is highly technical and mathematical, so to open the black box we would need to dive into the mathematical details, and that is beyond the scope of the book. We will focus on the process of model building with Python, giving only a high-level, intuitive explanation of how the learning models work. This is an option in the middle of the two options (black box versus white box); I call this option a **gray box approach**.

From here, when we refer to ML, we will be talking about how to use it for solving the kinds of predictive analytics problems we are dealing with in this book.

Tasks in supervised learning

There are two types of general tasks in supervised learning; the distinction is straightforward and it is based on the kind of target or output we have. We already mentioned this distinction back in `Chapter 2`, *Problem Understanding and Data Preparation*, when we were defining our problems for the diamond and credit card default datasets. These are the two types of tasks that we can have:

- **Regression**: When the target is a numerical feature. Examples include predicting house prices, the number of people clicking an ad, income, sales, crime rates, stock prices, and, of course, diamond prices.
- **Classification**: When the target is a categorical feature. Examples of classification tasks are everywhere: in the field of direct marketing when you are trying to predict if a customer will be a buyer or a non-buyer; in medicine, you can predict whether a patient is healthy or is sick; in insurance, we can try to classify clients by risk level as low, average, or high risk; and of course we are dealing with a classification task if we are trying to predict whether a customer will default or pay his credit card next month. There are three main types of classification problems:
  - **Binary classification**: The target has only two categories, which is the case for our credit card default problem.
  - **Multiclass classification**: When the target has more than two classes.

- **Multilabel classification**: The problem of assigning more than one category or label to an observation. A popular example could be to predict the subject of a news article based on its contents. Many news articles don't fall into just one category; one article could be simultaneously about the broad topics of *World News*, *Politics*, and *Finance*.

Creating your first ML model

In this section, we will build and implement the code in our first ML model. We will use the diamond prices dataset. Before moving on, let's load the libraries we will use in this notebook:

```
import numpy as np
import pandas as pd
import matplotlib.pyplot as plt
import seaborn as sns
import os
%matplotlib inline
```

Now, load the diamonds dataset and apply the transformations we have done before:

```
DATA_DIR = '../data'
FILE_NAME = 'diamonds.csv'
data_path = os.path.join(DATA_DIR, FILE_NAME)
diamonds = pd.read_csv(data_path)
## Preparation done from Chapter 2
diamonds = diamonds.loc[(diamonds['x']>0) | (diamonds['y']>0)]
diamonds.loc[11182, 'x'] = diamonds['x'].median()
diamonds = diamonds.loc[~((diamonds['y'] > 30) | (diamonds['z'] > 30))]
diamonds = pd.concat([diamonds, pd.get_dummies(diamonds['cut'],
prefix='cut', drop_first=True)], axis=1)
diamonds = pd.concat([diamonds, pd.get_dummies(diamonds['color'],
prefix='color', drop_first=True)], axis=1)
diamonds = pd.concat([diamonds, pd.get_dummies(diamonds['clarity'],
prefix='clarity', drop_first=True)], axis=1)
```

Our first model will be very simple, but the point is to explain the two most theoretical concepts we will see in this book: hypothesis set and learning algorithm. When you hear or read something about ML, you will often hear the terms *model* and *algorithm* a lot, frequently used interchangeably; my goal here is to clarify the potential confusion about these terms. In theory, what is an ML model? Technically, an ML model is a combination of two things:

- **A hypothesis set**: A proposed generic relationship between target and features. It is essentially how we are going to represent the connection between the values of the features, to produce the values of the target. This is a mathematical set whose elements are the particular representations of the relationship between features and target.
- **A learning algorithm**: A procedure that uses data to select *one* element from the hypothesis set. This selected element is what people usually call the **model**.

There is another important term connected with those abstract concepts: the concept of *training*. Training the ML model means to use the learning algorithm to select the model from the hypothesis set. These definitions are abstract and hard to grasp at a first read. Let's provide a concrete example using the diamonds dataset; we will create our first ML model:

- **Hypothesis set**: We propose a relationship between features and target to be given by the following equation:

$$\text{(H)} \quad price = w \times carat$$

Here, w is any positive number. So, our mathematical set is the set of all the possible equations of the form *(H)* where $w > 0$.

OK, so the model or the relationship we are proposing basically predicts the price by multiplying the number, w, by the value of carat. The following are examples of particular models that meet the condition; the following are three *elements* of our hypothesis set:

- $price = 3 \times carat$
- $price = 658.1 \times carat$
- $price = 2535 \times carat$

In fact, there is an infinite number of these particular examples; in other words, our hypothesis set has infinite elements. How do we select one element out of this infinite set?

- **Learning algorithm:** To get the value of w for all observations in the dataset, divide the price by the corresponding carat and average the results. Now, let's implement this learning algorithm; here is where we are using the data to *train* our model:

```
w = np.mean(diamonds['price']/diamonds['carat'])
```

The value we get is 4008.024. Great! So, from a set of infinite possible models that we had of the form $price = w \times carat$, we have used the data and implemented our learning algorithm to choose *one* model:

$$price = 4008.024 \times carat$$

We have produced our first ML model!

Now, we can use this model to make predictions; all we need is the `carat` value. Here is our ML model implemented as a Python function:

```
def first_ml_model(carat):
    return 4008.024 * carat
```

Now, we can use it to make predictions for some example values of `carat`:

```
carat_values = np.arange(0.5, 5.5, 0.5)
preds = first_ml_model(carat_values)
pd.DataFrame({"Carat": carat_values, "Predicted price":preds})
```

Here, we have the results:

	Carat	Predicted price
0	0.5	2004.012
1	1.0	4008.024
2	1.5	6012.036
3	2.0	8016.048
4	2.5	10020.060
5	3.0	12024.072
6	3.5	14028.084
7	4.0	16032.096
8	4.5	18036.108
9	5.0	20040.120

Congratulations! Finally, we have developed our first predictive analytics model; recall the definition of predictive analytics we gave back in Chapter 1, *The Predictive Analytics Process*:

> *"an applied field that uses a variety of quantitative methods that make use of data in order to make predictions"*

That is exactly what we did. Do those predictions seem reasonable to you? How good are they? By the end of this chapter, you will be able to answer those questions (and you will realize how awful the predictions of this model are).

Two important questions come to mind after this simple example:

- Where did this hypothesis set and learning algorithm come from?
- Are we supposed to come up with a hypothesis set and then invent a learning algorithm?

The answer for the first question is easy: I invented that ML algorithm (hypothesis set + learning algorithm) earlier. Of course, this model lacks many desirable and standard elements of a formal ML model, but again the point was to illustrate the theoretical concepts of the hypothesis set and learning algorithm.

The answer for the second question is also easy and simple: NO. You are not supposed to come up with your own ML algorithms; that is what researchers do and what they have been doing for decades: they create these hypothesis sets, study their theoretical properties, and propose learning algorithms that theoretically will extract *the best* (or at least a very good) model form for that hypothesis set.

Likewise, we won't implement any learning algorithms in Python, because the generous developers of scikit-learn have implemented, developed, and tested all of the most commonly used ML models in that fantastic library, which all of us can use.

The goal of ML models – generalization

In predictive analytics, what we would like to do is predict unknown events. When using the ML approach, what we are doing is using the data that we have to find out or learn how the features relate to the target; in fact, that is what ML models aim to discover: we suppose that there is a true but unknown function that maps the values of the features to the target. If we have only one feature, it would look something like this:

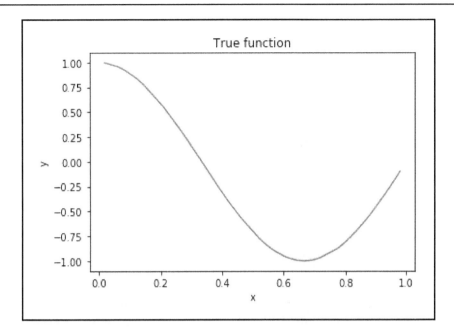

In reality, since this function is unknown, what we observe are some data points like this (if we knew the function, there is no point in trying to learn it with ML because we already know it!):

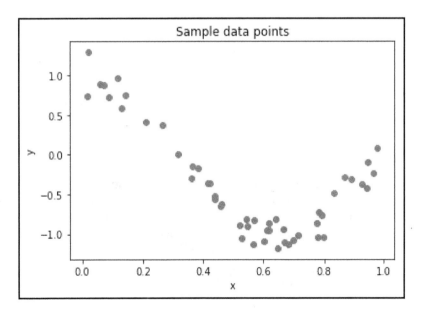

The goal of ML models is to approximate, as accurately as possible, this unknown function using the sample data points.

Now, back to our diamond prices example: we will use ML to discover what the function is that takes as inputs the features of the diamonds and returns their prices. We will try to approximate that function as accurately as possible using the sample of diamonds that we have. Once we have learned that relationship using the sample we have, we can use it with new diamonds, diamonds outside our sample, whose features are known, to predict unknown prices. This is what we mean by generalization. We want to be able to apply what the algorithm has learned from the data we have to data points we have not seen yet. This is very important, so important that I will be deliberately redundant: we want to generalize what we have learned from the data we have to points outside our sample, that is, data that we don't have.

OK, so in the case of the diamonds, do we have to wait until someone brings us a new diamond to see what our model predicts, and then wait for the diamond to be sold on the market to see how good the prediction is? No, that would be very impractical. What we want is to simulate that situation, and the way to do it is cross-validation, which is a set of methods for dividing a dataset into different subsets in order to give a good estimation of how good the model will generalize to data outside the sample. In this chapter, we will be using only the simplest form of cross-validation, which is the **hold-out** method. It simply involves dividing your dataset into two parts:

- **Training set**: Here is where learning happens; this is the portion of the data we use to *train* our model.
- **Test set**: Here is where evaluation happens; these observations play the role of the data outside our sample, which means data that the learning algorithm has not seen yet. How well the model does here will be an indication of how well the model will do with new data, in other words, how well learning will generalize.

Overfitting

Closely connected with the goal of generalization, we have the concept of overfitting. This is the situation where the model adapts too well to the training set and starts learning noise that is not related at all to the true relationship between features and target. Let me illustrate this concept with an example from the scikit-learn documentation, illustrated in the following diagram. In this example, we are doing it by modeling the relationship with polynomials of different degrees. Each plot shows a different situation; underfitting (left), good learning (center), and overfitting (right):

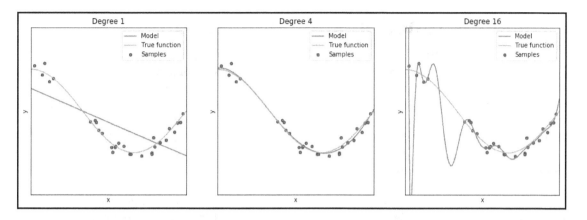

- **Underfitting**: This is the first situation, illustrated in the left-hand plot. We are trying to use a model that is too simplistic, a linear model, to capture the non-linear relationship (function) between feature and target. This simple model where the relationship is modeled by a polynomial of degree 1 (a line) won't be able to accurately predict new data points.
- **Good learning**: This is the perfect situation, where our model has the right level of complexity and is a very good approximation to the true function. For this example, a polynomial of degree 4 will be just right.
- **Overfitting**: The last plot shows the situation of overfitting; we are trying a model that is so complex that it has the possibility of learning the noise in the training dataset. This is affecting its ability to approximate the true function well. In this situation, we will also have trouble generalizing. Given the availability of very complex models, nowadays this is a common situation. The main symptom of overfitting is that the performance of the model in the training set is very good while its performance in the test set is bad.

Regularization is a set of techniques that will allow us to avoid overfitting. Some models such as lasso regression and ridge regression are actually defined by the regularization elements that will try to avoid overfitting.

Evaluation function and optimization

These are the last theoretical concepts we will discuss before going to back to writing code. All ML models have what is known as an evaluation function, objective function, or scoring function. A simplified explanation would be that this is a mathematical function that assigns a number to every element in the hypothesis set, usually based on how good the element is in predicting the target. This function is thus used by the learning algorithm to distinguish the good models from the bad models, and it also gives information on searching for the good models. The search for the best model within the elements in the hypothesis set is often performed with the help of optimization techniques.

A good optimization technique is key to the efficiency of the learning algorithm. Intuitively, an optimization procedure is a way to find the *best* element from a set of elements. During training, ML models run optimization routines to search for the final model. For example, the learning algorithm may choose the model that minimizes the evaluation function. An evaluation function and an optimization technique are what our simple first ML model lacks; I just decided arbitrarily to use the mean of the ratios between price and carat to find w. I don't know if that is the procedure that will find the best model, because I did not even define what being a good model means; this is the job of the evaluation function, and because my model lacks an evaluation function, I cannot use an optimization technique to find the best model.

I know this is perhaps too theoretical for a first read, but believe me, it is necessary to have a firm grasp of these concepts if you want to use ML correctly and successfully for doing predictive analytics.

Practical considerations before modeling

We now have a basic understanding of some of the most important conceptual and theoretical aspects of ML. In this section, we will talk about some of the practical things we need to do before building a model; this includes some further data processing that is needed for feeding the data for model training. We will also introduce our main tool for model building: scikit-learn.

Introducing scikit-learn

If you go to the main web page of scikit-learn, the first things you will read are the following statements about it:

- Simple and efficient tool for data mining and data analysis

- Accessible to everybody, and reusable in various contexts
- Built on NumPy, SciPy, and matplotlib
- Open source, commercially usable—BSD license

With the Python libraries we have used so far, we have been loading them before starting our work. With scikit-learn, it is different: we only load the different objects and classes as we need them. We will explain how to use some of the tools available in scikit-learn with the aid of the official documentation (`https://scikit-learn.org/stable/`). The scikit-learn is more than a library to build ML models; it is truly a kit with a lot of useful tools for the task of model building. Besides the implementation of dozens of the most popular and widely used ML models, it offers tools for related tasks such as these:

- Model selection
- Model evaluation
- Dataset transformations
- Loading utilities for datasets

Further feature transformations

Although we have talked about data preparation and already done some preparation and feature transformation back in `Chapter 2`, *Problem Understanding and Data Preparation*, remember that the predictive analytics process is not a linear process where the steps are completed in a strict sequence; you will find yourself going back and forth between stages. Although back in `Chapter 2`, *Problem Understanding and Data Preparation*, we transformed our dataset to be ready for analysis, there are still some recommended and useful transformations we may need to do in order to have the dataset ready for modeling. Different models can be affected in different ways depending on how we use the data, which is why it is important to not only import the data to the model but to give it in a way such that the model can perform at its best. For example, transformations that smooth the skewness of predictors or that take care of outliers can be very beneficial for the model to learn. In getting the data ready for modeling, there are two approaches: unsupervised pre-processing involves those techniques that do not consider the target when performing the calculations, and when we use the target, we are talking about *supervised* pre-processing. In this section, we will perform the first type of pre-processing: unsupervised.

Now, in order for us to use standard ML notation, we will create one matrix that contains the feature values, commonly called x, and instead of calling our target diamond prices, we will call it y. Before creating these objects, I want to let you know that one additional reason for using the one-hot-encoding format for the categorical variables is that scikit-learn only accepts numerical values. We can't provide categorical data directly to scikit-learn. Since the information in these categorical features is already in the one-hot-encoded columns, the original columns won't be included in our x matrix:

```
X = diamonds.drop(['cut','color','clarity','price'], axis=1)
y = diamonds['price']
```

Now, we are ready for the next step.

Train-test split

This is not exactly a transformation of the features, but is the first thing we have to do before modeling. Remember that we need to hold on to a portion of the dataset for testing how well our model will generalize to unseen data. In some sense, every transformation we do to the data before modeling is also part of the model; since the test dataset plays the role of the unseen data, we need perform all transformations in the training dataset and only then use them on the test dataset. This is the reason why the first step is to split our dataset into training and test datasets before performing any transformations, so we don't contaminate the test dataset with information we got from the training dataset.

When using the hold-out cross-validation method, commonly practitioners split the dataset by keeping 60-85% for training and the rest for testing; a common value is 80%. Why these values? It is mostly a custom. In reality, the goal of the test set is to be used to measure the performance of the model on unseen data, so if the dataset is very small, say fewer than 1,000 observations (as was the case when the ML field was born), then an 80-20 split makes sense, but with the massive datasets we work with now in predictive analytics, it is better to think about the split proportions before blindly applying the 80-20 rule.

The more data we have for training, the better; in fact, it is sort of folk knowledge that simple algorithms with lots of data often perform better than complex algorithms with less data. So, it is important to keep as much as we can for training. For instance, if you have a dataset of 5 million observations, you don't really need 20% for testing, as 1 million observations are too many. In that case, keeping only 1-2% (100,000-200,000) for testing will actually make much more sense.

We will use a 90-10 split. scikit-learn provides one function to perform this random split:

```
from sklearn.model_selection import train_test_split
X_train, X_test, y_train, y_test = train_test_split(X, y, test_size=0.1,
random_state=123)
```

Before performing this split, it is usually a good idea to shuffle the observations in the dataset (in case they present some kind of pattern); fortunately for us, the `tran_test_split` function does this internally before performing the split. As you can see, we used a test size of 10% (0.1), which means that we will have 5,392 observations for testing, enough to evaluate the performance of our models.

You will see the `random_state` parameter in many scikit-learn classes, methods, and functions that involve some kind of randomness. It is to make the operations and code reproducible, which means in this case that using `random_state=123` will give us exactly the same observations assigned to the training and test sets every time we use that value in that parameter.

Now that we have our dataset for training, (`X_train, y_train`), everything that we do will be done in this dataset.

Dimensionality reduction using PCA

Dimensionality reduction techniques are procedures that take a number of features and generate a smaller number of features that seek to preserve the majority of the information from the original ones. Say, for example, that you have data about the socioeconomic dimensions of a household: income level, wealth, taxes paid, years of education of the mother, years of education of the father, size of the house, and so on. Many of these features will have a strong correlation because they reflect many aspects of the socioeconomic status of the household. Suppose that you have 20 such features; you can use dimensionality reduction techniques to create a set of, say, two features that will preserve, for example, 85% of the information contained in the original 20 features. I like to think of these techniques as basically a good deal—85% of the value (information) at a small fraction of the cost (using two features instead of 20).

Recall that, when doing EDA on this dataset, we detected the problem of high correlation between x, y, and z. This is precisely the same situation as in the household example; these three features are a measure of the same thing, the size of the diamond, which is why we observe such a high correlation. They essentially have almost the same information:

```
sns.pairplot(X_train[['x','y','z']], plot_kws={"s": 3});
```

This gives us the following output:

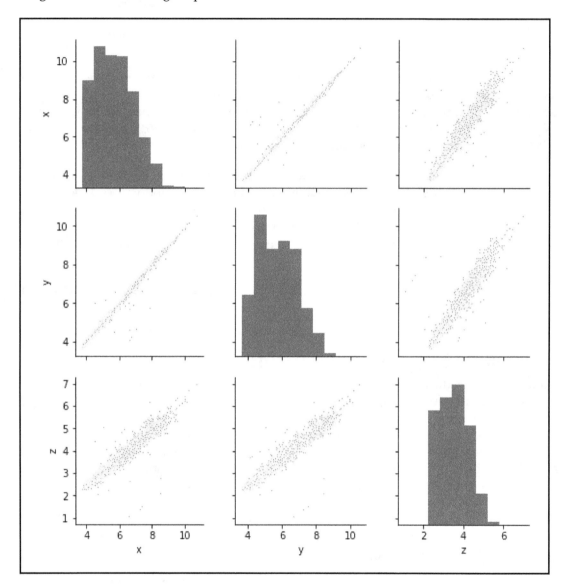

The most popular dimensionality reduction technique is **principal component analysis (PCA)**. It is a reduction technique that uses linear algebra techniques to transform the original features into another set of features that are linearly uncorrelated, which are called **principal components (PC)**. The first PC is the one that captures the most information from all features; the second PC captures most of the information left after considering the first component; the third PC captures most of the information left after considering the first and second components, and so on for the following components. If we start with k features, then k (or fewer) PCs are produced by this method, and then we must decide how many of these PCs we are going to use to reduce the dimension of the original k features.

Before doing this transformation, we will introduce the **transformers**, which are scikit-learn classes built to perform data preparation. To use transformers, you always follow these four steps:

1. Import the class you will use
2. Create an instance of the class (instantiate the object); here, you provide any extra parameters
3. Use the `fit` method of the instance; this will perform the internal calculations necessary for the next step
4. Use the `transform` method to perform the transformation

The PCA class is a transformer, so let's apply the step we just gave:

```
# 1. Import the class you will use
from sklearn.decomposition import PCA
# 2. Create an instance of the class
pca = PCA(n_components=3, random_state=123)
# 3. Use the fit method of the instance
pca.fit(X_train[['x','y','z']])
# 4. Use the transform method to perform the transformation
princ_comp = pca.transform(X_train[['x','y','z']])
```

Using the method, we can check out, in terms of proportion, how much variance (or information) is captured by each of the three components produced:

```
pca.explained_variance_ratio_.round(3)
```

We get the following output:

```
array([0.997, 0.003, 0.001])
```

So, 99.7% of the variance on the original three features is captured by the first principal component; the rest of the variance is captured mostly by the second component (0.2%), and the third one captures virtually nothing. Given these results, I think it would be a good idea to preserve only the first PC, which will be a sort of size index of the diamond. Before producing this new feature, I would like to show you that the three principal components are indeed uncorrelated:

```
princ_comp = pd.DataFrame(data=princ_comp, columns=['pc1', 'pc2', 'pc3'])
sns.pairplot(princ_comp, plot_kws={"s": 3});
```

This gives us the following output:

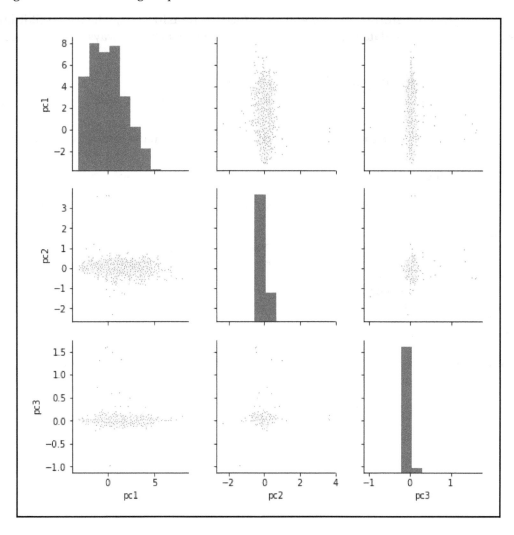

Take a look at the correlation coefficients; they are all 0:

```
princ_comp.corr().round(4)
```

This gives us the following output:

	pc1	pc2	pc3
pc1	1.0	0.0	0.0
pc2	0.0	1.0	0.0
pc3	0.0	0.0	1.0

Since we know we will preserve only the first component, let's run the same code but now using the n_components=1 parameter, then add the new feature to our dataset, and finally get rid of x, y, and z:

```
## Get only the first principal component
pca = PCA(n_components=1, random_state=123)
## Train the pca transformer
pca.fit(X_train[['x','y','z']])
# Add the new feature to the dataset
X_train['dim_index'] = pca.transform(X_train[['x','y','z']]).flatten()
# Drop x, y, and z
X_train.drop(['x','y','z'], axis=1, inplace=True)
```

Great, now we have reduced the three features to a single one, ready for the next step.

Standardization – centering and scaling

Standardization is perhaps the most commonly used transformation done in preparation for modeling. Although many learning algorithms will perform equally well without applying this transformation, it will improve the numerical stability and speed of most algorithms, and many of them (such as KNN) actually require this step to give sensible answers. There are some ways to standardize features; one involving scikit-learn is the most common.

Many ML estimators require the standardization of datasets when implemented in scikit-learn. When these features do not look like normally distributed data, they may behave badly. In practice, we usually look beyond the shape of the distribution and settle for transforming the data to center it. This is achieved by removing the mean value of each feature, and is followed by scaling it by dividing non-constant features by their standard deviation.

So, for every numerical feature, we will subtract the mean (so the new mean is 0) and divide every value by the standard deviation. After this, all of our features will have a mean of 0 and a standard deviation (and variance) of 1, so they will be on the same scale. We, of course, don't perform this transformation for the one-hot-encoded features.

For this operation, we will use another transformer, StandardScaler.

Let's perform the calculation:

```
numerical_features = ['carat', 'depth', 'table', 'dim_index']
# 1. Import the class you will use
from sklearn.preprocessing import StandardScaler
# 2. Create an instance of the class
scaler = StandardScaler()
# 3. Use the fit method of the instance
scaler.fit(X_train[numerical_features])
# 4. Use the transform method to perform the transformation
X_train.loc[:, numerical_features] =
scaler.transform(X_train[numerical_features])
```

These are some of the standardized values for the numerical features:

```
X_train[numerical_features].head()
```

This gives us the following output:

	carat	depth	table	dim_index
30066	-0.840293	1.429309	-0.205642	-0.918724
17608	0.677534	0.383359	-2.001069	0.848719
42508	-0.629484	0.034709	-0.205642	-0.568908
22842	0.719696	-0.662591	0.243215	0.908842
25957	2.553737	-1.987460	2.487499	2.147581

Finally, by running the following code, you can quickly check that the means and the standard deviations are indeed practically 0 and 1, respectively:

```
X_train[numerical_features].describe().round(4)
```

This gives us the following output:

	carat	depth	table	dim_index
count	48537.0000	48537.0000	48537.0000	48537.0000
mean	-0.0000	-0.0000	-0.0000	0.0000
std	1.0000	1.0000	1.0000	1.0000
min	-1.2619	-13.0745	-6.4896	-1.8151
25%	-0.8403	-0.5231	-0.6545	-0.9077
50%	-0.2079	0.0347	-0.2056	-0.0236
75%	0.5089	0.5228	0.6921	0.7115
max	8.8780	12.0283	9.6692	4.4957

It is important that you perform this as your last step in your preparation for modeling; if you perform other feature transformations or create new ones, then the features may no longer be standardized.

Now, our dataset is finally ready for modeling.

MLR

In scikit-learn, ML models are implemented in classes known as **estimators**, which include any object that learns from data, mainly models or transformers. All estimators have a `fit` method, which is used with a dataset to train the estimator like this: `estimator.fit(data)`.

It is important to note that the estimator has two kinds of **parameters**:

- **Estimator parameters**: All the parameters of an estimator can be set when it is instantiated or by modifying the corresponding attribute. Some of these estimator parameters correspond to the ML model **hyperparameters**. We will talk about model hyperparameters more later.
- **Estimated parameters**: When data is fitted with an estimator, parameters are estimated from the data at hand. All the estimated parameters are attributes of the estimator object, ending with an underscore.

Since scikit-learn has a very consistent API using estimators, it is very similar to using transformers. To use estimators, you always follow these four steps:

1. Import the estimator class you will use.
2. Create an instance of the class (instantiate the object). Here, you provide any extra parameters; some of them are model hyperparameters.
3. Use the `fit` method of the instance; this step trains the model.
4. Use the `predict` method to get the predictions.

MLR is the mother of all models, simple and straightforward. In this model, the target is modeled simply as a linear combination of the input variables, so our prediction is of the following form:

$$y\_pred = w_0 + w_1 x_1 + w_2 x_2 + \ldots + w_k x_k$$

For this model, what the learning algorithm (called **ordinary least squares (OLS)**) does is to identify the best combination of w (or weights) such that the **residual sum of squares (RSS)** will be minimized:

$$RSS = \sum_{i=1}^{N} (y_i - y\_pred_i)^2$$

N is the number of points in the training set, y_pred are the predicted values, and y, of course, represents the actual values of the target. Intuitively, training this model means finding the best combination of weights that will make the predicted values as close as possible to the actual values of the target. What is the procedure that this model follows to find that optimal combination of coefficients? I am afraid we won't explain that part here; if you are interested, please take a look at the references.

Finally! It is time for us to train our first real ML predictive analytics model:

```
# 1. Import the Estimator class you will use
from sklearn.linear_model import LinearRegression
# 2. Create an instance of the class
ml_reg = LinearRegression()
# 3. Use the fit method of the instance
ml_reg.fit(X_train, y_train)
# 4. Use the predict method to get the predictions
y_pred_ml_reg = ml_reg.predict(X_train)
```

The model has been trained and the predictions for the training dataset have been calculated. First, let's take a look at the weights, also known as the coefficients of the linear model:

```
pd.Series(ml_reg.coef_,
    index=X_train.columns).sort_values(ascending=False).round(2)
```

The output is as follows:

```
carat            5422.04
clarity_IF       5384.93
clarity_VVS1     5040.24
clarity_VVS2     4993.61
clarity_VS1      4616.93
clarity_VS2      4303.06
clarity_SI1      3704.82
clarity_SI2      2740.18
cut_Ideal         856.23
cut_Premium       756.77
cut_Very Good     756.17
cut_Good          609.70
table             -59.04
depth             -80.63
color_E          -217.07
color_F          -276.78
color_G          -489.66
color_H          -991.01
dim_index       -1235.23
color_I         -1480.56
color_J         -2384.35
dtype: float64
```

These are the coefficients that multiply each of the features in our model, the w from the former equation that defines our model. No other combination of coefficients makes the RSS smaller.

The fact that all the features have been scaled implies that we can interpret the coefficients as a measure of *variable importance*. Carat and clarity seem to be the features that appear to have the greatest influence on the price. The sign of the coefficient can also tell us something about the direction of the relationship between the target and the corresponding feature; in general, positive coefficients can be interpreted as having a positive impact on the price, and negative coefficients as having a negative impact on the price. First, the interpretation we develop only makes sense *within the model we are training and with the features we are using.* If we remove one feature, we will get different coefficients:

```
ml_reg.fit(X_train.drop('carat', axis=1), y_train)
pd.Series(ml_reg.coef_, index=X_train.drop('carat',
axis=1).columns).sort_values(ascending=False).round(2)
```

The output is as follows:

```
clarity_IF        5148.67
clarity_VVS1      4790.55
clarity_VVS2      4598.87
dim_index         4037.32
clarity_VS1       4006.20
clarity_VS2       3711.01
clarity_SI1       2975.99
clarity_SI2       2210.70
cut_Premium        934.69
cut_Ideal          923.11
cut_Very Good      811.81
cut_Good           607.89
depth              136.90
table               -6.19
color_E           -212.55
color_F           -361.49
color_G           -503.53
color_H           -814.98
color_I          -1111.87
color_J          -1876.45
dtype: float64
```

As you can see, the biggest change is the `dim_index` feature; its coefficient went from negative to positive. That doesn't make sense! The first model gave us a negative coefficient, so larger values of `dim_index` were associated with a lower price. Now, this model is giving the opposite information. What is going on? What is happening is that carat is closely related with `dim_index`, and when the two are together in the model, the best way the algorithm found to use the information contained in both features was to assign a large positive coefficient to carat and a relatively small negative coefficient to `dim_index`. When carat was removed, the best way to use the information contained in `dim_index` was to assign it a large positive coefficient. So, when the features show some relationship between them, don't be too dogmatic about the standard interpretation of the coefficients.

OK, with that point of confusion hopefully clear, let's retrain the model object with all the features:

```
ml_reg.fit(X_train, y_train)
```

Now, it is time to examine how good the predictions are. For this, we need a metric, a function that will take as inputs the predictions and the true values of the target, and will give us an estimation of how close they are. All standard metrics for regression models follow the same basic principle: *a model is better evaluated if predicted and actual values are close*. In this chapter, we will introduce perhaps the most commonly used standard metric for regression models: the **mean squared error** (**MSE**), defined as follows:

$$MSE = \frac{1}{N} \sum_{i=1}^{N} (y_i - y\_pred_i)^2$$

As you can see, the MSE is the average of the squared difference between the actual values and the predictions; *smaller values of MSE are associated with better predictions and thus are better*. Scikit-learn provides a function to calculate this quantity:

```
from sklearn.metrics import mean_squared_error
mse_ml_reg = mean_squared_error(y_true=y_train, y_pred=y_pred_ml_reg)
print('{:0.2f}M'.format(mse_ml_reg/1e6))
```

The result is 1.28 million. How big is this number? Is it large or small? We need a reference point to compare the value against. To get this reference point, try answering this question: in the absence of any information about a diamond's characteristics, what would be your best guess as to its price? It can be shown mathematically that, when we are completely ignorant about the characteristics of the diamond (or any variable), the guess that will minimize the MSE is to guess the mean. Predicting that all the values of the target are equal to the mean is called the null model, a model without predictors. The performance of this null model is the first reference point that we have to compare the performance of our models. Let's calculate the MSE for the null model:

```
y_pred_null_model = np.full(y_train.shape, y_train.mean())
mse_null_model = mean_squared_error(y_true=y_train,
y_pred=y_pred_null_model)
mse_null_model
```

Note that we used only the training values of the target to get the mean. We get an MSE of around 16.0 million. So, in the absence of any information, our best guess (the mean) would give us an MSE of 15.9 million, while our model that uses the information in the features gave us 1.28 million. Now, we have some perspective on this number. At least we can say that our model is doing much better than just guessing the mean, which is great for our first real ML model!

Lasso regression

Lasso is a clever modification to the multiple regression model that automatically excludes features that have little relevance to the accuracy of predictions. It performs a regularization strategy to perform variable selection in order to try to enhance the prediction accuracy of the multiple regression model. The equation that the lasso regression model uses to make the predictions is the same as in the multiple regression case: a linear combination of all the features, that is, each of them multiplied by a single coefficient. The modification is made in the quantity that the algorithm is trying to minimize; if we have P predictors, then the problem now is to find the combination of weights (w) that will minimize the following quantity:

$$\frac{1}{2N} \sum_{i=1}^{N} (y_i - y\_pred_i)^2 + \alpha \sum_{k=1}^{P} |w_k|, \alpha \geq 0$$

Note that the first part of the quantity is almost the same as in the case of the MLR (except for the constant multiplying the RSS); the key change is in the second term, which is the sum of the absolute values of the coefficients multiplied by a non-negative number, alpha, which is called the regularization coefficient. The intuition of the mathematics behind this model is that, by adding this penalty on the absolute size of the coefficients, the learning algorithm will shrink some of the coefficients to have a value of 0, thereby eliminating the corresponding features from being considered when making the prediction. For larger values of alpha, the model will assign zero coefficients to more features.

This model is very useful when we have dozens or hundreds (or even more) of features, but we would like to select only a small subset to actually make the prediction. Since in our problem we have relatively few features, *I would not recommend using lasso regression for this problem*. However, with the growing availability of data, the situation of having a dataset with hundreds of features is becoming more common, which is why I would like you to have this model in your predictive analytics toolbox. This is the true reason why we are using it here.

Now, let's use it for our regression problem to see what we have got:

```
# 1. Import the Estimator class you will use
from sklearn.linear_model import Lasso
# 2. Create an instance of the class
lasso = Lasso(alpha=10)
# 3. Use the fit method of the instance
lasso.fit(X_train, y_train)
# 4. Use the predict method to get the predictions
y_pred_lasso = lasso.predict(X_train)

## MSE calculation
mse_lasso = mean_squared_error(y_true=y_train, y_pred=y_pred_lasso)
print('{:0.2f}M'.format(mse_lasso/1e6))
```

The MSE of the lasso regression model is 1.52 million, which is not better than the MLR model because, as we said before, this would not be a recommended model for this problem. However, I would like to show you the coefficients of this model:

```
carat             4766.29
clarity_IF        1348.44
clarity_VVS2      1213.08
clarity_VVS1      1194.84
clarity_VS1        860.32
clarity_VS2        616.93
cut_Ideal          169.10
cut_Very Good       89.01
cut_Premium         55.05
clarity_SI1         33.97
cut_Good            -0.00
color_F             -0.00
color_E              0.00
table             -103.99
color_G           -124.79
depth             -145.90
color_H           -609.87
dim_index         -708.54
clarity_SI2       -768.25
color_I          -1001.55
color_J          -1780.44
dtype: float64
```

As you can see, three features were given zero coefficients; the rest of the features are the ones selected by the model. Since the zeros were given to the dummy features that represent some categories of our categorical variables, the interpretation would be the following: for color, our base category (the one not shown) is *D,* so the fact that the features representing the colors *F* and *E* got a zero coefficient tells us that, for this model, a diamond with the color *E* or *F* is the same as it having the color *D*; it basically does not add or subtract anything to/from the price. On the other hand, a diamond with the color *J* will have a negative impact on the price of 1,780 dollars on average. The last two words are important: on average.

KNN

The KNN method is a method that can be used for both regression and classification problems. It belongs to the class of non-parametric models, because, unlike parametric models, the predictions are not based on the calculation of any parameters. Examples of parametric models are the regression models that we just discussed. The weights in the case of the former regression models are the parameters. KNN belongs to the family of non-parametric models, and despite its simplicity (or perhaps because of it), it frequently produces very good results, comparable to those produced by more complex and elaborate models. In its most basic implementation, it is easy understand how to it works: for a fixed number, K, which is the number of neighbors, and a given observation whose target value we want to predict, do the following:

- Find the K data points that are closest in their feature values to the given data point
- Calculate the average target value for those K data points
- That calculated average is the prediction for the given data point

To understand how this basic KNN works a bit better, and why it makes sense, let's see how this procedure will work in our diamonds example. Say $K=12$; to predict the value of a given diamond d, do the following:

- Find the 12 diamonds that are most similar to d in terms of their characteristics: `carat`, `color`, `size`, and so on.
- Calculate the average price at which those 12 diamonds were sold.
- That calculated average is the prediction for our diamond, d.

Of course, this simple procedure makes a lot of sense; it is a sensible strategy to predict that the price of a given diamond will be close to the price of very similar diamonds. What we have described is KNN in its most basic form. There are many variations; a popular one is to use different weights in the calculation of the average.

The basic nearest neighbors regression uses uniform weights:

- Each point contributes uniformly in the local neighborhood to a query point's classification.
- In specific scenarios, there is an advantage to weighting points such that there is more contribution to the regression from nearby points than points far away.

To accomplish this, use the `weights` keyword. `weights = 'uniform'`, the default value, weights all points equally. `weights = 'distance'` assigns weights proportionally to the inverse of the distance from the query point. A user-defined function of the distance can be supplied as an alternative in order to compute the weights.

The key aspect of this algorithm is the concept of *closeness*, which intuitively corresponds to how similar the data points are. To measure similarity, we need to specify a mathematical metric of distance between data points, and this choice will have an impact on the performance of the model; see Weinberger, et al. (2006) for an in-depth discussion of this topic. Since we are introducing this model, we will use the Minkowski distance, which is the most widely known and perhaps most commonly used distance metric. In fact, it is the default used in scikit-learn. Now, let's fit this third model to our data to see how it performs:

```
# 1. Import the Estimator class you will use
from sklearn.neighbors import KNeighborsRegressor
# 2. Create an instance of the class
knn = KNeighborsRegressor(n_neighbors=12)
# 3. Use the fit method of the instance
knn.fit(X_train, y_train)
# 4. Use the predict method to get the predictions
y_pred_knn = knn.predict(X_train)
```

And now, let's calculate the MSE in our training dataset:

```
mse_knn = mean_squared_error(y_true=y_train, y_pred=y_pred_knn)
print('{:0.2f}M'.format(mse_knn/1e6))
```

We get 0.67 million, much better than the other two models! Looks like the KNN model is doing much better. But wait, not so fast; so far, we have been using the same data (`X_train, y_train`) for training and evaluation. We have to use (`X_test, y_test`) for evaluation.

Although the KNN algorithm is easy to understand and use, it is a victim of a technical problem known as the **curse of dimensionality**. This problem basically states that the samples needed for some algorithms to learn effectively grow exponentially with the number of dimensions (features) that we have. This is especially true for KNN models, so you should use it only with datasets with relatively few features.

Training versus testing error

The point of splitting the dataset into training and testing sets was to simulate the situation of using the model to make predictions on data the model has not seen. As we said before, the whole point is to generalize what we have learned from the observed data. The training MSE (or any metric calculated on the training dataset) may give us a biased view of the performance of our model, especially because of the possibility of overfitting. The metrics of performance we get from the training dataset will tend to be too optimistic. Let's take a look again at our illustration of overfitting:

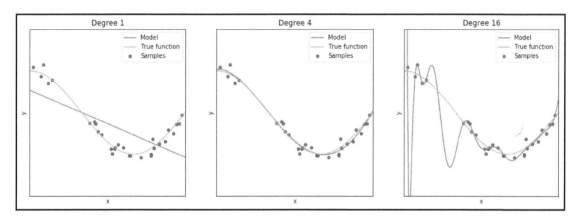

If we calculate the training MSE for these three cases, we will definitely get the lowest one (hence the best) for the third model, the polynomial with 16 degrees; as we see, the model touches many points, making the error for those points exactly 0. However, the curve that it is producing is far away from the true function the model is supposed to learn. In this case, we can observe the classic symptom of overfitting: good performance in the training set and poor performance in the test dataset. If the model is not overfitting, then the performance metrics for both the training and test datasets should be similar. In general, you will observe better performance in the training dataset than in the test dataset; this is because the model has been optimizing for observations in the training dataset, so, commonly, you will find a better performance for training data compared with the metrics calculated in the test dataset.

When evaluating the model, it is useful to get performance metrics on the training dataset; however, you should never trust them as a true indicator of the real performance of the model. Let's take a look at this extreme example:

```
perfect_knn = KNeighborsRegressor(n_neighbors=1)
perfect_knn.fit(X_train, y_train)
mean_squared_error(y_true=y_train, y_pred=perfect_knn.predict(X_train))
```

Here, we have trained a KNN model with only one neighbor, and as you can see by running the code, we got an MSE of 0; perfect performance! Well, not so fast... can you spot the problem here? Why are we getting no errors? Please think about it as an exercise.

Now, it is time for us to use the test dataset to properly evaluate our models. One important point here: all transformations we did in our training set, we must do to our testing set. What we did was the following:

- Scale our numerical features so they have zero mean and a variance of 1
- Reduce the features x, y, and z to a single feature, dim_index, using PCA
- Remove x, y, and z from the dataset

Let's perform these same transformations on our test dataset:

```
## Replacing x, y, z with dim_index using PCA
X_test['dim_index'] = pca.transform(X_test[['x','y','z']]).flatten()

# Remove x, y and z from the dataset
X_test.drop(['x','y','z'], axis=1, inplace=True)

## Scale our numerical features so they have zero mean and a variance of
one
X_test.loc[:, numerical_features] =
scaler.transform(X_test[numerical_features])
```

It is important to point out that, in these transformations, we have used the transformers we trained with our training dataset. Both `scaler` and `pca` have been trained before and we are using them to transform the test dataset, so there's no need to retrain the transformers. This is the proper way to do it.

Now that the test dataset has been transformed, we are ready to use it for making predictions and evaluating those predictions. For that, we will create a little pandas DataFrame and use it to store the MSE metrics for both training and test datasets:

```
mse = pd.DataFrame(columns=['train', 'test'], index=['MLR','Lasso','KNN'])
model_dict = {'MLR': ml_reg, 'Lasso': lasso, 'KNN': knn}
for name, model in model_dict.items():
    mse.loc[name, 'train'] = mean_squared_error(y_true=y_train,
y_pred=model.predict(X_train))/1e6
    mse.loc[name, 'test'] = mean_squared_error(y_true=y_test,
y_pred=model.predict(X_test))/1e6

mse
```

The output is as follows:

	train	test
MLR	1.28101	1.20721
Lasso	1.52062	1.40893
KNN	0.670249	0.780698

It is evident that the testing performance of the KNN model is better. A little visualization will be really useful here:

```
fig, ax = plt.subplots()
mse.sort_values(by='test', ascending=False).plot(kind='barh', ax=ax,
zorder=3)
ax.grid(zorder=0)
```

It gives us the following output:

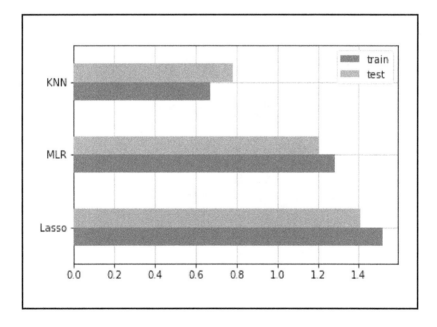

Judging by testing performance, the KNN model has the best MSE, so we have a winner. Note that its performance is better in the training set than in the test set, which is what is usually expected. For the multiple regression and lasso models, the situation is the opposite: the performance in the testing test is actually better compared with the performance in the training dataset. This is uncommon, but possible; what is happening here is that, since we have dedicated only 10% of the data for testing, most of the extreme errors in predictions are found in the training dataset. Since the MSE is an average of squared errors, these big errors tend to be magnified, thereby affecting the MSE. However, as you can see, the values are pretty close, so, although uncommon, there is nothing wrong with this. When working with real-world data, you will find things that are not shown in traditional textbooks.

As we stated before, in general, you should expect to find better performance metrics in the training dataset than in the test dataset. However, this is not a mathematical theorem that must always be true. If the performance in training is much better than the performance in testing, then the model is very likely overfitting. If the metrics are both really bad and close to each other, the model is underfitting, not learning well (or perhaps there is no pattern to learn). Another case is what we found in the MLR and lasso models here. This is uncommon, but as long as the difference is not too much, then it is OK; if the difference is too big, then you must take a look at the splitting procedure or the pre-processing steps.

Finally, to make this a bit more concrete, let's take a look at some of the predictions and actual prices (from the testing set) that are produced by our models:

```
demo_pred = X_test.iloc[:10].copy()
pred_dict = {'y_true':y_test[:10]}
for name, model in model_dict.items():
    pred_dict['pred_'+name] = model.predict(demo_pred).round(1)

pd.DataFrame(pred_dict)
```

The output is as follows:

	y_true	pred_MLR	pred_Lasso	pred_KNN
8549	4434	4638.0	4993.4	4172.9
27123	17313	15503.2	14918.2	14771.3
40907	1179	1603.1	1611.9	1092.5
1375	2966	3063.0	3299.2	2915.8
41673	1240	1859.6	1567.7	978.0
35461	901	1700.1	1329.1	1158.1
30655	736	1086.4	689.6	754.6
10271	4752	6010.9	6042.6	4970.2
28928	684	904.1	762.3	753.5
26351	645	704.7	651.4	722.9

What do you think of these predictions? Are they good? Do you think we can improve them? Is MSE a clear enough metric or do we need a more understandable performance metric? What about the skewness of the target we detected in the previous chapter? What can be done about it? Why did we choose *K=12* for our KNN model; why not 10 or 15? Please think about these questions; we will answer them in Chapter 8, *Model Tuning and Improving Performance*.

Summary

This was a dense chapter! We introduced some of the most important concepts of ML; we know that ML has three main branches, supervised, unsupervised, and reinforcement learning, and that we will be using only supervised learning in this book. Supervised learning has two types of tasks, regression and classification, whose only difference is the type of target we want to predict. We also talked about the very abstract concepts of hypothesis set and learning algorithm, and we even invented our (very bad) pseudo-ML model.

We also talked about the very important concept of generalization, which is the whole point of building ML models: to be able to learn how to map the features to the target using the data we have, and then use this knowledge to make predictions with data that we don't have yet. Cross-validation is a set of techniques to evaluate models; the most basic form of cross-validation is the train-test split we used in this chapter. This technique allows us not only to correctly evaluate our model, but also to avoid overfitting.

Then, we went on to the practical application of the concepts. After introducing scikit-learn, we performed some of the most commonly used transformations, standardizing the features and performing dimensionality reduction with PCA. We then proceeded with our gray box approach and explained how three of the foundational and most commonly used ML algorithms work: MLR, lasso regression, and KNN regression. Although in reality lasso would not be useful for the example of the diamonds dataset, it is an important tool you should know about.

Finally, we evaluated our models in the test dataset and declared KNN as the winner. However, there are still some pending questions that we will answer later in the book.

Further reading

- Friedman, J., Hastie, T., & Tibshirani, R. (2001). *The elements of statistical learning.* Springer series in statistics.
- Kuhn, M., & Johnson, K. (2013). *Applied predictive modeling.* Springer.
- Pedregosa, F. et. al. (2011). Scikit-learn: Machine learning in Python. In *Journal of machine learning research.*
- Raschka, S., & Mirjalili, V. (2017). *Python machine learning.* Packt Publishing.
- Weinberger, K. Q., Blitzer, J., & Saul, L. K. (2006). Distance metric learning for large margin nearest neighbor classification. In *Advances in neural information processing systems* (pp. 1473-1480).

5
Predicting Categories with Machine Learning

In the previous chapter, we learned the basics of machine learning. In this chapter, we will build models that predict categories. This class of machine learning problems is known as classification tasks. Classification models are the ones that are the most useful in practice, and in this chapter we will talk about some of the most popular and foundational classification models.

We begin the chapter by providing an overview of the classification tasks and some of their applications. Then we bring back our credit card default dataset and start preparing it for modeling. After that, we introduce one of the most popular models for classification—logistic regression, which is similar in spirit to the multiple regression models we discussed in the previous chapter. The next model we present is classification trees. We present this model because it is very popular and easy to understand and, besides, it is the basis for one of the most popular and power models used in predictive analytics—random forests.

As we did in the previous chapter, we explain at a high level how these models work and we use scikit-learn to train models in our credit card default dataset. After training the models, we compare their performance on the testing set. Finally, because the credit card default dataset is a binary classification problem, we finish the chapter with a brief section that contains an example of the multiclass classification problem.

These are the learning outcomes for this chapter:

- Learn about classification tasks and why classification models are so important
- Review the credit card default dataset
- Learn about the logistic regression model
- Understand the classification trees model

- Learn the random forest model
- Provide a simple example of multiclass classification
- Learn the basics of Naive Bayes classifiers

Technical requirements

The technical requirements for this chapter are as follows:

- Python 3.6 or higher
- Jupyter Notebook
- Recent versions of the following Python libraries: NumPy, pandas, matplotlib, Seaborn, and scikit-learn

Classification tasks

Classification tasks belong to the supervised learning branch of ML. These kinds of tasks are the most widely used in applications in industry and academia. Here are just a few examples of classification tasks in some domains of application:

- **Direct marketing**: Predict whether a customer will give a positive or a negative response to a campaign
- **Medicine**: Predict whether a patient is healthy or is sick; or, for example, which kind of cancer the patient has
- **Insurance**: Classify clients by risk level; for instance, low, average, or high risk
- **Telecommunication and other industries**: Churn models are classification models that predict which customers will switch to another provider
- **Education**: Predict which students will drop out from a program
- **Email services**: Classify emails that go to different places such as inbox, spam, social, and promotions

Of course, our credit card default problem is a classification task because we are trying to predict if a customer will default or pay his credit card next month.

To review what we mentioned in the previous chapter, there are mainly three types of classification problems:

- **Binary classification**: The target has only two categories, which is the case for our credit card default problem.
- **Multiclass classification**: When the target has more than two classes.
- **Multilabel classification**: The problem of assigning more than one category or label to an observation. A popular example could predict the subject of a news article based on its contents. Many news articles hardly fall into just one category; one article could be simultaneously about the broad topics of *World News*, *Politics*, and *Finance*.

Predicting categories and probabilities

ML classification models can output two types of predictions:

- **Predicted classes**: For every observation, the model will directly give the prediction of the class.
- **Probabilities for each class**: For every observation and every class, the model will output probabilities of that observation belonging to that class. Say, for example, we have three classes—*A*, *B*, and *C*—then the output of the model would be a triple of numbers such as [0.2, 0.7, 0.1], meaning the probabilities of the observation belonging to A, B, and C respectively. Note that, since we are dealing with probabilities, the values should add up to 1.

In the case of models that output the probability for every class, the classification is done by predicting the category with the highest probability. This is like the default rule; however, we can (and sometimes should) change this method of using the probabilities for predicting classes based on the goals we set for our predictive analytics project.

For binary classification models, we often name one of the classes "the positive class" and label the class with a 1 and the other class becomes "the negative class", labeled often with a 0 (many people like using a –1 as well, but I don't like it). The positive class *is the class around which the analysis is made*. Keep in mind that in this context the term "positive" has nothing to do with the regular use of the word, indicating that something is "good"—for instance, in the credit card default, our positive class will be "default", which of course from the point of view of the financial institution is not "positive" at all.

Credit card default dataset

OK, time to get our hands dirty with the credit card default data. We saw the descriptions of the features back in Chapter 2, *Problem Understanding and Data Preparation*:

- SEX: Gender (1 = male; 2 = female).
- EDUCATION: Education (1 = graduate school; 2 = university; 3 = high school; 4 = others).
- MARRIAGE: Marital status (1 = married; 2 = single; 3 = others).
- AGE: Age (year).
- LIMIT_BAL: Amount of the given credit (New Taiwan dollar)—it includes both the individual consumer credit and his/her family (supplementary) credit.
- PAY_1 - PAY_6: History of past payment. We tracked the past monthly payment records (from April, 2005, to September, 2005) as follows: 0 = the repayment status in September, 2005; 1 = the repayment status in August, 2005; . . .; 6 = the repayment status in April, 2005. The measurement scale for the repayment status is: -1 = pay duly; 1 = payment delay for one month; 2 = payment delay for two months; . . .; 8 = payment delay for eight months; 9 = payment delay for nine months and above.
- BILL_AMT1-BILL_AMT6: Amount of bill statement (New Taiwan dollar). X12 = amount of bill statement in September, 2005; X13 = amount of bill statement in August, 2005; . . .; X17 = amount of bill statement in April, 2005.
- PAY_AMT1-PAY_AMT6: Amount of previous payment (New Taiwan dollar).
- Default payment next month.

Now it is time for us to load the dataset and perform the transformations we have done back in Chapter 3, *Dataset Understanding – Exploratory Data Analysis*, to get this data ready for analysis. Remember that due to some strange values and lack of information, and for the sake of simplicity, we performed some transformations to simplify the dataset and get it ready for analysis. In summary, this is what we are doing in the following block of code:

1. Load the dataset and rename the columns so it is easier to work with.
2. Since this dataset consists of some group of features, it will be helpful to have some lists with the names of the related features.
3. Then we create some binary features—note here that we are not producing (the line is commented) the binary feature for "high school education", as we are considering just three categories for education—"high school and others" (the base category), "university", and "graduate school".

4. Then we simplify some features so they have a simpler interpretation:
   - `pay_i` features: Transform the -1 and -2 to 0, which means that the customer paid duly on the month `i`. Other integers indicate the number of delayed months.
   - `delayed_i`: These features are a simplification of the `pay_i` features; these are indicating just if a customer is delayed (1) or not in the month `i`.

5. Finally, we are creating a new feature, `month_delayed`, which is just the sum of how many months the customer has been delayed:

```
# Loading the dataset
DATA_DIR = '../data'
FILE_NAME = 'credit_card_default.csv'
data_path = os.path.join(DATA_DIR, FILE_NAME)
ccd = pd.read_csv(data_path, index_col="ID")
ccd.rename(columns=lambda x: x.lower(), inplace=True)
ccd.rename(columns={'default payment next month':'default'},
inplace=True)

# getting the groups of features
bill_amt_features = ['bill_amt'+ str(i) for i in range(1,7)]
pay_amt_features = ['pay_amt'+ str(i) for i in range(1,7)]
numerical_features = ['limit_bal','age'] + bill_amt_features +
pay_amt_features

# Creating binary features
ccd['male'] = (ccd['sex'] == 1).astype('int')
ccd['grad_school'] = (ccd['education'] == 1).astype('int')
ccd['university'] = (ccd['education'] == 2).astype('int')
#ccd['high_school'] = (ccd['education'] == 3).astype('int')
ccd['married'] = (ccd['marriage'] == 1).astype('int')

# transform the -1 and -2 values to 0
pay_features= ['pay_' + str(i) for i in range(1,7)]
for x in pay_features:
    ccd.loc[ccd[x] <= 0, x] = 0

# creating delayed features
delayed_features = ['delayed_' + str(i) for i in range(1,7)]
for pay, delayed in zip(pay_features, delayed_features):
    ccd[delayed] = (ccd[pay] > 0).astype(int)
# creating a new feature: months delayed
ccd['months_delayed'] = ccd[delayed_features].sum(axis=1)
```

Note that, since the `delayed_i` features are just a simplification of the `pay_i` features, we should not use them together in a model.

Now, let's prepare this dataset for modeling (I will leave it as an exercise to perform EDA on this dataset). For now, we will use just a subset of the features—we will exclude the `pay_i` and `delayed_i` features and include only `months_delayed`, which is a kind of summary of the former features:

```
numerical_features = numerical_features + ['months_delayed']
binary_features = ['male','married','grad_school','university']
X = ccd[numerical_features + binary_features]
y = ccd['default'].astype(int)
```

Now, let's split the dataset into training and testing sets. We have 30,000 observations; let's use 5,000 for testing and the rest for training:

```
from sklearn.model_selection import train_test_split
X_train, X_test, y_train, y_test = train_test_split(X, y, test_size=5/30,
random_state=101)
```

Finally, just as we did in the previous chapter, it is always a good idea to standardize the numerical features, so they are in the same scale with a mean of 0 and a standard deviation of 1:

```
# 1. Import the class you will use
from sklearn.preprocessing import StandardScaler
# 2. Create an instance of the class
scaler = StandardScaler()
# 3. Use the fit method of the instance
scaler.fit(X_train[numerical_features])
# 4. Use the transform method to perform the transformation
X_train.loc[:, numerical_features] =
scaler.transform(X_train[numerical_features])
```

Great! We are ready to start modeling.

Logistic regression

This is a mandatory model to know if you are performing a classification task using machine learning, because it is simple and is often used as a first benchmark to evaluate the performance of more complicated models. For binary classification, this model produces the *conditional probability* of the target belonging to the positive class. This model is another example of a parametric model; the learning algorithm will try to find the best combination (vector) of parameters $w = [w_0, w_1, w_2, \ldots, w_p]$ such that the estimated probabilities produced by the equation are as follows:

$$P(y = 1|X) = \frac{1}{1 + exp(-w^t X)}$$

We are close to 1 when the target belongs to the positive class and close to 0 when the target belongs to the negative class. So, by definition, this model predicts probabilities, and then we use this probability to predict classes. To understand it better, let's produce our first simple logistic regression model using just one feature.

A simple logistic regression model

To understand better how this model produces the probabilities, let's create a simple model using only a single feature, the one we created called `months_delayed`:

```
from sklearn.linear_model import LogisticRegression
simple_log_reg = LogisticRegression(C=1e6)
simple_log_reg.fit(X_train['months_delayed'].values.reshape(-1, 1),
y_train)
```

All scikit-learn estimators expect the X matrix containing the features to be a two-dimensional object (NumPy array or a pandas DataFrame), which is why if you are using only one feature it is necessary to reshape so X has two dimensions: the `reshape(-1,1)` method will do the trick. The same happens with the predict method if you are using only one observation you would need to use the method like so: `reshape(1,-1)`.

The logistic regression implementation of scikit-learn is actually more sophisticated than the model I just described. It includes a regularization term (which helps to avoid overfitting); I don't want to use regularization in this example, which is why I set the `C` parameter to a big number.

After fitting the model, we get the calculated parameters of `W`:

```
print("W0: {}, W1: {}".format(simple_log_reg.intercept_[0],
simple_log_reg.coef_[0][0]))

W0: -1.3814542479409055, W1: 0.8190226651901202
```

We now have all we need to implement the equation that will give us the probabilities of default for a value of `months_delayed`:

```
def get_probs(months_delayed):
    m = scaler.mean_[-1]
    std = scaler.var_[-1]**.5
    x = (months_delayed - m)/std
    prob_default = 1/(1+np.exp(-simple_log_reg.intercept_[0] + -
simple_log_reg.coef_[0][0]*x))
    return prob_default
```

Note that, if we want to use the original values of the feature (say two or three months), we need to standardize those values using the values calculated by the trained `scaler` object. Let's take a look at the probabilities produced by this model:

```
months = np.arange(13)
pred_probs = get_probs(months)
pd.DataFrame({'months': months, 'pred_probs':pred_probs})
```

The following screenshot shows the output:

	months	pred_probs
0	0	0.139067
1	1	0.214219
2	2	0.315119
3	3	0.437107
4	4	0.567208
5	5	0.688658
6	6	0.788722
7	7	0.863022
8	8	0.914041
9	9	0.947220
10	10	0.968040
11	11	0.980813
12	12	0.988542

This probability makes sense, right? If someone has not been delayed at all in the last six months, the model predicts a chance of 13.9% of this customer defaulting—in other words, according to this model about 14% of the costumers who have not delayed in the last six months will default. Likewise, about 79% of the customers who have been delayed for six of the past six months will default in their payment next month.

 Note that our original feature had values from 0 to 6. As we used the model for values beyond 6, we need to be careful when doing these extrapolations; the model may not work when we used values too far away from the range of our observed data.

Perhaps a plot would be helpful here to visualize the probabilities produced by this simple model as a function of the months delayed:

```
fig, ax = plt.subplots()
ax.plot(months, pred_probs)
ax.set_xlabel('Months delayed')
ax.set_ylabel('Probability of default')
ax.grid()
```

The output is shown in the following screenshot:

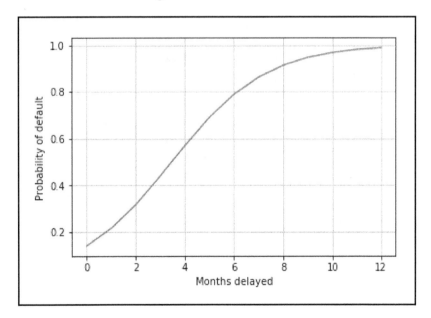

Hopefully, this example clarified a bit how the logistic regression model produced the probabilities.

A complete logistic regression model

Now, let's train a model using all the selected features:

```
log_reg = LogisticRegression(C=1e6)
log_reg.fit(X_train, y_train)
```

The model has been trained using all the features we have in X_train. We know that this model produces probabilities as outputs; to get these probabilities for such models we have the `predict_proba` method, which will produce a two-dimensional NumPy array with each column giving the probability of the observation belonging to the respective class. In this case, the first column corresponds with the probability associated with the negative class (labeled as 0) and the second column corresponds with the probabilities for the positive class. Here, we have the first 10 predicted probabilities for the training data:

```
prob_log_reg = log_reg.predict_proba(X_train)
prob_log_reg[:10]
```

The output is shown in the following screenshot:

```
array([[0.80546441, 0.19453559],
       [0.89230804, 0.10769196],
       [0.80288351, 0.19711649],
       [0.85899725, 0.14100275],
       [0.19901693, 0.80098307],
       [0.82373747, 0.17626253],
       [0.70903546, 0.29096454],
       [0.79648631, 0.20351369],
       [0.81846397, 0.18153603],
       [0.73849053, 0.26150947]])
```

Since those are probabilities, as you can see the two columns add up to 1. If we don't want the probabilities but we want the labels, then we could use the `predict` method which we have used before:

```
y_pred_log_reg = log_reg.predict(X_train)
y_pred_log_reg[:10]
```

This outputs the following:

```
array([0, 0, 0, 0, 1, 0, 0, 0, 0, 0])
```

As we said before, these labels are produced by using probabilities—the label for which the probability is larger, or equivalently—predict 1 when the second column of `pred_log_reg` is greater than 0.5. You verify this by running the following code:

```
np.all(y_pred_log_reg == (prob_log_reg[:,1] > 0.5))
# True
```

Congratulations! You have produced your first complete classification model! Here, we have the coefficients associated with each of the features used:

```
pd.Series(data=log_reg.coef_[0],
index=X_train.columns).sort_values(ascending=False).round(2)
```

The output is shown in the following screenshot:

```
months_delayed      0.75
bill_amt2           0.22
bill_amt3           0.18
married             0.17
grad_school         0.13
male                0.11
university          0.11
age                 0.06
pay_amt3           -0.00
pay_amt4           -0.02
bill_amt5          -0.03
pay_amt5           -0.03
pay_amt6           -0.04
bill_amt4          -0.06
bill_amt6          -0.06
bill_amt1          -0.16
limit_bal          -0.18
pay_amt1           -0.23
pay_amt2           -0.31
dtype: float64
```

A crude interpretation of these coefficients is that features with positive ones are positively associated with the probability, meaning that larger values of them will increase the probabilities of default and smaller values will tend to decrease the probability of default. For features with negative coefficients, the relationship would be negative—larger values of the feature would be associated with a smaller probability of default and vice versa. Of course, these interpretations are valid if there are no strong correlations between the features, but we know there are, so, as I said in the previous chapter, do not be too dogmatic about the simple interpretation. However, in this case, the model identifies the `months_delayed` feature, like the one having the largest positive effect on the probability of default. That makes sense! In addition, remember that this feature was engineered by us—we created it and it turns out that it gave us valuable information about the credit card default, which is great!

Now that we have trained our first model, let's introduce our first performance metric for classification models—accuracy. This is the simplest metric we have to evaluate classification. It is defined as the proportion (or percentage) of predictions that are *correct*. A correct prediction is, of course, when our model predicts the same category that is observed:

```
from sklearn.metrics import accuracy_score
accuracy_log_reg = accuracy_score(y_true=y_train, y_pred=y_pred_log_reg)
accuracy_log_reg
```

We get a training accuracy of 0.80372, or, in other words, 80.37% of the predictions made in the training set are correct. Does this look right? Think about it. We will get back to this point. Now it is time for us to take a look at another popular model—classification trees.

Classification trees

Classification trees are also very popular because they are very transparent and easy to understand and it is straightforward to explain how they produce the predictions. They belong to the category of non-parametric methods, and they can be used for regression and classification tasks. The way they produce the predictions is by creating a series of rules that are applied consecutively until we arrive at a "leaf" node in the tree that contains the classification. An example will make this more clear.

For visualizing scikit-learn trees in your Jupyter Notebook, you will have to install `graphviz`. In the Anaconda prompt with your virtual environment activated, install the `graphviz` and `pydotplus` **packages:** `conda install graphviz` and `conda install pydotplus`. In addition (in Windows), you will have to add the `C:\Users\<user>\Anaconda3\envs\<env_name>\Library\bin\ graphviz` root to the PATH environment variable.

Let's import the necessary class and train our classification tree. For now, don't worry about the parameters we are using for creating the `class_tree` instance:

```
from sklearn.tree import DecisionTreeClassifier
class_tree = DecisionTreeClassifier(max_depth=3)
class_tree.fit(X_train, y_train)
```

Now let's import everything we need to visualize the classification tree in our Jupyter Notebook:

```
from sklearn.externals.six import StringIO
from sklearn.tree import export_graphviz
from IPython.display import Image
import pydotplus
```

Now let's visualize the classification tree—the main function we just imported is `export_graphviz`, which exports the decision tree in a file with DOT format. This function generates a GraphViz representation of the decision tree, which is then written into `out_file` (which in this case is an instance of the `StringIO` class). Finally, the `Image` function is used to display the tree.

 For more information on GraphViz, refer to `https://www.graphviz.org/`.

Here is the code to display the graphical representation:

```
dot_data = StringIO()
export_graphviz(decision_tree=class_tree,
                out_file=dot_data,
                filled=True,
                rounded=True,
                feature_names = X_train.columns,
                class_names = ['pay','default'],
                special_characters=True)
graph = pydotplus.graph_from_dot_data(dot_data.getvalue())
```

```
Image(graph.create_png())
```

The result is the following:

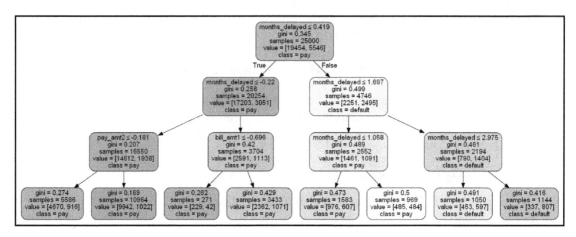

This is the graphical representation of the rules produced by the model: for every observation, start at the top and then, based on the truth value of the proposition, go left if it is `True` and right if it is `False`. It's like answering a series of yes/no questions with the information of a client. Suppose you have the data for one observation, then you start answering in the following manner:

1. Is `months_delayed` <= 0.419? Answer: `True` => go left
2. Is `months_delayed` <= -0.22? Answer: `False` => go right
3. Is `bill_amt1` <= -0.696? Answer: `True` => go left and predict that this customer will pay

In the tree, we can see that the node predicts `pay` because, out of 271 customers whose answers were the same, 229 ended up paying their credit card the next month.

Perhaps you will find it more useful to print the proportions instead of the counts. We can easily do it by setting the `proportion=True` parameter:

```
dot_data = StringIO()
export_graphviz(decision_tree=class_tree,
                out_file=dot_data,
                filled=True,
                rounded=True,
                proportion=True,
                feature_names = X_train.columns,
                class_names = ['pay','default'],
                special_characters=True)
```

```
graph = pydotplus.graph_from_dot_data(dot_data.getvalue())
Image(graph.create_png())
```

The output will be as follows:

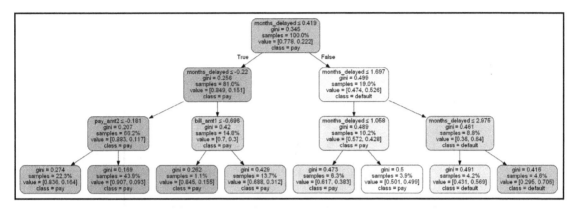

As we can see in the leftmost leaf node, only 16.4% of the clients ended up defaulting, compared to the rightmost node, where 70.5% are defaults. No doubt this model is very useful in generating important information about the possible causes of credit card default.

How trees work

Now that we know how it works, let's talk at a high level about how it produces these rules. Essentially, trees produce their predictions by partitioning the feature space into rectangular regions. In the case of classification, it finds those splits that make the regions as homogeneous as possible. The method commonly used is called recursive binary splitting. Suppose we have two categories, purple and yellow, that we would like to classify. Let's say that we have two features and you would like to split one of them such that the space is divided into two regions. The goal is to make the two regions as "pure" or homogeneous as possible; you have to answer two questions:

1. Which feature should you split?
2. At which point should the split be done?

Answering these two questions will give us the first rule of the top of the tree:

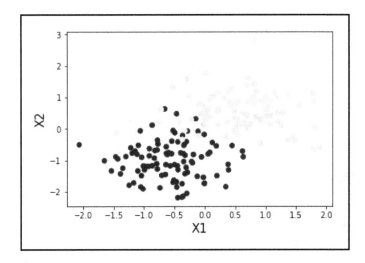

Just by looking at the plot, a good guess for answering the questions might be the following:

1. Which feature should you split? Answer: X2
2. At which point should the split be done? Answer: -0.6

There we have our first split: X2 >= -0.6.

Now the feature space has been split into two regions:

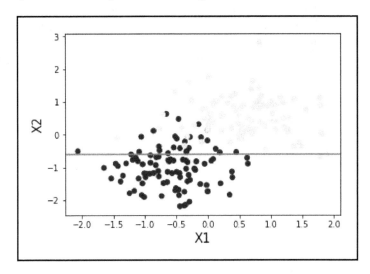

Now, for each region, let's recursively ask the same two questions. For the top region we ask the following:

1. Which feature should you split? Answer: X1
2. At which point should the split be done? Answer: -0.1

The space will now look like this:

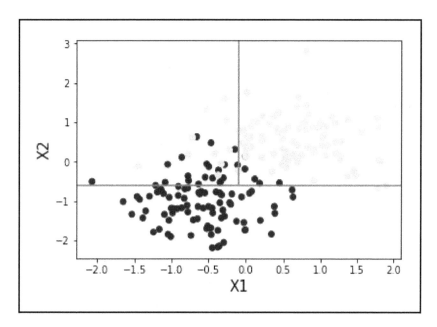

Now for the bottom region, we ask the following:

1. Which feature should you split? Answer: X1
2. At which point should the split be done? Answer: 0.7

The result is as follows:

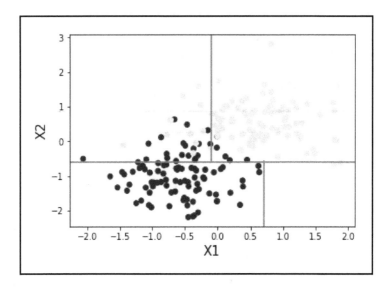

Now we have a small tree that can be represented as follows:

Is X2 >= -0.6?

- If `True`: Is X1 >= -0.1?
    - if `True`: (upper-right) predict yellow
    - if `False`: (upper-left) predict purple
- If `False`: is X1 >= 0.7?
    - If `True`: predict yellow
    - If `False`: predict purple

This approach of recursively partitioning the feature space continues until some stopping criteria are reached, such as the maximum size of the tree or the minimum number of samples that we consider in a node ("box") for doing a split. To control the size of the tree, the simplest three parameters you can change in scikit-learn (`https://scikit-learn.org/stable/modules/generated/sklearn.tree.DecisionTreeClassifier.html`) are the following:

- `max_depth`: The maximum depth of the tree. If nothing, then nodes are expanded until all leaves are pure or till all leaves contain fewer than `min_samples_split` samples.

- `min_samples_split`: (default=2) The minimal number of samples required to split an internal node:
  - If `int`, then considers `min_samples_split` the minimal number.
  - If `float`, then `min_samples_split` is a percentage and `ceil`(`min_samples_split * n_samples`) are the minimal number of samples for each split.
- `min_samples_leaf`: (default=1) The minimal number of samples required to be at a leaf node:
  - If `int`, then considers `min_samples_leaf` the minimal number.
  - If `float`, then `min_samples_leaf` is a percentage and ceil (`min_samples_leaf * n_samples`) are the minimal number of samples for each node.

There are other parameters for controlling the size and the splitting criteria of the trees, but we would need a bit more technical knowledge to adjust them.

Of course, this is just a simple example. I just visually decided on the features and the splits; the algorithm in scikit-learn does the split by calculating a quantity called the Gini index or another called the **entropy**. The technical details are outside the scope of this book, but you can take a look at the references.

Finally, please keep in mind that there are many types and variations of "tree" models that researchers have published (such as ID3, C4.5, C5.0, and CART), each with different techniques and theoretical reasons for building the trees in one way or another. Take a look at *Loh, W. Y. (2008)* for a more in-depth discussion of tree-based models. The explanation we just gave is a generic one.

The good and the bad of trees

Here are some of the advantages of using classification tree models:

- They are very easy to understand and explain
- The rules produced are easy to implement
- It is computationally efficient to produce predictions with them
- Little pre-processing is needed—classification trees are not affected by skewed predictors, or the predictors being in different scales

The main drawbacks of these models are the following:

- Their predictive power is often less than that of other models, so you can't expect highly accurate predictions.
- They may be unstable: even small changes in the dataset can lead to very different rules. Technically, this is known as the model having **high variance**.
- They can easily overfit.
- Because of the simplicity of the if-then rules, there are some complex interactions that these models cannot learn.

On the other hand, the scikit-learn documentation (`https://scikit-learn.org/stable/modules/tree.html#tree`) contains very useful tips for practical use; I encourage you to take some time to read them.

Training a larger classification tree

Now that we have a good idea about how classification trees work, let's train a larger tree. For simplicity, we will go with the default scikit-learn parameters and we will just control the size of the tree using `max_depth` and `min_samples_split`:

```
class_tree = DecisionTreeClassifier(max_depth=6, min_samples_split=50)
class_tree.fit(X_train, y_train)
y_pred_class_tree = class_tree.predict(X_train)
```

When calculating the training accuracy score of this model, we use the following:

```
accuracy_class_tree = accuracy_score(y_true=y_train,
y_pred=y_pred_class_tree)
accuracy_class_tree
```

We get 0.80824 or 80.8%, which is similar to the logistic regression model.

Finally, another nice feature of this model is that we can get a (normalized) score of feature importance, using the `feature_importances_` method:

```
pd.Series(data=class_tree.feature_importances_,
index=X_train.columns).sort_values(ascending=False).round(3)
```

The output is shown in the following screenshot:

```
months_delayed    0.828
pay_amt2          0.042
bill_amt1         0.022
limit_bal         0.020
pay_amt1          0.018
bill_amt2         0.015
bill_amt6         0.011
pay_amt4          0.010
bill_amt5         0.007
pay_amt3          0.007
age               0.006
pay_amt6          0.004
pay_amt5          0.003
bill_amt3         0.003
grad_school       0.002
bill_amt4         0.002
male              0.000
married           0.000
university        0.000
dtype: float64
```

The model gives by far the most importance to months_delayed, and virtually no importance to gender, being married, or education. Perhaps a plot will make this more clear:

```
pd.Series(data=class_tree.feature_importances_,
    index=X_train.columns).sort_values(ascending=False).plot(kind='bar');
```

The output is shown in the following screenshot:

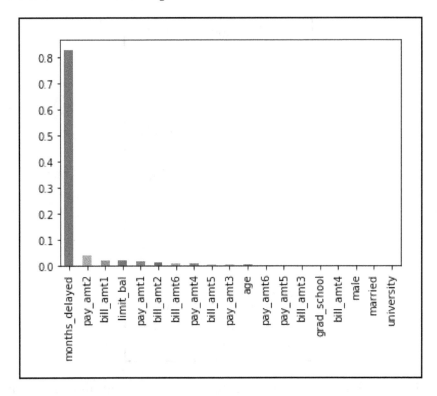

Now we know about trees. They are the basis for one of the most powerful models there is for making accurate predictions: random forests.

Random forests

As we discussed when talking about trees, one of their advantages is their simplicity; but that is also the cause of their problems—their performance is often worse than other models, especially if the tree is small, in which case we will have what is known as a *weak predictor*. By the end of the 1980s, two researchers, Kearns and Valiant (1988, 1989), posted the question *"Can a set of weak learners create a single strong learner?"* This question gave rise to a lot of research on what is known as **Ensemble methods** or **Ensemble Learning**. The core idea of Ensemble Learning is simple—instead of using just one model to make predictions, use many individual models and combine their predictions. This simple idea has been one of the keys in the success of machine learning in producing very accurate models. Ensemble Learning is, of course, a whole sub-area of machine learning research and we won't talk much about it. We will only introduce some of the concepts needed for having a high-level understanding of how random forests work:

- **Bootstrap sample**: If you have a dataset D of n observations, then a *bootstrap sample* of the dataset will consist of n samples randomly chosen with replacement from D. Suppose $D = [1,2,3,4,5]$; a bootstrap sample would be $D*=[5,5,1,2,2]$. We see repeated values because the sampling process was done with replacement.

- **Bagging**: This word comes from *bootstrap aggregating* and it is the procedure of taking, say, K bootstrap samples of a dataset and then fitting K models, one in each of the K bootstrap sample datasets; this means that we would have K models. Then we can aggregate (combine) their individual predictions, by averaging in the case of regression, or in the case of classification by applying the **majority vote** rule. For example, if $K=100$ and for some observation 75 out of the 100 models classify the observation as "default", then the final classification of the Bagging method would be "default". Bagging is the basis for the random forest method that applies a small variation to **decorrelate** the individual predictors.

They are called *forests* because the individual predictors are trees. The rationale is the following—if your $K=100$ models will give you a very similar prediction, or (in the extreme case) the same prediction for all observations, then there is no point in using 100 models because they are giving you the same opinion. It's like inviting 100 people to debate a topic about which they all have the same opinion—there is no debate. Decorrelating the individual predictors means to make them a bit distinct from one another, so they can offer a different perspective on the data. The basic mechanism that random forest implements to perform this decorrelation is to use only a *random sample* of the features when splitting trees (this is where the *Random* in the random forest name comes from).

When a node is split during the construction of the tree, the chosen split is no longer the best split among all features; instead, the split that is picked is the best split among a random subset of the features. So, let's say we have 15 predictors and the `max_features` parameter is 5, then only five randomly chosen features will be considered for the split. Once all the individual trees have been fit, then the majority vote rule is applied to give the final prediction. Of course, there are more technical details, but I hope this explanation is enough to give you an idea of how these models work.

Now, since the individual predictors are trees when using these models we need to provide hyperparameters for both the individual trees and the ensemble itself. This makes the random forest a bit tricky to optimize; however, the good people of scikit-learn usually give us good default parameters.

Let's fit our first random forest model:

```
from sklearn.ensemble import RandomForestClassifier
rf = RandomForestClassifier(n_estimators=99,
                            max_features=5,
                            max_depth=4,
                            min_samples_split=100,
                            random_state=85)
rf.fit(X_train, y_train)
y_pred_rf = rf.predict(X_train)
```

Now, let's take a look at the training accuracy score:

```
accuracy_rf = accuracy_score(y_true=y_train, y_pred=y_pred_rf)
```

We get 0.80744 or 80.7%; not very far from what we got from the other models.

These models also give us a measure of variable importance:

```
pd.Series(data=rf.feature_importances_,
          index=X_train.columns).sort_values(ascending=False).round(3)
```

The output is shown in the following screenshot:

```
months_delayed    0.828
pay_amt2          0.042
bill_amt1         0.022
limit_bal         0.020
pay_amt1          0.018
bill_amt2         0.015
bill_amt6         0.011
pay_amt4          0.010
bill_amt5         0.007
pay_amt3          0.007
age               0.006
pay_amt6          0.004
pay_amt5          0.003
bill_amt3         0.003
grad_school       0.002
bill_amt4         0.002
male              0.000
married           0.000
university        0.000
dtype: float64
```

All of this, as you can see, more or less agrees with the results of the classification trees.

Training versus testing error

Now that we have presented three very useful classifiers, it is time for us to evaluate their accuracy on the testing set; in the training set, the three models appear to give us about the same accuracy of about 80%. However, before calculating testing accuracy, recall what we said in the previous chapter about the need for a reference point to know if this 80% is good or bad. Back in the previous chapter, we answered a version of this question—in the absence of any information about the customer, what would be our best guess for his payment status next month? In this case, we have only two choices: pay or default, and since most of the clients in our sample paid, in the absence of any information our best guess would be to always predict pay. This simple strategy (always predict pay) will be in this case called the **null model**, the model without predictors. Logically, since 77.9% of the observations in our dataset belong to the pay category, the null model will be correct about 77.9% of the time. We can verify this using the testing data:

```
y_pred_null = np.zeros_like(y_test)
accuracy_score(y_true=y_test, y_pred=y_pred_null)
```

Indeed, we get 78.2%. In the light of this result, the 80% we got in our models does not look very good. However, that does not mean that our models are useless. Perhaps we are not judging fairly, or perhaps we are not evaluating them properly; we will delve deeper into the evaluation of classification models in Chapter 8, *Model Tuning and Improving Performance*. For now, just for the sake of completeness, let's calculate training and testing accuracy for our three models:

```
## Remember to also standardize the numerical features in the testing set
X_test.loc[:, numerical_features] =
scaler.transform(X_test[numerical_features])
## Calculating accuracy
accuracies = pd.DataFrame(columns=['train', 'test'],
index=['LogisticReg','ClassTree','RF'])
model_dict = {'LogisticReg': log_reg, 'ClassTree': class_tree, 'RF': rf}
for name, model in model_dict.items():
    accuracies.loc[name, 'train'] = accuracy_score(y_true=y_train,
y_pred=model.predict(X_train))
    accuracies.loc[name, 'test'] = accuracy_score(y_true=y_test,
y_pred=model.predict(X_test))

accuracies
```

The output is shown in the following screenshot:

	train	test
LogisticReg	0.80372	0.7794
ClassTree	0.80824	0.3098
RF	0.80744	0.7854

As we can see, the three models are performing virtually equally when we evaluate them only on accuracy in both training and testing sets:

```
fig, ax = plt.subplots()
accuracies.sort_values(by='test', ascending=False).plot(kind='barh', ax=ax,
zorder=3)
ax.grid(zorder=0)
```

The output is as follows:

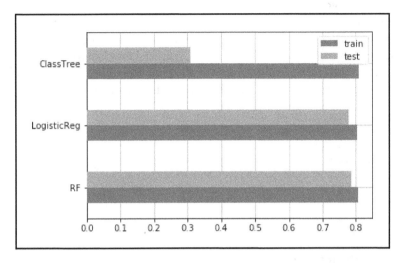

We will stop for now with these models, but keep in mind that our job is not done yet. There are many things we can do to make these models better:

- Use PCA with correlated features (`bill_amt` and `pay_amt`)
- Look for hyperparameters that produce better predictions: this is called **hyperparameter tuning**
- Change the classification threshold, which is by default 0.5
- Go beyond accuracy: perform a more complete and better model evaluation

We will do some of these things in `Chapter 8`, *Model Tuning and Improving Performance*.

Multiclass classification

This is a brief section about multiclass classification. This is the situation when we have more than two classes in our target. Models such as classification trees can handle this case using basically the same logic that we explained. For other models such as logistic regression, which is defined only for two classes, the most common approach is called **One-vs-the-Rest** or **One-versus-All**. This strategy can only be used with models that produce probabilities or other scores that can be interpreted as *confidence* of the classification. This method consists of fitting one classifier per class (that class versus the rest); the observations in that class will be considered the positive class and the rest the negative class. After all models have been trained, the class that is assigned to the observations is that of the model that produced the highest probability (or score).

Let's provide a little example: we will use the iris dataset, the most overused dataset in human history. In case you don't know it (which I doubt), it's a little set of 150 flowers that contains four measurements of the flower, each of which belongs to one of three categories: Setosa, Versicolour, or Virginica. If we use the four measurements as features and the species of the flower as the target, then we have a multiclass classification problem. Let's fit a logistic regression model that will (automatically) use the One-vs-All method to produce the classifications. Let's load the dataset, fit the model, and make predictions:

```
# Loading the iris dataset
from sklearn.datasets import load_iris
iris = load_iris()
# Training the logistic regression model
iris_log_reg = LogisticRegression(C=1e5)
iris_log_reg.fit(iris.data, iris.target)
# Making predictions
iris_probs = iris_log_reg.predict_proba(iris.data)
iris_pred = iris_log_reg.predict(iris.data)
```

Now, take a look at the results:

```
iris_pred_df = pd.DataFrame(iris_probs, columns=iris.target_names).round(4)
iris_pred_df['predicted_class'] = iris.target_names[iris_pred]
iris_pred_df.sample(12)
```

The output is shown in the following screenshot:

	setosa	versicolor	virginica	predicted_class
17	0.9400	0.0600	0.0000	setosa
109	0.0000	0.0332	0.9668	virginica
10	0.9512	0.0488	0.0000	setosa
78	0.0000	0.9974	0.0026	versicolor
22	0.9582	0.0418	0.0000	setosa
42	0.8494	0.1506	0.0000	setosa
148	0.0000	0.0497	0.9503	virginica
140	0.0000	0.0907	0.9093	virginica
83	0.0000	0.4270	0.5730	virginica
15	0.9959	0.0041	0.0000	setosa
133	0.0000	0.7520	0.2480	versicolor
55	0.0000	0.9998	0.0002	versicolor

As you can see, the predicted class corresponds with the one with the highest probability. This little example shows that doing multiclass classification in scikit-learn is no more complicated than binary classification.

Naive Bayes classifiers

Naive Bayes classifiers is a family of classifiers based on the famous Bayes theorem. This section will take us a bit off topic (which is why I am including it at the end), but it is worth having this family of models in your predictive analytics toolbox. We will briefly review some important probability concepts and will discuss the intuition behind this classifier; then we will use it in our problem.

Conditional probability

This section is by no means a mathematically rigorous discussion of probability concepts: we will focus on the intuition and will make some calculations to make the concepts more concrete.

In this section, we will use the same dataset we have been using and assume that we can accurately estimate the probabilities of different events by calculating relative frequencies in our sample of 30,000 customers, which is a reasonable assumption. For example, suppose we define the following events:

- **Event A**: A customer is a default
- **Event B**: A customer is male
- **Event C**: A customer with an age between 30 and 39

If you choose one customer at random from the population of all customers of the bank, we are assuming that we can get the respective probabilities of these events by performing the following calculations:

```
N = ccd.shape[0]
Prob_A = (ccd['default']==1).sum()/N
Prob_B = (ccd['male']==1).sum()/N
Prob_C = ((ccd['age']>=30) & (ccd['age']<=39)).sum()/N
print("P(A) = {:0.4f}; P(B) = {:0.4f}; P(C) = {:0.4f}".format(Prob_A,
Prob_B, Prob_C))
# Which gives:
P(A) = 0.2212; P(B) = 0.3963; P(C) = 0.3746
```

Now let's review the concept of **conditional probability**: as the name suggests, a conditional probability is the probability of an event given that some condition (or event) is taken to be true. Mathematically, the "probability of A *given* B" is defined as follows:

$$P(A|B) = \frac{P(A \cap B)}{P(B)}$$

In the context of our example, it would be as follows:

$$P(default|male) = \frac{P(default\ and\ male)}{P(male)}$$

This can be read as: if you are looking only at male customers (*male* is the event that is taken to be true), the probability of default is given by the ratio of those two probabilities:

1. `numerator`: The probability of both events happening simultaneously
2. `denominator`: The probability of male

Let's perform this calculation:

```
numerator = ((ccd['default']==1) & (ccd['male']==1)).sum()/N
denominator = Prob_B
Prob_A_given_B = numerator/denominator
print("P(A|B) = {:0.4f}".format(Prob_A_given_B))
## Which gives:
P(A|B) = 0.2417
```

Of course, we could obtain the same result by filtering the dataset to include only males and then calculating the proportion of defaults in this filtered DataFrame:

```
only_males = ccd.loc[ccd['male']==1]
only_males['default'].value_counts(normalize=True)
## Which gives:
0.2417
```

Bayes' theorem

Bayes' theorem is a formula that expresses the relationship between conditional probabilities—mathematically, it is almost trivially easy to deduce it given the definition of conditional probabilities. Here we have its most basic form:

$$P(A|B) = \frac{P(B|A)P(A)}{P(B)}$$

The formula does not look very complicated; however, it is very useful, although it's not that obvious how. The first thing you should understand is that this probability formula gives us the link between *P(A|B)* and *P(B|A)*, which are definitely different things. So, in our example, the following would apply:

- *P(A|B)* = *P(default | male)* = probability that a *male* customer is a *default*
- *P(B|A)* = *P(male | default)* = probability that a *default* customer is *male*

Still confused? Don't worry, that happens to all of us. In the first conditional probability, we are only looking at males, and then we calculate the probability of default; in the second one, we look only at defaults, and then calculate the probability of male. Let's calculate both probabilities to show that they are not the same. First let's do it for *P(default | male)*:

```
only_males = ccd.loc[ccd['male']==1]
Prob_default_given_male =
(only_males['default']==1).sum()/only_males.shape[0]
Prob_default_given_male
## Which gives:
0.2417
```

This can be interpreted as follows, if I know the customer is *male,* then there is a 24.17% chance that this customer is a *default.*

Now let's calculate *P(male | default)*:

```
only_defaults = ccd.loc[ccd['default']==1]
Prob_male_given_default =
(only_defaults['male']==1).sum()/only_defaults.shape[0]
Prob_male_given_default
## Which gives:
0.4329
```

In other words, if I know a customer is a default, then there is a 43.29% chance that it is male.

Bayes' theorem gives us a way to link these probabilities, like so:

$$P(default|male) = \frac{P(male|default)P(default)}{P(male)} = \frac{0.4392 \times 0.2212}{0.3963} \approx 0.2417$$

You can make this calculation directly:

```
Prob_default = Prob_A
Prob_male = Prob_B
Prob_male_given_default * Prob_default / Prob_male
## Which gives:
0.24167227456
```

This is the same number we got from our direct calculation.

The usefulness of Bayes' theorem comes when we only know one conditional probability, say P(A | B), and we would like to know the "reverse" conditional probability P(B | A).

Using Bayesian terms

In the context of Bayesian statistics, the terms in the following formula are as follows:

$$P(default|male) = \frac{P(male|default)P(default)}{P(male)}$$

They are described using the following terminology:

- *P(default | male)*: **Posterior probability** or simply posterior, this is the probability of the event of interest *after* we know some fact or information, in this case, the "information" is the second event: the customer is *male*
- *P(default)*: **Prior probability** or simply prior, the probability of the event before we consider any information
- *p(male | default)*: **Likelihood,** the "reverse" conditional probability, if the event of interest is true, the probability that the information (second event) is true
- *p(male)*: the probability of the information or second event, this is sometimes referred to as the probability of the **evidence** of the second event

The formula then becomes the following:

$$posterior = \frac{likelihood \times prior}{evidence}$$

Back to the classification problem

If you think about it, what we are trying to do when doing classification is to know the posterior probability of an event given that we have some new information: if I know nothing about a particular customer, the only thing I can say about his probability of being a default is the previous calculation: *P(default)* = 0.2212 or 22.12%. What if I have additional information about this customer? What if now we know that the customer is 35 years old? Bayes's theorem tells us how we should update our probability of the event of interest (default) given this new information:

$$P(default|age = 35) = \frac{P(age = 35|default)P(default)}{P(age = 35)}$$

What if we had an additional piece of information? Say that now we know that the limit balance of this customer is 150K; how can we use these two pieces of information simultaneously? We do it just as we did before:

$$P(default|age = 35, limit\_bal = 150K) = \frac{P(age = 35, limit\_bal = 150K|default)P(default)}{P(age = 35, limit\_bal = 150K)}$$

The term $P(age = 35, limit\_bal = 150K)$ is an example of a joint probability, or the probability of both events to be simultaneously true.

The previous formula looks a bit complicated and, in fact, it is more complicated, and this is where the **naive** part of the Naive Bayes classifier comes into play: we suppose that the features (information) are **independent**, in other words, there is no relationship between *age* and *limit balance*. This is a naive assumption since in almost all datasets the features have some degree of dependency. The point of accepting this naive assumption is that it allows us to simplify the formula because the joint probability of independent events is the product of the probabilities of the events we have:

$$\frac{P(age = 35, limit\_bal = 150K|default)P(default)}{P(age = 35, limit\_bal = 150K)} = \frac{P(age = 35|default) \times P(limit\_bal = 150K|default) \times P(default)}{P(age = 35, limit\_bal = 150K)}$$

Now we have to calculate quantities such as *P(age = 35 | default)*. Here is where the second (perhaps equally naive) assumption of the Naive Bayes classifier comes into play: in the case of continuous features, we assume that we can obtain the probabilities of events such as *P(age = 35 | default)* assuming that *P(age | default)* is a normal (Gaussian) distribution. Let's take a look at the actual data:

```
## This dataframe contains only defaults:
sns.distplot(only_defaults['age'], hist=False)
plt.title("P(age | default)");
```

The output is shown in the following screenshot:

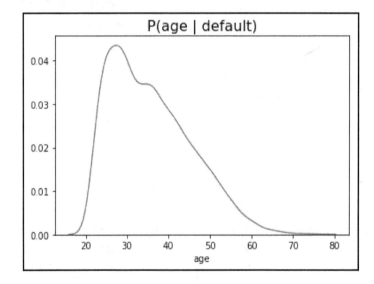

It does not look normal, but the assumption is not that crazy. We use the same assumption for all the features to be able to calculate the respective probabilities. This member of the Naive Bayes family is called **Gaussian Naive Bayes**.

Gaussian Naive Bayes

This is a classifier we use when we have only continuous predictors (features). Remember that we assume two things:

- Given any value of the target, every pair of features has an independent distribution
- The features follow a Gaussian distribution

Despite these naive assumptions, this type of classifier is very effective in many tasks such as document classification and spam filtering.

Now the general formulation: say we have k features; since we are considering a binary classification problem, we have two relevant posterior probabilities we would like to calculate, one of which is the posterior probability of *default*:

$$P(default|x_1, x_2, \ldots, x_k) = \frac{P(x_1, x_2, \ldots, x_k|default)P(default)}{P(x_1, x_2, \ldots, x_k)}$$

The other is the posterior probability of *pay*:

$$P(pay|x_1, x_2, \ldots, x_k) = \frac{P(x_1, x_2, \ldots, x_k|pay)P(pay)}{P(x_1, x_2, \ldots, x_k)}$$

The classification rule is simple: given the values of $x_1, x_2, \ldots, x_k$, predict the category with the highest posterior probability; that is, the value of y (*default* of *pay*) that maximizes the following quantity:

$$Q = \frac{P(x_1, x_2, \ldots, x_k|y)P(y)}{P(x_1, x_2, \ldots, x_k)}$$

Now, using the independence assumption, we get the following:

$$P(x_1, x_2, \ldots, x_k|y) = P(x_1|y)P(x_2|y)\ldots P(x_k|y) = \prod_{i=1}^{k} P(x_i \mid y)$$

Since the denominator Q does not depend on y, we can ignore and use only the denominator to give the following classification rule:

$$y\_pred = \arg\max_{y} P(y) \prod_{i=1}^{k} P(x_i \mid y)$$

Gaussian Naive Bayes with scikit-learn

What scikit-learn will do internally is to estimate the parameters for the Gaussian distributions of the features and then calculate the quantity:

$$P(y) \prod_{i=1}^{k} P(x_i \mid y)$$

It will finally give us a prediction the y that maximizes that quantity. This rule works for binary or multiclass classification.

Let's train this algorithm using only the numerical features from our dataset:

```
from sklearn.naive_bayes import GaussianNB
gnb = GaussianNB()
gnb.fit(X_train[numerical_features], y_train)
y_pred_gnb = gnb.predict(X_test[numerical_features])
```

Now let's get the accuracy score:

```
accuracy_score(y_true=y_test, y_pred=y_pred_gnb)
## Which gives
0.4182
```

A pretty bad result, at least from the point of view of accuracy! Perhaps Gaussian Naive Bayes is not a good classifier for our problem. That is OK; not all that you will try in predictive modeling will work.

If you had only binary or categorical features, you could use other members of this family such as Multinomial Naive Bayes or Bernoulli Naive Bayes. But, what if you had a mixture of continuous and categorical features, as we do in our problem? In principle, you could use the Naive Bayes approach: the mathematical formulation remains the same, just assume a Gaussian distribution for the continuous features and a Bernoulli distribution (https://en.wikipedia.org/wiki/Bernoulli_distribution) for the binary features. However, one of the limitations of the scikit-learn implementations is that you can only use one type of features. This is why this algorithm is constrained to certain kinds of problems such as text classification.

Despite its limitations, Naive Bayes can give you very good results and, as I said before, it is worth having in your predictive analytics toolbox.

Summary

In this chapter, we introduced important models for classification tasks and we used them in practice with the credit card default dataset. We covered the most commonly used models in the application and research industry, looking at three types of classification tasks—binary, multiclass, and multilabel classification. We learned about the logistic regression model, which tries to estimate the conditional probability of an observation belonging to the positive class. Toward the end of the chapter, we learned how multiclass classification is done automatically by scikit-learn models using the One-versus-All method.

Now that we have learned the basic models for regression and classification tasks, it is time for us to take a look at a family of models that have become very popular in the last years, not only for doing predictive analytics but for their success in artificial intelligence: deep learning models.

In the next chapter, we will explore neural nets for predictive analytics.

Further reading

- Friedman, J., Hastie, T., & Tibshirani, R. (2001). *The elements of statistical learning*. Springer series in statistics
- Loh, W. Y. (2008). Classification and regression tree methods. Encyclopedia of statistics in quality and reliability, 1, 315-323
- Pedregosa, F. et. al. (2011). *Scikit-learn: Machine learning in Python*. Journal of machine learning research
- Raschka, S., & Mirjalili, V. (2017). *Python Machine Learning*, Packt Publishing

6
Introducing Neural Nets for Predictive Analytics

In the last two chapters, we have presented some of the most basic and popular models for regression and classification tasks. In this chapter, we introduce a family of models based on neural networks. This family of models is the basis for the field of deep learning—an approach to machine learning behind some of the most exciting and recent advances in the field of artificial intelligence.

This chapter will give you enough knowledge to be able to use neural networks for predictive analytics; the point here is to present the fundamental concepts about these models and learn to train the most fundamental type of neural network—the **multilayer perceptron (MLP)**.

First, we will cover the main concepts of neural networks when talking about the anatomy of an MLP; then we will discuss how these models learn to make predictions. After covering the conceptual material, we will learn about TensorFlow, and especially about Keras, which will be our main tools for building and training models in this chapter. We will use the two datasets we have been working with in the book, and we will see whether neural network models can make better predictions. We conclude the chapter by discussing some of the issues associated with training neural network models and talk about important techniques such as early stopping and dropout regularization.

After finishing this chapter, we will be able to include MLPs in your predictive analytics toolbox and use them to make predictions.

The following topics will be covered in this chapter:

- Introducing neural networks
- Introducing Keras and a brief overview of TensorFlow
- Regression models with neural networks
- Classification models with neural networks
- Learning some important tips when using neural networks

Technical requirements

- Python 3.6 or higher
- Jupyter Notebooks
- Recent versions of the following Python libraries: NumPy, pandas, matplotlib, Seaborn, and scikit-learn
- Recent installations of TensorFlow and Keras

Introducing neural network models

There is no question that lately neural networks and deep learning are terms that have attracted a lot of attention. Although there is definitely a lot of hype and misunderstanding of these technologies, they are behind some of the most important developments and breakthroughs in the field of artificial intelligence—self-driving cars, language translators, speech recognition, super-human level players in many board games, computer vision, and many other achievements are directly related to different kinds of deep learning models.

In this chapter, we will learn about one basic type of neural network model—the MLPs will use these models to solve predictive analytics problems, in particular, we will apply them to solve the two examples we have been working on within the book. After finishing this chapter, we will be able to include MLPs in your predictive analytics toolbox.

Deep learning

Back in Chapter 4, *Predicting Numerical Values with Machine Learning*, we introduced machine learning as a subfield of computer science and an approach to artificial intelligence that studies the methods for using data to give computer systems the ability to learn to perform a task without being explicitly programmed. So, machine learning is an approach to producing intelligent systems. Deep learning is a subset of machine learning methods that are based on models called generically **neural networks**—these are models that are built as a series of *layers;* we can think of these layers as a *representation* of the input features. Each successive layer in a neural network model can be viewed as an *increasingly meaningful representation* of the input features. The *deep* in deep learning has to do with the number of layers that are used in the neural network model. Some model architectures require dozens, or even hundreds, of layers, and these types of models are able to learn very complex tasks such as speech recognition, image classification, language processing, image captioning, automatic translation, and other artificial intelligence applications. The success of these models comes from their ability to learn automatically useful representations from unstructured data, such as videos, audio, images, text, and so on. However, to train these models, huge amounts of data are required. What is considered *deep* has changed with the arrival of different models and architectures, and it remains fairly arbitrary; there is no line dividing deep-form shallow models; at the time of this writing, my own estimation is that a model of say 24 layers or more would be considered by most people as a deep learning model.

Neural network models are inspired by the biological brain—the analogy is that just as the neurons in brains calculate something and are connected, **neurons** in artificial neural networks also calculate and are connected, forming networks of interconnected neurons, also called **units**. In reality, the analogy ends there; biological brains are complicated structures, and there is still a lot that we don't know about how they work. So, if someone asks you whether your neural network model works like a brain, the answer is an emphatic, *No.*

Since the datasets we are working with are relatively small, we won't be building deep learning models; our models will have only a few layers; however, the point here is to present the fundamental concepts about these models and learn to train the most fundamental type of neural network—the MLPs.

Anatomy of an MLP – elements of a neural network model

When you enter the world of neural networks or deep learning, you encounter many new terms that can be confusing at first. Some of these new terms have to do with the neural network models themselves, and some of them with the training process. Let's introduce the components of the neural network models that we will use in this chapter—the MLP. This is the most basic type of neural network. Before giving a definition, it is a good idea to clarify the hierarchy that defines this model—neural networks are made of layers, and layers are made of neurons.

Neurons: These are also called **artificial neurons** and are the computational units on neural network models, which is why they are also sometimes called **units**. The neurons we will learn about in this chapter are mathematical functions that receive n inputs, or a vector of inputs—$\mathbf{x} = [x_1, x_2, x_3, \ldots, x_n]$ and return one output; mathematically, they are defined like this:

$$output = g(w_1 x_1 + w_2 x_2 + w_3 x_3 + \ldots + w_n x_n + b) = g(\sum_{i=1}^{n} w_i x_i + b)$$

The almost-universal visual representation of a neuron looks something like this (a neuron with two inputs):

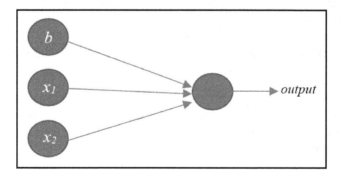

These types of neurons have three elements:

- **Weights**: The set of w's you see in the equation multiplying each of the inputs.
- **Bias**: In our equation, it is the b that is added to the summation; there are technical reasons why this constant will make the model better.

- **Activation function**: This is the g in our equation. It is the component that introduces the nonlinearity in the neural network models. There are standard activation functions such as `Sigmoid`, `Hyperbolic Tangent`, or the `ReLU`. Here, you have the plot of these very commonly used activation functions:

```
x = np.linspace(-5, 5, 200)

fig, ax = plt.subplots(nrows=1, ncols=3, figsize=(10,4))
ax[0].plot(x, 1/(1+np.exp(-x)))
ax[0].set_title('Sigmoid')
ax[1].plot(x, np.tanh(x))
ax[1].set_title('Hyperbolic Tangent')

ax[2].plot(x, np.maximum(0, x))
ax[2].set_title('ReLU')

for p in ax:
    p.grid()
```

The output is as follows:

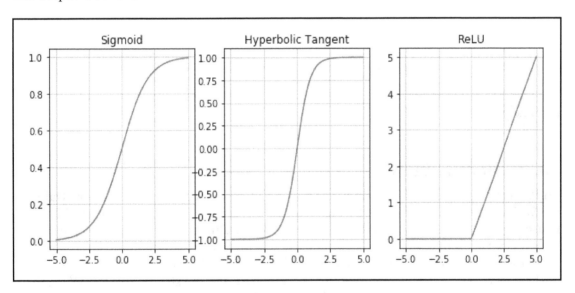

Layers: The layers are made of neurons. A layer is like a data-processing module of the model—it receives inputs and produces outputs; mathematically, a layer can be considered a function that receives k inputs and returns m outputs. Layers are the components that extract useful representations from the data. There are different kinds of layers; the types of layers we will use are called **dense** or **fully connected** layers.

Neural network: This is a model that consists of a number of successive layers. By their position, we can have different types of layers:

- **Input layer**: This is the layer consisting of the features in our dataset.
- **Hidden layers**: The internal layers of the neural network; this is where processing and learning takes place.
- **Output layer**: The layer that produces the outputs. In the case of a regression task, it would be the prediction, and in the case of a classification, it would usually be the probabilities for each of the categories.

The usual visual representation that you will find of an MLP is something such as this:

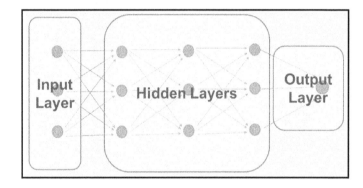

Now that we know about the basic components of an MLP, let's talk about how they learn to make predictions.

How MLPs learn

MLPs can be considered to be parametric models; just like the multiple regression, training the MLP means to find the correct set of weights (w's) and biases such that the model learns to use the input features to produce the target. In the multiple regression model, the set of weights that are found are the best in the sense that no other combination of weights will make the sum of quadratic errors smaller. With MLPs, we try to do a similar thing—find the best set of weights; however, due to the complexity and the structure of the MLPs, there are technical reasons why it is not possible to find the best set of weights, so training the MLP means finding a set of weights and biases that are "good enough" so that the model produces good predictions.

Now, we will explain at a high level the training loop of an MLP, which is the sequence of steps by which we train an MLP model. Before entering the loop, we need to initialize the weights of the network randomly, and the biases usually occur with the value of 1. There are rules and best practices for the random initialization, and these best practices are built into the libraries for deep learning. So, for now, don't worry about how this is done. We perform this step before entering the training loop. Now, we will outline the steps in the loop:

1. **Get a batch**: Get a batch of training samples and corresponding targets. Before moving on, one important thing to be aware of is that, generally, neural network models deal with very large datasets, and because of the way they are trained, they do not process the whole training dataset at once; instead, the data is divided into **batches**, and then the data is passed to the neural network one batch at a time. The **batch size** is the amount of samples in a batch. By convention, batch sizes are usually powers of 2: 32, 64, 128, 256, or 512, but, of course, you can use other values, such as 100.

2. **Forward pass**: Feed the batch to the MLP and get the predictions. The second step in the loop is called a forward pass, and it is simply to take the batch of samples, feed them to the network, and get the outputs (predictions).

3. **Calculate the loss**: Compute the loss using the **loss function**. Now that we have the predictions, it is time to use the loss function—a function that will measure how good the predictions are. It produces the signal that will tell the network how close the predictions are to the target values. This function will take the predictions and the target values and will output one number called the **loss**. So, in this step, we compute the loss of the network on the batch—a measure of the mismatch between the predicted and the observed values.

4. **Update the weights**: Update all weights of the network simultaneously in such a way that reduces the loss on the current batch. This is the job of the **optimizer**—this is the element of the model in charge of taking the signal from the loss function and adjust (update) the weights to reduce the loss. The usual mechanism by which this task is done is called **backpropagation**.

This training loop is completed within an **epoch**—which is one complete pass over the training dataset. Suppose your training set is of size 6,400 and the batch size is 64; then the training loop we just described will run for 100 iterations to complete one epoch. Usually, it takes many epochs to train a neural network. In the example we just gave, if the network is trained for 10 epochs, then the initial weights will be updated 100 times per epoch, multiplied for 10 epochs, and this will give us a total of 1,000 updates.

Introducing TensorFlow and Keras

Now we know that neural networks are a special type of machine learning model. Although, usually these models need huge amounts of data to start outperforming other machine learning approaches, one big advantage is that the process of training neural networks can make use of parallelization in hardware such as **graphical processing units (GPUs)**, which do the operations needed for training neural networks faster than traditional CPUs. This is the reason that in the past few years, new specialized software frameworks have been developed with the capacity to make use of GPUs; examples of these frameworks are Theano, Caffe, and TensorFlow. These frameworks have allowed the deep learning models to be used for professionals outside specialized academic circles, thus democratizing the use of these powerful models. In this section, we introduce the two software tools we will use in this chapter—TensorFlow and Keras.

TensorFlow

As we pointed out in Chapter 1, *The Predictive Analytics Process*, TensorFlow is Google's specialized library for deep learning; open sourced in November 2015, it has become the main library for deep learning for both research and production applications in many industries.

From the library's official website (https://www.tensorflow.org/), we get the following description:

> *"TensorFlow™ is an open source software library for high-performance numerical computation. Its flexible architecture allows the easy deployment of computation across a variety of platforms (CPUs, GPUs, TPUs), and from desktops to clusters of servers to mobile and edge devices. Originally developed by researchers and engineers from the Google Brain team within Google's AI organization, it comes with strong support for machine learning and deep learning, and the flexible numerical computation core is used across many other scientific domains.*

There are two versions of TensorFlow:

- A GPU
- A CPU version

From the documentation, we read the following:

- **TensorFlow with CPU support only**. If your system does not have an NVIDIA® GPU, you must install this version. Note that this version of TensorFlow is typically much easier to install (typically, in 5 or 10 minutes), so even if you have an NVIDIA GPU, we recommend installing this version first.
- **TensorFlow with GPU support**. TensorFlow programs typically run significantly faster on a GPU than on a CPU. Therefore, if your system has an NVIDIA® GPU meeting, the prerequisites shown next, and you need to run performance-critical applications, you should ultimately install this version.

So, training neural network models is usually faster in a GPU, and if you are working with very large datasets, it would be absolutely necessary to use the GPU version; of course, you will need to have the corresponding hardware to work with. If you don't have a GPU in your machine, there are now services such as `FloydHub` and `PaperSpace` that basically rent you hardware so you can train and deploy your deep learning models. If you have a GPU in your machine, you could install the TensorFlow-GPU version; however, the installation is still tricky, and very platform-dependent; since we are just introducing the topic (this is not a book about deep learning), we will follow the recommendation given by the TensorFlow guys and install the CPU-only version. If you are interested, you can view the requirements for the GPU version on the `official website`. To install TensorFlow (if using Anaconda) with your virtual environment activated, run the following command in the Anaconda prompt:

```
pip install --ignore-installed --upgrade tensorflow
```

TensorFlow includes many advanced computing capabilities, and it is based on a dataflow programming paradigm—TensorFlow programs work by first building a computational graph and then running the computations described in the graph within specialized objects called **sessions**, which are in charge of placing the computations on to devices such as CPUs or GPUs. This computing paradigm is not as straightforward to use and understand, which is why we won't use TensorFlow directly in our examples. In the examples presented in this chapter, TensorFlow will act as a backend, and it will be the software that will perform all the calculations behind the scenes. The library we will use as an interface to build our neural network models is Keras.

Keras – deep learning for humans

Instead of using TensorFlow directly, we will use Keras to build our neural network models. Keras is a great, user-friendly library that serves as a frontend for TensorFlow (or other deep learning libraries such as Theano). The main goal of Keras is "deep learning for humans." In my opinion, Keras fulfills this goal because it makes the development of deep learning models easy and intuitive. From the official website (`https://keras.io/`), we read the following:

> *"Keras is a high level neural networks API, written in Python and capable of running on top of* TensorFlow, CNTK, *or* Theano. *It was developed with a focus on enabling fast experimentation. Being able to go from idea to result with the least possible delay is key to doing good research."*

Let's install Keras in our Anaconda virtual environment. Keep in mind that **the installation of TensorFlow must be done first**. Just run the following command in your Anaconda prompt:

```
pip install keras
```

That's it! We are finally ready to start building our neural network models, and we will learn how to use Keras in the process.

Regressing with neural networks

We will again use our diamonds dataset. Although this is a small dataset and MLP is perhaps a model that is too complicated for this problem, there is no reason we could not use an MLP to solve it; in addition to this, remember that back when we defined the hypothetical problem, we established that the stakeholders wanted a model that was as accurate as possible in their predictions, so let's see how accurate we can get with an MLP. As always, let's import the libraries we will use:

```
import numpy as np
import pandas as pd
import matplotlib.pyplot as plt
import seaborn as sns
import os
%matplotlib inline
```

Now, since we are beginning from scratch, load and prepare the dataset:

```
DATA_DIR = '../data'
FILE_NAME = 'diamonds.csv'
data_path = os.path.join(DATA_DIR, FILE_NAME)
diamonds = pd.read_csv(data_path)
## Preparation done from Chapter 2
diamonds = diamonds.loc[(diamonds['x']>0) | (diamonds['y']>0)]
diamonds.loc[11182, 'x'] = diamonds['x'].median()
diamonds.loc[11182, 'z'] = diamonds['z'].median()
diamonds = diamonds.loc[~((diamonds['y'] > 30) | (diamonds['z'] > 30))]
diamonds = pd.concat([diamonds, pd.get_dummies(diamonds['cut'],
prefix='cut', drop_first=True)], axis=1)
diamonds = pd.concat([diamonds, pd.get_dummies(diamonds['color'],
prefix='color', drop_first=True)], axis=1)
diamonds = pd.concat([diamonds, pd.get_dummies(diamonds['clarity'],
prefix='clarity', drop_first=True)], axis=1)
```

Now, let's apply the transformations we did to this dataset before modeling:

Split these into training and testing sets:

```
X = diamonds.drop(['cut','color','clarity','price'], axis=1)
y = diamonds['price']
from sklearn.model_selection import train_test_split
X_train, X_test, y_train, y_test = train_test_split(X, y, test_size=0.1,
random_state=123)
```

Perform dimensionality reduction on x, y, and z with PCA:

```
from sklearn.decomposition import PCA
pca = PCA(n_components=1, random_state=123)
pca.fit(X_train[['x','y','z']])
X_train['dim_index'] = pca.transform(X_train[['x','y','z']]).flatten()
X_train.drop(['x','y','z'], axis=1, inplace=True)
```

And here is the last step—standardize the numerical features:

```
numerical_features = ['carat', 'depth', 'table', 'dim_index']
from sklearn.preprocessing import StandardScaler
scaler = StandardScaler()
scaler.fit(X_train[numerical_features])
X_train.loc[:, numerical_features] =
scaler.transform(X_train[numerical_features])
```

We are ready to build our neural network model.

Building the MLP for predicting diamond prices

As we said before, neural network models consist of a number sequential layers, which is why Keras has a class called `Sequential` that we can use to instantiate a neural network model:

```
from keras.models import Sequential
nn_reg = Sequential()
```

Good! We have created an empty neural network called `nn_reg`. Now, we have to add layers to it. We will use what is known as fully connected or **dense layers**—these are layers made of neurons that are connected with all neurons from the previous layer. In other words, every neuron in a dense layer receives the output of all the neurons from the previous layer. Our MLP will be made of dense layers. Let's import the `Dense` class:

```
from keras.layers import Dense
```

As we discussed in our conceptual section, the first layer in an MLP is always the input layer, the one that will receive the data of the features and pass it to the first hidden layer. However, in Keras, there is no need to create an input layer, because this layer is basically the features. So, you will not explicitly see the input layer in the code, but conceptually it is there. With that point clear, the first layer we will add to our empty neural network is the first hidden layer; this is a special layer, because we need to specify (as a tuple) the shape of the input; from the Keras documentation, we read that the first layer in a sequential model (and only the first, because the following layers can do automatic shape inference) needs to receive information about its input shape. Now, we will add this first layer:

```
n_input = X_train.shape[1]
n_hidden1 = 32
# adding first hidden layer
nn_reg.add(Dense(units=n_hidden1, activation='relu',
input_shape=(n_input,)))
```

Let's understand each of the parameters:

- `units`: This is the number of neurons in the layer; we are using 32
- `activation`: This is the activation function that will be used in each of the neurons; we are using ReLU
- `input_shape`: This is the number of inputs the network will receive, which is equal to the number of predictive features in our dataset; we don't need to specify how many samples the network will receive, as it can deal with any number of them

Our neural network now has one hidden layer; since this is a relatively simple problem and we have a relatively small dataset, we will add only two more hidden layers, for a total of three. Few people would call this a deep learning model, since we have only three layers, but the process of building and training is essentially the same with three or with 300 hidden layers. This is our first neural network model, so I consider it to be a good start. Let's add the next two hidden layers:

```
n_hidden2 = 16
n_hidden3 = 8
# add second hidden layer
nn_reg.add(Dense(units=n_hidden2, activation='relu'))
# add third hidden layer
nn_reg.add(Dense(units=n_hidden3, activation='relu'))
```

Notice the number of units we are using in our successive layers—32, 16, and 8. First, we are using powers of 2, which is a common practice in the field, and second we are shaping our network as a funnel—we are going from 32 units to 8 units; there is nothing special about this shape but, empirically, sometimes it works very well. Another common approach would be to use the same number of neurons in each hidden layer.

To finish our neural network, we need to add the final layer—the output layer. Since this is a regression problem for each sample, we want only one output—the prediction for the price, so we need to add a layer that connects the 8 outputs from the previews layer to one output that will give us the price prediction. In this last layer, there is no need for an activation function, since we are getting the final prediction:

```
# output layer
nn_reg.add(Dense(units=1, activation=None))
```

Great! Our model architecture has been defined—our neural network, just like the other models we built before, is a function that will take the values of 21 features and will produce one number as output—the predicted price.

Our neural network has been built. In fact, if you feed it data, you will get price predictions; here, you have the predictions for the first 5 diamonds in the training set:

```
nn_reg.predict(X_train.iloc[:5, :])
```

The output will be as follows:

```
array([[ 0.01396593],
       [-0.07197536],
       [-0.07281694],
       [ 0.10343548],
       [ 0.22442862]], dtype=float32)
```

These are the price predictions, and they are, of course, very bad predictions. Why is this? Because every neuron in our network has randomly initialized weights, and biases are all initialized as 1's. Keras, by default, uses an initialization procedure called **Glorot uniform initializer**, also called **Xavier uniform initializer** (Glorot & Bengio, 2010), which is one of the most popular ways of initializing neural networks and that has been proven very useful in practice. There are other initialization schemes, but a discussion about those is outside our scope. We are going to trust the good and smart developers of Keras and use their defaults.

Now, it is time to start modifying these random weights and biases, little by little, using our training data, and now we will enter the training loop.

Training the MLP

Now, we will use data for training our neural network so it learns how to map the values of the features to predict the prices. I will repeat some of the things I have already said in the conceptual section, so excuse me for being a bit redundant, but the goal is to present the concepts as clearly as possible.

There are four decisions we have to make at this stage:

- **Batch size**: The number of observations the network will see at each step of the training loop. This decision is actually not very complicated; for a problem such as ours, we can try a batch size of 32, 64, or 128. There is good evidence that it is better to use small numbers, no bigger than 512 (Shirish et al., 2017).
- **Number of epochs**: How many times the network will see the entire training dataset to adjust the weights. Here, we need to be a bit more careful, because if there are too few the network will not learn well; if there are too many networks will overfit to our training data. Let's try 50. Why? Well, it is just my first guess, because it is a relatively simple problem. We can try other values of course, and we'll do this later.

- **Loss function**: As we said before, the loss function produces the signal that will tell the network how good the predictions are. In the case of regression problems, the most commonly used loss function is the MSE, the one that we have used before in other models to measure their performance. Of course, there are other loss functions that we can use, but for the moment we will stick to MSE.
- **Optimizer**: This is the element by which the network will use the signal produced by the loss function and update the weights and biases of the network. There are many choices of optimizers, and researchers keep making progress in this area, but essentially all optimizers are variations of the gradient descent (https://en.wikipedia.org/wiki/Gradient_descent) optimization algorithm. Again, this is a very technical issue, and we will use the Adam optimizer, which has become very popular because it has been shown to work well for a variety of problems. Please refer to the *Further reading* section for more resources about optimizers.

Once we have made these four decisions, we can **compile** our model—this is telling Keras both the loss function and the optimizer we want to use:

```
nn_reg.compile(loss='mean_squared_error', optimizer='adam')
```

If you want to take a look at the architecture and the number of parameters in your model, you can use the `summary` method:

```
nn_reg.summary()
```

The output will be as follows:

Layer (type)	Output Shape	Param #
dense_1 (Dense)	(None, 32)	704
dense_2 (Dense)	(None, 16)	528
dense_3 (Dense)	(None, 8)	136
dense_4 (Dense)	(None, 1)	9

Total params: 1,377
Trainable params: 1,377
Non-trainable params: 0

We have a total of 1,377 weights and biases in our model. Now, we are ready to train our model using the `fit` method:

```
batch_size = 64
n_epochs = 50
nn_reg.fit(X_train, y_train, epochs=n_epochs, batch_size=batch_size)
```

In the training process, you will see something such as this:

```
Epoch 1/50
48537/48537 [==============================] - 1s 17us/step - loss: 14830316.2529
Epoch 2/50
48537/48537 [==============================] - 1s 11us/step - loss: 1737586.2522
Epoch 3/50
48537/48537 [==============================] - 1s 11us/step - loss: 1222372.8833
Epoch 4/50
48537/48537 [==============================] - 1s 12us/step - loss: 1033083.3758
Epoch 5/50
48537/48537 [==============================] - 1s 12us/step - loss: 917965.2226
Epoch 6/50
48537/48537 [==============================] - 1s 12us/step - loss: 829952.7295
Epoch 7/50
48537/48537 [==============================] - 1s 12us/step - loss: 762489.6997
Epoch 8/50
48537/48537 [==============================] - 1s 11us/step - loss: 714690.7879
Epoch 9/50
```

This mainly shows, with every epoch, how the training loss is reduced. Remember that the training loop we talked about was previously done in every epoch, in our case, 50 times. This is great! We have trained our first neural network!

Making predictions with the neural network

It is time to evaluate how good the predictions are that the network makes. We will compare both the training and the testing performances using MSE. But first, remember we have to perform the same transformations we did in our training set to our testing set:

```
## PCA for dimentionality reduction:
X_test['dim_index'] = pca.transform(X_test[['x','y','z']]).flatten()
X_test.drop(['x','y','z'], axis=1, inplace=True)
## Scale our numerical features so they have zero mean and a variance of
one
X_test.loc[:, numerical_features] =
scaler.transform(X_test[numerical_features])
```

Now, make predictions using the `predict` method and calculate the MSE:

```
from sklearn.metrics import mean_squared_error
y_pred_train = nn_reg.predict(X_train)
y_pred_test = nn_reg.predict(X_test)
train_mse = mean_squared_error(y_true=y_train, y_pred=y_pred_train)
test_mse = mean_squared_error(y_true=y_test, y_pred=y_pred_test)
print("Train MSE: {:0.3f} \nTest MSE: {:0.3f}".format(train_mse/1e6,
test_mse/1e6))
```

This will give us the following output:

```
Train MSE: 0.320
Test MSE: 0.331
```

You may get different values due to the randomness involved in the training process, but the values shouldn't be too far away.

This is very impressive! Here, we have the results of the models we introduced in the previous chapter:

	train	test
MLR	1.28101	1.20721
Lasso	1.52062	1.40893
KNN	0.670249	0.780698

We reduced the best testing MSE by more than half using a relatively small network!

Neural networks are very powerful indeed; although there has been a lot of hype around them, there is something truly remarkable about these models.

Classification with neural networks

Now, let's perform our classification task using a neural network. As you will see, the only change necessary in an MLP for it to be able to perform classification is in the output layer:

```
import numpy as np
import pandas as pd
import matplotlib.pyplot as plt
import seaborn as sns
import os
%matplotlib inline
```

As always, let's start from scratch and import and prepare our data:

```
# Loading the dataset
DATA_DIR = '../data'
FILE_NAME = 'credit_card_default.csv'
data_path = os.path.join(DATA_DIR, FILE_NAME)
ccd = pd.read_csv(data_path, index_col="ID")
ccd.rename(columns=lambda x: x.lower(), inplace=True)
ccd.rename(columns={'default payment next month':'default'}, inplace=True)

# getting the groups of features
bill_amt_features = ['bill_amt'+ str(i) for i in range(1,7)]
pay_amt_features = ['pay_amt'+ str(i) for i in range(1,7)]
numerical_features = ['limit_bal','age'] + bill_amt_features +
pay_amt_features

# Creating creating binary features
ccd['male'] = (ccd['sex'] == 1).astype('int')
ccd['grad_school'] = (ccd['education'] == 1).astype('int')
ccd['university'] = (ccd['education'] == 2).astype('int')
#ccd['high_school'] = (ccd['education'] == 3).astype('int')
ccd['married'] = (ccd['marriage'] == 1).astype('int')

# simplifying pay features
pay_features= ['pay_' + str(i) for i in range(1,7)]
for x in pay_features:
    ccd.loc[ccd[x] <= 0, x] = 0

# simplifying delayed features
delayed_features = ['delayed_' + str(i) for i in range(1,7)]
for pay, delayed in zip(pay_features, delayed_features):
    ccd[delayed] = (ccd[pay] > 0).astype(int)
# creating a new feature: months delayed
ccd['months_delayed'] = ccd[delayed_features].sum(axis=1)
```

Now, split and standardize the dataset:

```
numerical_features = numerical_features + ['months_delayed']
binary_features = ['male','married','grad_school','university']
X = ccd[numerical_features + binary_features]
y = ccd['default'].astype(int)

## Split
from sklearn.model_selection import train_test_split
X_train, X_test, y_train, y_test = train_test_split(X, y, test_size=5/30,
random_state=101)

## Standarize
```

```
from sklearn.preprocessing import StandardScaler
scaler = StandardScaler()
scaler.fit(X_train[numerical_features])
X_train.loc[:, numerical_features] =
scaler.transform(X_train[numerical_features])
```

Building the MLP for predicting credit card default

We are ready; let's create our empty neural network:

```
from keras.models import Sequential
nn_classifier = Sequential()
```

For the architecture of this network, instead of a funnel shape, we will try another approach; let's give every layer the same number of units. Here, we have the first hidden layer:

```
from keras.layers import Dense
n_input = X_train.shape[1]
n_units_hidden = 64
nn_classifier.add(Dense(units=n_units_hidden, activation='relu',
input_shape=(n_input,)))
```

For now, let's use another four layers for a total of five:

```
# add 2nd hidden layer
nn_classifier.add(Dense(units=n_units_hidden, activation='relu'))
# add 3th hidden layer
nn_classifier.add(Dense(units=n_units_hidden, activation='relu'))
# add 4th hidden layer
nn_classifier.add(Dense(units=n_units_hidden, activation='relu'))
# add 5th hidden layer
nn_classifier.add(Dense(units=n_units_hidden, activation='relu'))
```

The last part of our network is the output layer. Since we are doing binary classification, for the output layer, we would like to have the probability of a default; since we want a probability, the output has to be a single number between 0 and 1. This is the reason we are using one unit (the output), and we are using the sigmoid as an activation function, which, as you can see in the image from the previous section, takes any real number and maps this number to a value in the interval $(0,1)$, which can be interpreted as a probability:

```
# output layer
nn_classifier.add(Dense(units=1, activation='sigmoid'))
```

Now, we can proceed with the compilation step:

```
nn_classifier.compile(loss='binary_crossentropy', optimizer='adam')
```

We are using a new loss function—binary_crossentropy—this is a special case of the general cross entropy concept coming from an information theory, which measures the distance between two probability distributions; this loss function is low when the model produces values close to 1 when y_true=1 and values close to 0 when y_true=0. This is the most popular and standard loss function for binary classification problems, so we will use it in this example.

Here is the summary of the model:

```
nn_classifier.summary()
```

The output will be as follows:

```
Layer (type)                    Output Shape               Param #
=================================================================
dense_1 (Dense)                 (None, 64)                 1280

dense_2 (Dense)                 (None, 64)                 4160

dense_3 (Dense)                 (None, 64)                 4160

dense_4 (Dense)                 (None, 64)                 4160

dense_5 (Dense)                 (None, 64)                 4160

dense_6 (Dense)                 (None, 1)                  65
=================================================================
Total params: 17,985
Trainable params: 17,985
Non-trainable params: 0
```

We see that we have many more parameters to train, compared to the regression model, that is, 17,985 parameters. Before moving on and running the training step, let's save the initial weights of our network. You will see why in a moment:

```
nn_classifier.save_weights('class_initial_w.h5')
```

Now, for training, let's try with 150 epochs and a batch size of 64. Now we are ready to train the model:

```
batch_size = 64
n_epochs = 150
nn_classifier.fit(X_train, y_train, epochs=n_epochs, batch_size=batch_size)
```

Evaluating predictions

Once the network is done with the training process, it is time for us take a look at the predictions, and we will calculate the estimated probabilities for both training and testing datasets; then we will use the default threshold of 0.5 to make the predictions:

```
## Getting the probabilities
y_pred_train_prob = nn_classifier.predict(X_train)
y_pred_test_prob = nn_classifier.predict(X_test)

## Classifications from predictions
y_pred_train = (y_pred_train_prob > 0.5).astype(int)
y_pred_test = (y_pred_test_prob > 0.5).astype(int)
```

Now, take a look at the accuracy score for both sets:

```
from sklearn.metrics import accuracy_score
train_acc = accuracy_score(y_true=y_train, y_pred=y_pred_train)
test_acc = accuracy_score(y_true=y_test, y_pred=y_pred_test)
print("Train Accuracy: {:0.3f} \nTest Accuracy: {:0.3f}".format(train_acc,
test_acc))
```

This is what we get:

```
Train Accuracy: 0.902
Test Accuracy: 0.728
```

Unlike our fantastic results in the diamond prices problem, here we are not getting great results. There is no guarantee that a more complicated model will give you better performance than a simple one. But maybe we are not using the correct neural network... Welcome to the dark art of training neural networks.

The dark art of training neural networks

From the results we got, we can see that there is a clear symptom of overfitting—the training accuracy looks great (91%), but the testing accuracy is lower than even random guessing. The most likely two causes for this are as follows:

- The model has too many parameters
- The model has been trained for too long

Since we are overfitting, we need to try some regularization technique; the simplest in the case of neural networks is training the model for fewer epochs. Now, let's get the initial weights and biases of the network back to the original values (the ones we saved in the a.h5 file):

```
nn_classifier.load_weights('class_initial_w.h5')
```

Now the weights have been reset, let's train our model again, this time only for 50 epochs:

```
batch_size = 64
n_epochs = 50
nn_classifier.compile(loss='binary_crossentropy', optimizer='adam')
nn_classifier.fit(X_train, y_train, epochs=n_epochs, batch_size=batch_size)
```

Now, again, calculate the results:

```
## Getting the probabilities
y_pred_train_prob = nn_classifier.predict(X_train)
y_pred_test_prob = nn_classifier.predict(X_test)

## Classifications from predictions
y_pred_train = (y_pred_train_prob > 0.5).astype(int)
y_pred_test = (y_pred_test_prob > 0.5).astype(int)

## Calculating accuracy
train_acc = accuracy_score(y_true=y_train, y_pred=y_pred_train)
test_acc = accuracy_score(y_true=y_test, y_pred=y_pred_test)
print("Train Accuracy: {:0.3f} \nTest Accuracy: {:0.3f}".format(train_acc,
test_acc))
```

These are the results:

```
Train Accuracy: 0.847
Test Accuracy: 0.629
```

It seems that the problem, although less extreme, is still there. Welcome to training neural networks—the dark art of guessing the correct configuration.

So many decisions; so little time

This is one of the main drawbacks of using neural networks in predictive analytics; there are so many decisions to make that you are very unlikely to guess a good configuration when solving a problem. For the model architecture (hidden layers, input, and output layers are fixed by the problem), you have to make decisions about the following:

1. The number of layers
2. The number of units in each layer
3. The activation function to use in each layer
4. The weight initialization method

For the compilation step, you have to make choices about the following:

5. The loss function
6. The optimizer
7. The parameters of the optimizer

For the training step you have to decide the following:

8. The batch size
9. The number of epochs

Finally, because neural networks are very susceptible to overfitting, you will almost always need to perform regularization, so there are two more decisions:

10. The type of regularization
11. The parameters of the regularization

Just for the sake of argument, and for a quick calculation, let's say that you have three options for each of your decisions. The total number of combinations is $3^{11} = 177,147$ possible configurations for your model. Let's say that you only consider 10% of those combinations; even if the network takes only 1 second to train and evaluate (a very unrealistic assumption), it would be really impractical to try so many configurations one by one to find the best, and even the best combination may not give very good results. The good news is that there are many practical tips, theoretical, and empirical results that will narrow your search space and that will make you choose good values for the configuration of your network. The bad news is that understanding some of these results and how to use them effectively requires some advanced technical knowledge, and even after getting that understanding there is still a lot of trial and error involved in the process of training neural networks.

Regularization for neural networks

In this section, we will talk about two methods to avoid overfitting in MLP. The first one has to do with the number of epochs you use. Remember that the training loop we explained earlier runs for every epoch; each step of the loop updates the weights of the network and decreases the loss, which leads to better predictions on the training data. However, if we run the network for too many epochs, the predictions will also start fitting to the noise in the training data; in other words, too many epochs can lead to overfitting. One way to address this problem is to stop the training of the network when the loss (or some other performance metric) stops improving. We must be careful here, as the training loss will (almost) always decrease, and in that sense, it does not stop improving. What we need to monitor is another quantity—the **validation loss.** This is a loss that is calculated on a **validation set**—which is a small subset of the training dataset that is not used for training, but it is used for **hyperparameter tuning**. We will talk more about hyperparameter tuning in the next chapter. In this case, we will use the validation set to monitor the loss in a set that is independent of the training set.

Using a validation set

Before implementing early stopping, let's see how easy it is in Keras to monitor a loss that is calculated in a validation set; here, we will build another neural network for the diamond prices dataset:

```
nn_reg2 = Sequential()
n_hidden = 64
# hidden layers
nn_reg2.add(Dense(units=n_hidden, activation='relu',
input_shape=(n_input,)))
nn_reg2.add(Dense(units=n_hidden, activation='relu'))
nn_reg2.add(Dense(units=n_hidden, activation='relu'))
nn_reg2.add(Dense(units=n_hidden, activation='relu'))
nn_reg2.add(Dense(units=n_hidden, activation='relu'))
nn_reg2.add(Dense(units=n_hidden, activation='relu'))
# output layer
nn_reg2.add(Dense(units=1, activation=None))
nn_reg2.compile(loss='mean_squared_error', optimizer='adam',
metrics=['mse', 'mae'])
nn_reg2.summary()
```

The output will be as follows:

```
Layer (type)                    Output Shape              Param #
=================================================================
dense_30 (Dense)                (None, 64)                1408
_____
dense_31 (Dense)                (None, 64)                4160
_____
dense_32 (Dense)                (None, 64)                4160
_____
dense_33 (Dense)                (None, 64)                4160
_____
dense_34 (Dense)                (None, 64)                4160
_____
dense_35 (Dense)                (None, 64)                4160
_____
dense_36 (Dense)                (None, 1)                 65
=================================================================
Total params: 22,273
Trainable params: 22,273
Non-trainable params: 0
```

For using a validation dataset, we simply have to use the `validation_split` parameter
when fitting the model, to indicate the fraction of the training data to be used for validation.
As explained before, the model will set apart this fraction of the training data, will not train
on it, and will evaluate the loss and any model metrics on this data at the end of each
epoch. In Keras, the validation data is selected from the last samples in the x and y data
provided, before shuffling. Now, let's use 10% of the training data for validation:

```
batch_size = 64
n_epochs = 300
history = nn_reg2.fit(X_train, y_train,
                      epochs=n_epochs,
                      batch_size=batch_size,
                      validation_split=0.1)
```

When we start the training process, Keras shows us the metrics and loss for both training and validation sets:

```
Train on 43683 samples, validate on 4854 samples
Epoch 1/200
43683/43683 [==============================] - 1s 34us/step - loss: 4055990.1263 - mean_squared_error: 4055990.1263 - mean_abs
olute_error: 956.1925 - val_loss: 858424.0533 - val_mean_squared_error: 858424.0533 - val_mean_absolute_error: 466.2541
Epoch 2/200
43683/43683 [==============================] - 1s 20us/step - loss: 663071.1309 - mean_squared_error: 663071.1309 - mean_absol
ute_error: 424.6258 - val_loss: 597554.1679 - val_mean_squared_error: 597554.1679 - val_mean_absolute_error: 401.7508
Epoch 3/200
43683/43683 [==============================] - 1s 19us/step - loss: 520859.1741 - mean_squared_error: 520859.1741 - mean_absol
ute_error: 382.6596 - val_loss: 507527.5170 - val_mean_squared_error: 507527.5170 - val_mean_absolute_error: 377.5142
Epoch 4/200
43683/43683 [==============================] - 1s 20us/step - loss: 436868.4289 - mean_squared_error: 436868.4289 - mean_absol
ute_error: 362.6997 - val_loss: 426952.9810 - val_mean_squared_error: 426952.9810 - val_mean_absolute_error: 354.5501
Epoch 5/200
43683/43683 [==============================] - 1s 19us/step - loss: 389967.3728 - mean_squared_error: 389967.3728 - mean_absol
ute_error: 347.0831 - val_loss: 416801.4770 - val_mean_squared_error: 416801.4770 - val_mean_absolute_error: 358.8682
```

The `history` object has a dictionary inside, also called `history` that records the different values for the metrics and losses during each epoch. We can use these values to visualize how the loss behaves with each epoch; we are taking the logarithm just for making the visualization clearer:

```
fig, ax = plt.subplots(figsize=(8,5))
ax.plot(np.log(history.history['loss']), label='Training Loss')
ax.plot(np.log(history.history['val_loss']), label='Validation Loss')
ax.set_title("log(Loss) vs. epochs", fontsize=15)
ax.set_xlabel("epoch number", fontsize=14)
ax.legend(fontsize=12)
ax.set_ylim(12,14)
ax.grid();
```

We will get the following output:

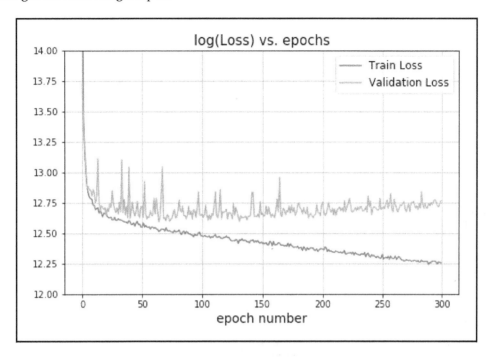

What we observe is something typical when training neural networks—as we mentioned before, the training loss always decreases with each epoch because that is what the training process is doing—adjusting the weights so that the loss is smaller. However, as we have said before, what really matters is generalization—how well the model can predict using unseen data; in this case, the unseen data is the 10% of validation data that we are using. We see that the validation loss decreases for the first few epochs and then it starts increasing, and this is an indication that the network has stopped learning the relationship between features and target and it is just learning the noise in the training data.

We can also monitor other metrics that we can set during the compilation step; here, we are using another popular metric for evaluating regression models—**mean absolute error** (**MAE**). As with other regression metrics, the smaller the better. We will talk more about this metric in the next chapter; for now, let's see how the training and validation loss vary with the number of epochs:

```
fig, ax = plt.subplots(figsize=(8,5))
ax.plot(history.history['mean_absolute_error'], label='Train MAE')
ax.plot(history.history['val_mean_absolute_error'], label='Validation MAE')
ax.set_title("MAE vs. epochs", fontsize=15)
ax.set_xlabel("epoch number", fontsize=14)
```

```
ax.legend(fontsize=12)
ax.set_ylim(200,500)
ax.grid();
```

We will get the following output:

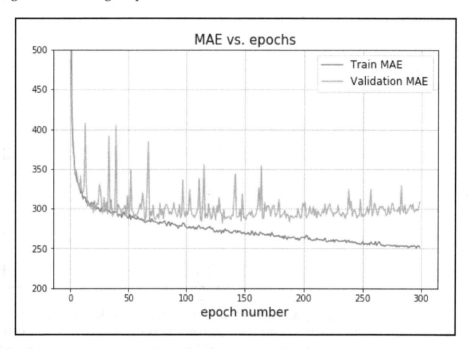

The behavior we see is the same for both plots—constant improvement in the training metrics; however, in the validation metrics, first we observe a decrease and then an increase. We are training this network for **300** epochs, and this is perhaps too much; according to the plots, we should stop training much earlier, and we should only be training for between 40 and 70 epochs. Now, let's implement early stopping.

Early stopping

For implementing early stopping in Keras, we will use an instance of a class of objects called **callbacks**; according to the documentation (https://keras.io/callbacks/), a callback is the following:

"A callback is a set of functions to be applied at given stages of the training procedure. You can use callbacks to get a view on internal states and statistics of the model during training. You can pass a list of callbacks (as the keyword argument callbacks) to the .fit() method of the Sequential or Model classes. The relevant methods of the callbacks will then be called at each stage of the training."

We will use one of these callbacks—`EarlyStopping`. First, we instantiate the object, and then we can use it to control training. The arguments we can configure are the following:

- `monitor`: Quantity to be monitored.
- `min_delta`: Minimum change in the monitored quantity to qualify as an improvement; that is, an absolute change of less than `min_delta`, will count as no improvement.
- `patience`: Number of epochs with no improvement after which training will be stopped.
- `verbose`: Verbosity mode.
- `mode`: One of the following: `auto`, `min`, `max`. In `min` mode, training will stop when the quantity monitored has stopped decreasing; in `max` mode, it will stop when the quantity monitored has stopped increasing; in `auto` mode, the direction is automatically inferred from the name of the monitored quantity.
- `baseline`: Baseline value for the monitored quantity to reach. Training will stop if the model doesn't show improvement over the baseline.
- `restore_best_weights`: Whether to restore model weights from the epoch with the best value of the monitored quantity. If false, the model weights obtained at the last step of training are used. Here is how we can use early stopping for our example:

```
from keras.callbacks import EarlyStopping
early_stoping =
EarlyStopping(monitor='val_mean_absolute_error',
                            min_delta=5,
                            patience=20,
                            verbose=1,
                            mode='auto')
```

We have configured early stopping in such a way that when the MAE stops improving by more than five units after 20 epochs, training will stop.

Since the network was already trained, we have to build it again (or we could have saved the initial weights) to retrain using early stopping:

```
nn_reg2 = Sequential()
n_hidden = 64
# hidden layers
nn_reg2.add(Dense(units=n_hidden, activation='relu',
input_shape=(n_input,)))
nn_reg2.add(Dense(units=n_hidden, activation='relu'))
nn_reg2.add(Dense(units=n_hidden, activation='relu'))
nn_reg2.add(Dense(units=n_hidden, activation='relu'))
nn_reg2.add(Dense(units=n_hidden, activation='relu'))
nn_reg2.add(Dense(units=n_hidden, activation='relu'))
# output layer
nn_reg2.add(Dense(units=1, activation=None))
# compilation
nn_reg2.compile(loss='mean_squared_error', optimizer='adam',
metrics=['mse', 'mae'])
```

All callbacks must be placed inside a list for passing them when fitting the network. Let's fit our network:

```
batch_size = 64
n_epochs = 300
history = nn_reg2.fit(X_train, y_train,
 epochs=n_epochs,
 batch_size=batch_size,
 validation_split=0.1,
 callbacks=[early_stoping])
```

When using early stopping, the network has stopped after just 59 epochs, meaning that after that we don't see much improvement in the validation metric we are tracking. Let's plot the MAE again:

```
fig, ax = plt.subplots(figsize=(8,5))
ax.plot(history.history['mean_absolute_error'], label='Train MAE')
ax.plot(history.history['val_mean_absolute_error'], label='Validation MAE')
ax.set_title("MAE vs. epochs", fontsize=15)
ax.set_xlabel("epoch number", fontsize=14)
ax.legend(fontsize=12)
ax.set_ylim(200,500)
ax.grid();
```

We will get the following output:

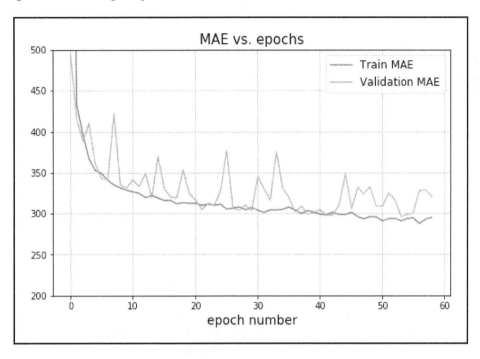

Now, our network is not overfitting anymore; both the training and validation MAEs are relatively close to each other.

Dropout

As you have noticed, neural networks have a huge number of trainable parameters (weights and biases). Even with small MLPs, such as the ones we are working with, we see that we have hundreds or thousands of parameters. In the network we are working with, we have more than 22,000 trainable parameters. This is one of the reasons neural networks overfit very easily, which is why we often have to use some kind of regularization technique.

One of the most popular techniques for neural network regularization is **dropout**, an intuitively simple approach proposed by Hinton et al. (2012). Geoffrey E. Hinton is one of the key researchers in the development of deep learning theory and techniques. The idea is simple—at each step of the training loop, every unit in our network (including input units, but excluding output units) has some fixed probability, say *p* (*p=dropout rate*), of being ignored or dropped during that training step. So, with a drop rate of 0.5, for every step in the training loop, it is like tossing one coin for every neuron in our network, and then, based on the result, deciding whether the weights in that neuron get updated. The logic behind this technique and why it works is as follows—since the units are constantly going on and off the training process, the units cannot rely on one another, reducing the dependency between them and therefore forcing each individual neuron to be as useful as possible for making good predictions. This is why dropout is not only a very useful regularization technique but also often improves the performance of the network.

Using dropout in Keras is also easy; we just add a dropout layer after the layer that we will apply dropout to. For this example, let's build a third network for our regression problem. First, let's import the `Dropout` class:

```
from keras.layers import Dropout
```

Now, let's build our network; notice that the first layer is a `Dropout` layer because we want to apply dropout to our input units. In other words, we are randomly selecting which features to use in every training step, and we are using a dropout rate of 0.3, or 30%:

```
nn_reg_dropout = Sequential()
n_hidden = 64
dropout_rate = 0.3

## Dropout for input layer
nn_reg_dropout.add(Dropout(rate=dropout_rate, input_shape=(n_input,)))

## Now adding four hidden layers + dropout for each of them
nn_reg_dropout.add(Dense(units=n_hidden, activation='relu',
input_shape=(n_input,)))
nn_reg_dropout.add(Dropout(rate=dropout_rate))

nn_reg_dropout.add(Dense(units=n_hidden, activation='relu'))
nn_reg_dropout.add(Dropout(rate=dropout_rate))

nn_reg_dropout.add(Dense(units=n_hidden, activation='relu'))
nn_reg_dropout.add(Dropout(rate=dropout_rate))

nn_reg_dropout.add(Dense(units=n_hidden, activation='relu'))
nn_reg_dropout.add(Dropout(rate=dropout_rate))
```

```
nn_reg_dropout.add(Dense(units=n_hidden, activation='relu'))
nn_reg_dropout.add(Dropout(rate=dropout_rate))

nn_reg_dropout.add(Dense(units=n_hidden, activation='relu'))
nn_reg_dropout.add(Dropout(rate=dropout_rate))

nn_reg_dropout.add(Dense(units=1, activation=None))
```

Take a look at the summary:

```
nn_reg_dropout.summary()
```

The output is given as follows:

```
Layer (type)                    Output Shape              Param #
=================================================================
dropout_7 (Dropout)             (None, 21)                0
_____
dense_26 (Dense)                (None, 64)                1408
_____
dropout_8 (Dropout)             (None, 64)                0
_____
dense_27 (Dense)                (None, 64)                4160
_____
dropout_9 (Dropout)             (None, 64)                0
_____
dense_28 (Dense)                (None, 64)                4160
_____
dropout_10 (Dropout)            (None, 64)                0
_____
dense_29 (Dense)                (None, 64)                4160
_____
dropout_11 (Dropout)            (None, 64)                0
_____
dense_30 (Dense)                (None, 64)                4160
_____
dropout_12 (Dropout)            (None, 64)                0
_____
dense_31 (Dense)                (None, 64)                4160
_____
dropout_13 (Dropout)            (None, 64)                0
_____
dense_32 (Dense)                (None, 1)                 65
=================================================================
Total params: 22,273
Trainable params: 22,273
Non-trainable params: 0
```

Here is the compilation step:

```
nn_reg_dropout.compile(loss='mean_squared_error', optimizer='adam',
metrics=['mse', 'mae'])
```

And, finally, let's train the network using early stopping again, but being more patient; because of dropout, the network will take longer to train, so we are setting `patience=40` for early stopping:

```
batch_size = 64
n_epochs = 300
early_stoping = EarlyStopping(monitor='val_mean_absolute_error',
 min_delta=5,
 patience=40,
 verbose=1,
 mode='auto')

history = nn_reg_dropout.fit(X_train, y_train,
 epochs=n_epochs,
 batch_size=batch_size,
 validation_split=0.1,
 callbacks=[early_stoping])
```

The network was trained for 60 epochs. Now, take a look at the training and validation MAE:

```
fig, ax = plt.subplots(figsize=(8,5))
ax.plot(history.history['mean_absolute_error'], label='Train MAE')
ax.plot(history.history['val_mean_absolute_error'], label='Validation MAE')
ax.set_title("MAE vs. epochs using dropout", fontsize=15)
ax.set_xlabel("epoch number", fontsize=14)
ax.legend(fontsize=12)
ax.grid();
```

We will get the following output:

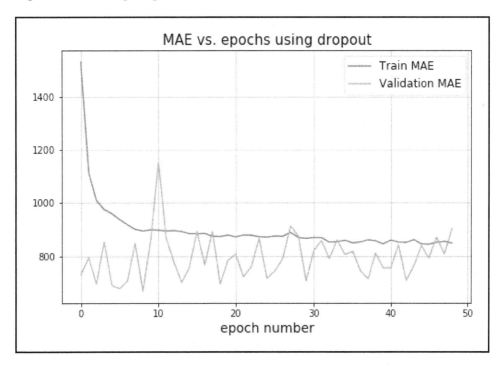

In our case, it looks as though dropout did not help with the validation accuracy of our network, as the validation MAE is much larger than the one we had with no dropout. This is not surprising, because dropout tends to work best for larger networks, those with dozens of layers and hundreds of thousands or millions of parameters. Although dropout was not useful for our example (at least with our network configuration), now you know about dropout regularization and how to use it.

Practical advice on training neural networks

In this section, we provide some practical tips that you may find useful when using and training neural networks, these are simple tips that can make a huge difference. Of course, there are more best practices and results that you can apply, but explaining them is outside the scope of this book:

- Standardize your features before feeding them to the model; MLPs are very sensitive to features in different scales, so always make sure that you do it.
- Start with the small network—use just a few layers with not too many units, and if the performance is not enough, grow the size of your network.
- In general, deeper networks tend to work better than shallow networks with many units per layer.
- Try not to use correlated features, as they can affect network performance.
- Use a validation split to monitor overfitting during training.
- For dropout rate, try values between 0.1 and 0.5.
- Use the Adam optimizer or RMSprop in Keras with the default parameters, choosing the right parameters for an optimizer can be a challenging job. Take a look at the *Further reading* section to learn more.
- Tweak one thing at at time: When you are in this trial-and-error process, tweak one thing at a time, whether you are adjusting the number of layers, number of units per layers, dropout rate, or any other aspect of the network, do it one thing at a time: If you move more than one thing at a time, you will not know what is causing the change in the performance of the network.
- Neural networks work best with large datasets: One of the factors associated with neural network popularity and effectiveness is the size of datasets researchers and companies use to train them, especially for very complicated tasks. Neural networks are very powerful when used with very large datasets. For relatively small datasets, such as the ones we are working within this book; MLPs may or may not be as useful.
- Be patient; these models are just complicated to work with.

Finally, please take into account that MLPs are truly black boxes; we feed data to the neural network and (hopefully) good predictions come out at the other side of the network. However, there is no easy way to know which features are important for predictions or how the network is using the different features.

Summary

In this chapter, we introduced the most fundamental type of deep learning model—the MLP. We covered a lot of new concepts related to this power class of models such as deep learning, neural network models, and the activation functions of neurons. We also learned about TensorFlow, which is a framework to train deep learning models; we used it as a backend for running the calculations necessary to train our models. We covered Keras, where we first build a network, and then we compile it (indicating the loss and optimizer), and finally, we train the model. Lastly, we covered dropout, which is a regularization technique that is often used with neural networks, although it works best with very large networks. To conclude, neural networks are hard to train because they involve making many decisions; a lot of practice and knowledge is needed to be able to use these models effectively for predictive analytics.

In the next chapter, we will learn about evaluation for regression models, evaluation for classification models and model evaluation.

Further reading

- Bengio, Y (2012). *Practical recommendations for gradient-based training of deep architectures. Neural networks: Tricks of the trade* (pp. 437-478).
- Chollet, F (2017). *Deep Learning with Python*, Manning Publications.
- Glorot, X, and Bengio, Y (2010, March). *Understanding the difficulty of training deep feedforward neural networks*. From the proceedings of the 13th international conference on artificial intelligence and statistics (pp. 249-256).
- Keskar, N. S., et al. (2016). *On large-batch training for deep learning: Generalization gap and sharp minima*. arXiv preprint arXiv:1609.04836.

Model Evaluation 7

So far, we have learned a lot about predictive analytics and the fundamentals of regression models—classification models—including simple models such as multiple linear regression and very complex models such as multilayer perceptrons. We know how to train models to make predictions and that it is very important to set apart a testing set for evaluation because we want to evaluate how the model will perform with data that it has not seen before, that is, we want the model to learn something that can be **generalized** to unseen data.

So far, we have been using generic metrics to evaluate model performance—**Mean Squared Error** (**MSE**) for regression problems and accuracy for classification problems. However, in every predictive analytics project, you have to think carefully about the metrics you are using for evaluating the model and the general evaluation strategy and how to connect this strategy with the business problem you are trying to solve.

This chapter is divided into three main sections. First, we talk about evaluation for regression models. Here, we talk about some of the most important and popular metrics for evaluating regression models, and we also present some very useful visualization techniques. Then we go back to our credit card default problem and talk about evaluation for classification models; here we also cover numerical metrics and visualization techniques. We end the chapter with the topic of k-fold cross-validation, which is very important for model evaluation as well as for hyperparameter tuning, which is the subject of the next chapter.

We have the following learning objectives for this chapter:

- Learn about different metrics for regression and classification models
- Learn about custom metrics relating to the business problem
- Learn about the different plots that are used for model evaluation
- Understand how to use different thresholds to produce different classifiers
- Understand the relationship between precision and recall

- Understand the process of k-fold cross-validation
- Learn how to evaluate a model metric using k-fold cross-validation and why it is a good practice

Technical requirements

- Python 3.6 or higher
- Jupyter Notebooks
- Recent versions of the following Python libraries: NumPy, pandas, matplotlib, Seaborn, and scikit-learn

Evaluation of regression models

When evaluating a model, we have numerical metrics and visualization techniques that are complementary ways to asses model performance. In this section, we will go back to our diamond prices problem and we will talk about the most common metrics and plots that are used to evaluate regression models. We will also define our own evaluation metric in the context of the business problem we are trying to solve.

Before we begin, I would like to make a clarification—in this section, we use interchangeably the terms errors and residuals in reference to the difference between actual and predicted value: *actual_price – predicted_price*. Technically, the term **error** refers to a population concept and has to do with a theoretical population value. So, although technically we should not use the term errors meaning residuals, for the sake of clarity we will do it (may the statistics gods forgive me).

As in previous chapters, let's begin by loading the data and doing all the necessary preparation. Perform the following steps:

1. Load the necessary libraries:

```
import numpy as np
import pandas as pd
import matplotlib.pyplot as plt
import seaborn as sns
import os

%matplotlib inline
```

2. Now, load the dataset:

```
DATA_DIR = '../data'
FILE_NAME = 'diamonds.csv'
data_path = os.path.join(DATA_DIR, FILE_NAME)
diamonds = pd.read_csv(data_path)
```

3. And perform all the preparation steps we have done in previous chapters:

```
## Preparation done from Chapter 2
diamonds = diamonds.loc[(diamonds['x']>0) | (diamonds['y']>0)]
diamonds.loc[11182, 'x'] = diamonds['x'].median()
diamonds.loc[11182, 'z'] = diamonds['z'].median()
diamonds = diamonds.loc[~((diamonds['y'] > 30) | (diamonds['z']
> 30))]
diamonds = pd.concat([diamonds, pd.get_dummies(diamonds['cut'],
prefix='cut', drop_first=True)], axis=1)
diamonds = pd.concat([diamonds,
pd.get_dummies(diamonds['color'], prefix='color',
drop_first=True)], axis=1)
diamonds = pd.concat([diamonds,
pd.get_dummies(diamonds['clarity'], prefix='clarity',
drop_first=True)], axis=1)

## Dimensionality reduction
from sklearn.decomposition import PCA
pca = PCA(n_components=1, random_state=123)
diamonds['dim_index'] =
pca.fit_transform(diamonds[['x','y','z']])
diamonds.drop(['x','y','z'], axis=1, inplace=True)
```

4. The dataset is ready now for the modeling process.

Metrics for regression models

In this section, we will use a simple multiple linear regression model. I know it is not the best model for this problem, but I am using it just for the sake of illustrating some points:

1. Let's split the data into training and testing datasets:

```
X = diamonds.drop(['cut','color','clarity','price'], axis=1)
y = diamonds['price']

from sklearn.model_selection import train_test_split
X_train, X_test, y_train, y_test = train_test_split(X, y,
test_size=0.1, random_state=1)
```

2. Now let's standardize the numerical features of our dataset:

```
numerical_features = ['carat', 'depth', 'table', 'dim_index']
from sklearn.preprocessing import StandardScaler
scaler = StandardScaler()
scaler.fit(X_train[numerical_features])
X_train.loc[:, numerical_features] =
scaler.fit_transform(X_train[numerical_features])
X_test.loc[:, numerical_features] =
scaler.transform(X_test[numerical_features])
```

3. Now let's build our model and get the predictions:

```
from sklearn.linear_model import LinearRegression
ml_reg = LinearRegression()
ml_reg.fit(X_train, y_train)
y_pred = ml_reg.predict(X_test)
```

4. Now that we have the predictions, we can calculate the evaluation metrics in the testing dataset.

Evaluating regression models is relatively simple, as the intuition behind almost all metrics is the same—if the predictions are close to the actual values then it is good, if they are far away then it is bad. Technically, the difference between the actual and predicted prices is called the **residual**, so most metrics just measure how small residuals are (in absolute terms).

MSE and Root Mean Squared Error (RMSE)

The metric we have been using is the MSE, defined as the following:

$$MSE = \frac{1}{N} \sum_{i=1}^{N} (y_i - y\_pred_i)^2$$

N is the number of samples in our testing dataset. Because we are taking the square, an underestimation of, say, 10 dollars is equivalent to an overestimation of 10 dollars. Another consequence of using the square is that large deviations will affect the MSE very badly—a deviation from the actual value of 10 dollars will be squared to 100, and a deviation of 50 dollars will be squared to 2,500, which will have a significant effect on this metric.

On the other hand, as you can see, this metric is an average of squared quantities; therefore, it is a squared quantity. In this case, our target values are prices measured in US dollars, so the difference between predicted and actual prices is also measured in dollars, but when we are averaging the squares of those differences we get dollars squared, hence MSE is in dollars squared. To make this number more interpretable, we usually take the square root to go back to the original units (dollars in this case). The metric we get is unsurprisingly called RMSE:

$$RMSE = \sqrt{MSE}$$

Let's calculate the RMSE for our model. Note that we are calculating MSE and then taking the square root:

```
from sklearn.metrics import mean_squared_error
rmse = mean_squared_error(y_true=y_test, y_pred=y_pred)**0.5
print("RMSE: {:,.2f}".format(rmse))
```

The result is as follows:

```
RMSE: 1,085.01
```

This is a measure of how far, on average, the predictions of the model are from the actual values. Some people try to interpret this metric as, on average, the error the model will make is 1,085.0 dollars. Although a valid interpretation may not be accurate, if you want to actually calculate the average of the absolute errors the model will make, it is better to use the **Mean Absolute Error** (**MAE**).

Finally, keep in mind that, for this metric, smaller values are better and the best value we can get (the perfect model) is 0.

MAE

This metric is much more interpretable because it is not an approximation to the average error the model makes; it is, by definition, the average of the absolute values of the deviations of predicted versus actual values:

$$MAE = \frac{1}{N} \sum_{i=1}^{N} |y_i - y\_pred_i|$$

Because we are taking the absolute value, for this metric (as with MSE) we are giving the same importance to underestimations and to overestimations of the actual value.

Here we have the calculation for our model:

```
from sklearn.metrics import mean_absolute_error
mae = mean_absolute_error(y_true=y_test, y_pred=y_pred)
print("MAE: {:,.2f}".format(mae))
```

The result is as follows:

```
MAE: 733.67
```

Now we can say that the error the model will make is, on average, 733.7 dollars.

As with the MSE and RMSE, for this metric, smaller values are better and the best value we can get (the perfect model) is 0.

R-squared (R^2)

When we are trying to make predictions, these are about a quantity that can vary—if all diamonds had the same price then there wouldn't be any need for developing a predictive model, as the price would be constant. In reality, diamond prices are different—we observe variation in the prices. When building a model, from some point of view, what we are trying to do with our model is to explain the variation in prices, by taking into consideration different factors (features) that can affect the diamond prices.

The R^2 or **coefficient of determination** is a metric that is often interpreted as the proportion of variation in the target that is predictable or explained by the model. It is a number that can go from 1 for a model that explains 100% of the variation in the target, to 0 (a model that just predicts the average), and it can get even worse, although a negative R^2 would indicate that the model is so bad that it would be better just to always predict the average.

Therefore, a coefficient of determination of 0.6 can be interpreted as 60% of the variation in the target being explained by the model and the other 40% being due to some other factors and, of course, randomness. This metric is usually calculated by squaring the Pearson correlation coefficient between the actual and predicted values. Keep in mind that this metric is a measure of how closely observed and predicted values vary together; it does not tell us directly about how close the predictions are to the actual values. Let's perform the calculation of the R^2 for our model:

```
from sklearn.metrics import r2_score
r2 = r2_score(y_true=y_test, y_pred=y_pred)
print("R-squared: {:,.2f}".format(r2))
```

The result is as follows:

```
R-squared: 0.92
```

So, 92% of the variability observed in the diamond prices is explained or captured by our model. From this perspective, the model looks really good.

Defining a custom metric

When delivering the results of a model to stakeholders, you want to be as clear as possible and to demonstrate that the model is actually useful from the perspective they care about. Very few business people will understand or care about a metric such as RMSE; for this reason, often you will need to define your own metrics based on the business problem you are trying to solve.

Let's say that you have been told by the **Intelligent Diamond Reseller** (**IDR**) management that, although more accurate price predictions are always better, because of their business model and how the diamond market works, what is really important for them is that the prediction error (difference between prediction and market price) is less than 15% of the actual price. So, as long as the absolute value of the error is not more than 15% of the actual price, the company will make money.

With that information, we can create a custom metric that we can use to evaluate how valuable our model is. We can define this metric as the percentage of predictions within acceptable error.

Before calculating this metric, let's create a pandas `DataFrame` that will be useful for this and for the next section:

```
eval_df = pd.DataFrame({"y_true": y_test, "y_pred": y_pred, "residuals":
y_test - y_pred})
```

In this `DataFrame`, we have the actual and predicted prices (of the test set) and also the residuals. Now, let's think about what we were told with one example—suppose that for some diamond the real price is 2,000 and our prediction is 2,250, then the residual is 2,000 - 2,250 = -250, or 250 dollars in absolute terms, which is 12.5% of the actual price (250/2,000). Note that this prediction will be good for the company because it is within the 15% of tolerance that they have determined.

Now that we understand the calculation we need to do, let's add a new column to this DataFrame—the percentage that the absolute value of the residual represents with respect to the actual price:

```
eval_df["prop_error"] = eval_df["residuals"].abs()/eval_df["y_true"]
```

Now we can easily calculate the percentage of predictions that are within 15%:

```
costum_metric = 100*(eval_df["prop_error"] < 0.15).mean()
print("Custom metric: {:,.2f}%".format(costum_metric))
```

This is what we get:

```
Custom metric: 39.22%
```

So, around 39.2% of the predictions we are making have an error that is less than 15% of the actual price.

Visualization methods for evaluating regression models

It is usually very helpful to complement the numeric analysis of metrics with visualizations that will help us understand the predictions and the mistakes the model is making. The first thing we can do is to take a look at the distribution of the residuals:

```
eval_df["residuals"].hist(bins=25, ec='k');
```

The output will be as follows:

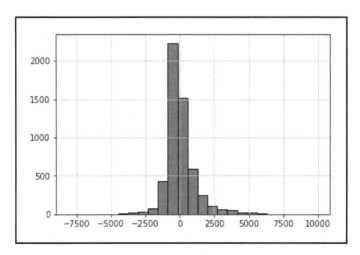

We see that most of the residuals are within 2,000 dollars and that they are more or less evenly distributed; however, we see that a high proportion of them are between -1,000 and 0. Let's calculate how many of the residuals are negative (meaning the model is overestimating the price):

```
(eval_df["residuals"] <=0).mean()
```

We get that 59% percent of the residuals are negative, so maybe the model is systematically overestimating the prices.

To investigate further, let's visualize the scatter plot of the actual versus the predicted values in the test set:

```
fig, ax = plt.subplots(figsize=(8,5))
ax.scatter(eval_df["y_true"], eval_df["y_pred"], s=3)
ax.plot(eval_df["y_true"], eval_df["y_true"], color='red')
ax.set_title('Predictions vs. observed values')
ax.set_xlabel('Observed prices')
ax.set_ylabel('Predicted prices')
ax.grid();
```

We will get the following output:

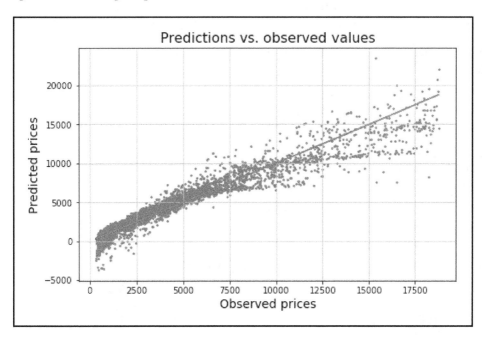

In the perfect model, all the points should be on the red line. The first thing that we notice is that, in general, the predictions follow the actual prices. That is good. However, when taking a closer look at the lower-left corner of the plot, we see something weird—this model is making a very stupid and nonsensical mistake—it is predicting negative prices! That is embarrassing! Imagine if we present this model to our client or boss. It is good that we realized this (see how important model evaluation is?). Here are some of the negative predictions:

```
eval_df["y_pred"].loc[eval_df["y_pred"]<0][:5]
```

The output is as follows:

```
39299    -312.643120
29808    -140.454585
31615    -283.365154
2714     -523.867542
5045     -569.694449
Name: y_pred, dtype: float64
```

In addition, we see that in the range of observed prices between 1,000 and 7,500 dollars the model is mostly overestimating the prices—most of the points are above the red line.

Another plot that can help us detecting some pattern in the residuals is visualizing these and the predicted values:

```
fig, ax = plt.subplots(figsize=(8,5))
ax.scatter(eval_df["y_pred"], eval_df["residuals"], s=3)
ax.set_title('Predictions vs. residuals', fontsize=16)
ax.set_xlabel('Predictions', fontsize=14)
ax.set_ylabel('Residuals', fontsize=14)
ax.axhline(color='k'); ax.axvline(color='k');
ax.grid();
```

This will give us the following output:

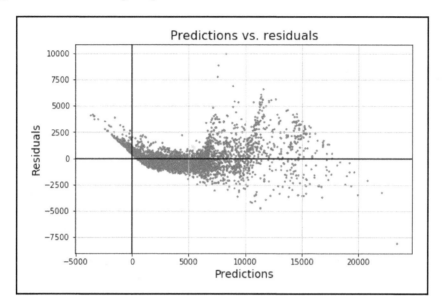

From this plot, we see that again the model overestimated prices (negative residuals). We also notice some kind of non-linear pattern between predictions and residuals. Ideally, we should not see any pattern in this plot; the presence of the pattern means that we are not using all the information in the features to predict the outcome. This means we have room for improvement.

Evaluation for classification models

So far, we have been using accuracy as the default metric for evaluating classification models. We used it because it is the most intuitive metric—it is just the proportion of cases correctly predicted by the classifier. So, an accuracy of 0.75 (or 75%) means that, on average, we should expect the classifier to make an accurate prediction 75% of the time. Although sometimes useful, this metric is very limited. Evaluating a classifier, even a binary classifier such as the one we are working with in the credit card default problem, is tricky.
In this section, we examine how we can make a more detailed evaluation of a binary classification model. We will use the credit card default dataset again, so we need to load and prepare everything again for this chapter. Let's run the code we have in one of the notebooks for this chapter. As always, we begin with the libraries we will use:

```
import numpy as np
import pandas as pd
```

```
import matplotlib.pyplot as plt
import seaborn as sns
import os

%matplotlib inline
```

Now load and prepare the data:

```
# Loading the dataset
DATA_DIR = '../data'
FILE_NAME = 'credit_card_default.csv'
data_path = os.path.join(DATA_DIR, FILE_NAME)
ccd = pd.read_csv(data_path, index_col="ID")
ccd.rename(columns=lambda x: x.lower(), inplace=True)
ccd.rename(columns={'default payment next month':'default'}, inplace=True)

# getting the groups of features
bill_amt_features = ['bill_amt'+ str(i) for i in range(1,7)]
pay_amt_features = ['pay_amt'+ str(i) for i in range(1,7)]
numerical_features = ['limit_bal','age'] + bill_amt_features +
pay_amt_features

# Creating creating binary features
ccd['male'] = (ccd['sex'] == 1).astype('int')
ccd['grad_school'] = (ccd['education'] == 1).astype('int')
ccd['university'] = (ccd['education'] == 2).astype('int')
ccd['married'] = (ccd['marriage'] == 1).astype('int')

# simplifying pay features
pay_features= ['pay_' + str(i) for i in range(1,7)]
for x in pay_features:
    ccd.loc[ccd[x] <= 0, x] = 0

# simplifying delayed features
delayed_features = ['delayed_' + str(i) for i in range(1,7)]
for pay, delayed in zip(pay_features, delayed_features):
    ccd[delayed] = (ccd[pay] > 0).astype(int)
# creating a new feature: months delayed
ccd['months_delayed'] = ccd[delayed_features].sum(axis=1)
```

Finally, split and standardize the numerical features:

```
numerical_features = numerical_features + ['months_delayed']
binary_features = ['male','married','grad_school','university']
X = ccd[numerical_features + binary_features]
y = ccd['default'].astype(int)

## Split
```

```
from sklearn.model_selection import train_test_split
X_train, X_test, y_train, y_test = train_test_split(X, y, test_size=5/30,
random_state=2)

## Standardize
from sklearn.preprocessing import StandardScaler
scaler = StandardScaler()
scaler.fit(X_train[numerical_features])
X_train.loc[:, numerical_features] =
scaler.transform(X_train[numerical_features])
# Standardize also the testing set
X_test.loc[:, numerical_features] =
scaler.transform(X_test[numerical_features])
```

We are ready for building a model and exploring the different ways in which we can evaluate it.

Confusion matrix and related metrics

First, we need a model to evaluate. Let's quickly build and train a random forest:

```
from sklearn.ensemble import RandomForestClassifier
rf = RandomForestClassifier(n_estimators=25,
                            max_features=6,
                            max_depth=4,
                            random_state=61)
rf.fit(X_train, y_train)
```

A confusion matrix is nothing but a table with four different cases that we have in a binary classification problem. In the case of the credit card default problem, we have defined *defaults* as the positive class. Considering this scenario, we get four possible cases in a binary classification problem.

First, when the model makes a correct prediction we have two possible cases:

- **True Positives (TP)**: The model predicts the positive class and the observation actually belongs to the positive class. In our problem the model predicts default and the customer actually defaults in his or her payment.
- **True Negatives (TN)**: The model predicts the negative class and the observation actually belongs to the negative class. In our problem the model predicts the customer will pay (no default) and the customer actually makes his or her next payment.

On the other hand, when the model makes a mistake, again we have two possible cases:

- **False Positives (FP)**: The model predicts the positive class and the observation actually belongs to the negative class. In our problem the model predicts default and the customer actually makes his or her next payment.
- **False Negatives (FN)**: The model predicts the negative class and the observation actually belongs to the positive class. In our problem the model predicts the customer will pay (no default) and the customer will actually default.

There is not a standard way to present the confusion matrix; people do it differently. The way I like to use it is in the following format:

		Predictions	
		Negative	Positive
Observations	Negative	TN	FP
	Positive	FN	TP

Now that we know the terminology, we can compute the confusion matrix, but to make it more understandable we will write a little function that will make it more readable:

```
from sklearn.metrics import confusion_matrix
def CM(y_true, y_pred):
    M = confusion_matrix(y_true, y_pred)
    out = pd.DataFrame(M, index=["Obs Paid", "Obs Default"], columns=["Pred
Paid", "Pred Default"])
    return out
```

Now, remember that the random forest model gives us the estimated probability of the observation belonging to the positive class (from now, we will refer to this estimation as the predicted probability or just the probability), then we need to use a **threshold** to decide which observations will be classified as positives (defaults) and which as negatives (no default). The default threshold is 0.5 and, using this, we can get the predictions:

```
threshold = 0.5
y_pred_prob = rf.predict_proba(X_test)[:,1]
y_pred = (y_pred_prob > threshold).astype(int)
```

Now let's see the confusion matrix for this model:

```
CM(y_test, y_pred)
```

Here we have it:

	Pred Paid	Pred Default
Obs Paid	3746	133
Obs Default	852	269

From the 5,000 observations in our testing dataset, we see that 3,746 are true negatives and 269 are true positives; those are the ones the model got correct. On the other hand, we have 133 false positives and 852 false negatives.

There are some metrics that we can calculate to make more sense of these numbers. Here we have some of the most important metrics we can get from the quantities we see in the confusion matrix:

- **Accuracy**: Proportion of cases correctly identified by the classifier (N represents the total number of observations in the testing set):

$$accuracy = \frac{TP + TN}{N}$$

- **Precision**: Proportion of correct positive predictions. In our problem, this is the proportion of cases when the model is correct when it predicts default:

$$precision = \frac{TP}{TP + FP}$$

- **Recall, sensitivity, or true positive rate**: Proportion of observed positives predicted correctly as positives. In our problem, this is the proportion of actual defaults that the model can correctly identify:

$$recall = \frac{TP}{TP + FN}$$

- **False positive rate, false alarm ratio**: Proportion of observed negatives predicted falsely as positives. In our problem, this is the proportion of people that will pay that the model is falsely accusing as defaults (false alarms):

$$fpr = \frac{TP}{TP + TN}$$

There are many other proportions that can be calculated from the confusion matrix (just take a look at the Wikipedia entry for confusion matrix). However, for almost every binary classification problem, these four metrics will help you understand which types of mistakes the model is making.

Now, let's calculate precision and recall for our model:

```
from sklearn.metrics import precision_score, recall_score

precision = precision_score(y_test, y_pred)
recall = recall_score(y_test, y_pred)
print("Precision: {:0.1f}%, Recall: {:.1f}%".format(100*precision,
100*recall))
```

The results are as follows:

```
Precision: 66.9%, Recall: 24.0%, Accuracy: 80.3%
```

When the model makes a positive prediction (default), it is correct almost 70% of the time (precision); that is not so bad. However, the model is able to identify only 24% of the actual defaults. These two metrics give us a useful picture of what is going on with our model.

Visualization methods for evaluating classification models

As with regression problems, it is always a good idea to complement the numerical analysis with some visualizations that can help us understand what is going on with the predictions our model is making. We can visualize the probabilities and the relationships between different metrics that come from the confusion matrix.

Visualizing probabilities

It is always a good idea to take a look at the distribution of predicted probabilities:

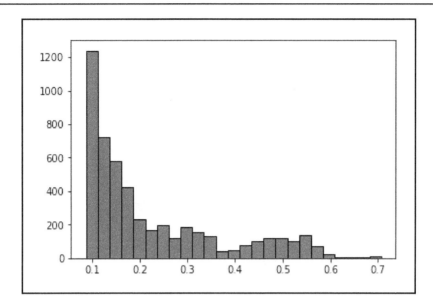

We see that in many cases the probabilities are close to 0, meaning that the model has confidence that those observations are not default; on the other hand, we don't see probabilities that are close to 1. This means that when we are classifying a customer as default, the model is not so sure.

Another plot that I find really useful is the distribution of probabilities separated by positive and negative classes:

```
fig, ax = plt.subplots(figsize=(8,5))
sns.kdeplot(y_pred_prob[y_test==1], shade=True, color='red',
label="Defaults", ax=ax)
sns.kdeplot(y_pred_prob[y_test==0], shade=True, color='green',
label="Paid", ax=ax)
ax.set_title("Distribution of predicted probabilities", fontsize=16)
ax.legend()
plt.grid();
```

We will get the following output:

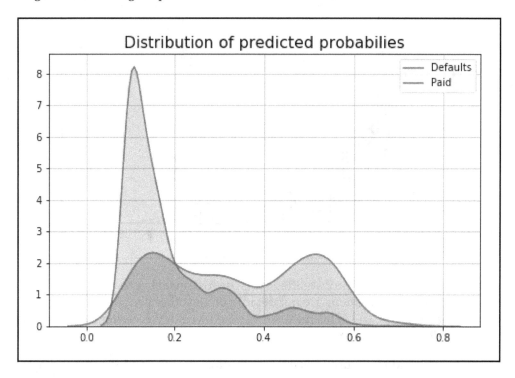

As we see, when the model predicts a low probability, it is much more likely that this customer is a no-default (paid), and when the model predicts a probability above 0.5, it is more likely that the customer is a default. However, there is a big overlap in the distributions—this is where the errors are coming from. Ideally, we would like to see these two distributions with as little overlap as possible.

Receiver Operating Characteristic (ROC) and precision-recall curves

As we mentioned before, to obtain the final predictions from the predicted probabilities we get from the model, we need a classification threshold. Therefore, if we change the threshold we will get a different classifier, a different confusion matrix, and, of course, different classification metrics. Let's see what happens if we use a threshold of 0.4:

```
threshold = 0.4
y_pred_prob = rf.predict_proba(X_test)[:,1]
y_pred = (y_pred_prob > threshold).astype(int)
```

```
precision = precision_score(y_test, y_pred)
recall = recall_score(y_test, y_pred)
print("Precision: {:0.1f}%, Recall: {:.1f}%".format(100*precision,
100*recall))
CM(y_test, y_pred)
```

We get the following results:

	Pred Paid	Pred Default
Obs Paid	3556	323
Obs Default	654	467

For making the comparison easier, here we have the former confusion matrix:

	Pred Paid	Pred Default
Obs Paid	3746	133
Obs Default	852	269

With a lower threshold (0.4 instead of 0.5), we now have more true positives (467 versus 269). That is a good thing, however, we also have more false positives (323 versus 133). So, we are finding more true positives, but the price we are paying is more false positives. What is happening is that, by lowering the classification threshold, we are lowering the bar for classifying a customer as a default; in other words, we are accusing more people of being defaults. Some of them will actually be defaults and some of them will actually pay, which is why we observe an increase in both TP and FP.

The classification metrics of course also change with this new confusion matrix:

```
precision = precision_score(y_test, y_pred)
recall = recall_score(y_test, y_pred)
accuracy = accuracy_score(y_test, y_pred)
print("Precision: {:0.1f}%, Recall: {:.1f}%, Accuracy:
{:0.1f}%".format(100*precision, 100*recall, 100*accuracy))
```

This is what we get:

```
Precision: 59.1%, Recall: 41.7%, Accuracy: 80.5%
```

The model has basically the same accuracy. We also observe a better recall (41.7 versus 24.0) but the precision has decreased (59.1 versus 66.9).

In summary, given some predicted probabilities, the choice of threshold will determine the predictions; these predictions together with the observed values will determine the confusion matrix and the performance metrics derived from it. So, there is a dependency between classification threshold and metrics such as precision and recall. We can actually see this relationship using the `precision_recall_curve` function:

```
from sklearn.metrics import precision_recall_curve
precs, recs, ths = precision_recall_curve(y_test, y_pred_prob)
```

Now we can visualize this quantity:

```
fig, ax = plt.subplots(figsize=(8,5))
ax.plot(ths, recs[1:], label='Precision')
ax.plot(ths, precs[1:], label='Recall')
ax.set_title('Precision and recall for different thresholds', fontsize=16)
ax.set_xlabel('Theshold', fontsize=14)
ax.set_ylabel('Precision, Recall', fontsize=14)
ax.set_xlim(0.1,0.7)
ax.legend(); ax.grid();
```

The output is as follows:

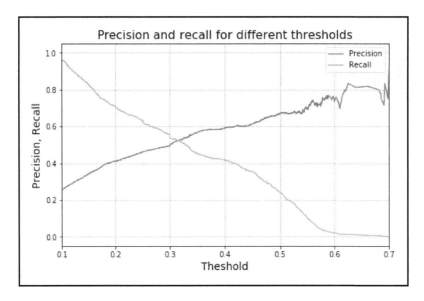

As we can see, there is an inverse relationship between precision and recall. Higher thresholds imply better precision but also lower recall. We can observe this directly by plotting the precision-recall curve:

```
fig, ax = plt.subplots(figsize=(8,5))
ax.plot(precs, recs)
ax.set_title('Precision-recall curve', fontsize=16)
ax.set_xlabel('Precision', fontsize=14)
ax.set_ylabel('Recall', fontsize=14)
ax.set_xlim(0.3,0.7)
ax.grid();
```

We will get the following output:

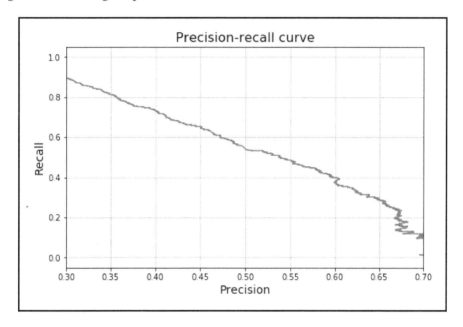

The relationship we observe in the former plot can be explained in two equivalent ways:

- If you want your positive predictions to be more reliable (better precision), then use a higher classification threshold. This will imply that the classifier will be more selective when assigning an observation to the positive class, which will increase the number of samples classified as negatives, which in turn will increase the number of false negatives, worsening the recall.

- If you want to be able to detect more actual positives, then use a lower classification threshold. This will imply that the classifier will be more willing to classify an observation as positive. In the case of our example, a lower probability will have the effect of easily accusing a customer of being a default; this will increase the number of samples classified as positives, which will increase the number of false positives, worsening the precision.

In summary, there is an inverse relationship between precision and recall.

Finally, sometimes it is useful to visualize the relationship between recall (true positive rate) and the false positive rate. This is again another perspective on the same reality – the inverse relation between FP and FN. In other words, given some predicted probabilities, for lowering one type of mistake we necessarily need to make the other higher.

When plotting the false positive rate against the recall, we get a plot called the **ROC curve**. Don't worry about the name or where it comes from, just make sure that you can interpret it. We can obtain it as follows:

```
from sklearn.metrics import roc_curve
fpr, tpr, ths = roc_curve(y_test, y_pred_prob)

fig, ax = plt.subplots(figsize=(8,5))
ax.plot(fpr, tpr)
ax.set_title('ROC curve', fontsize=16)
ax.set_xlabel('False positive rate', fontsize=14)
ax.set_ylabel('Recall, true negative rate', fontsize=14)
ax.grid();
```

We get the following output:

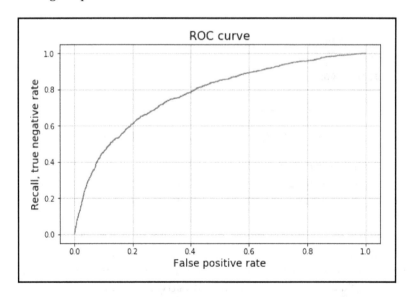

The curve begins at *(0,0)*. This is when all the samples are assigned to the negative class. Since there are no positives, we are identifying none of the actual positives (recall = zero) and there are no false alarms (false positive rate = zero). On the other extreme, if all samples are classified as positives, then we will identify 100% of the actual positives (if we accuse all the customers of defaulting, we will identify 100% of the actual defaulters, recall=1.0); however, all of the mistakes we will make will be false positives (false positive rate = 1.0).

So which curve should you use? The precision-recall curve or the ROC curve? That depends on the problem you are working with and the way you evaluate and analyze it.

Defining a custom metric for classification

In real-world applications, such as the one we are dealing with here, the two types of mistakes the classifier can make are not equally important and they almost always have different consequences and/or costs for the business problem we are dealing with. In our example, what do you think is worse? A false positive, saying that the customer will not pay when in fact he will pay? Or a false negative, saying that the customer will pay when in fact he will default?

When asking these types of questions, we are outside the ML field and inside the business or domain problem; don't forget that an effective predictive analytics solution is the one that solves the business problem (not the one with the fanciest ML model).

Sometimes, it would be possible to assign a cost to each of the mistakes the classifier can make. If that is the case, then we could assign some kind of cost to every classifier depending on the number of FP and FN it produces. Let's write a function that gives predicted and observed values and computes a normalized cost using the confusion matrix:

```
def class_cost(y_true, y_pred, cost_fn=1, cost_fp=1):
    M = confusion_matrix(y_true, y_pred)
    N = len(y_true)
    FN = M[1,0]
    FP = M[0,1]
    return (cost_fn*FN + cost_fp*FP)/N
```

Note that what we are doing is simply multiplying the respective costs of a false positive and a false negative by some fixed numbers. By default we are giving the same cost (1) to both mistakes. Note also that we are normalizing by the number of observations we are using to evaluate the model.

For example, for the last predictions we made (with a threshold of 0.4), we get the following cost:

```
class_cost(y_test, y_pred)
# 0.2048
```

Using this function and different thresholds, we could calculate the different associated costs for the different classifiers. In this example, we are assuming that a false negative costs three times as much as a false positive:

```
thresholds = np.arange(0.05, 0.95, 0.01)
costs = []
for th in thresholds:
    y_pred = (y_pred_prob > th).astype(int)
    costs.append(class_cost(y_test, y_pred, cost_fn=3, cost_fp=1))
costs = np.array(costs)
```

Here we have the corresponding plot:

```
fig, ax = plt.subplots(figsize=(8,5))
ax.plot(thresholds, costs)
ax.set_title('Cost vs threshold', fontsize=16)
ax.set_xlabel('Threshold', fontsize=14)
ax.set_ylabel('Cost', fontsize=14)
ax.grid();
```

The output will be as follows:

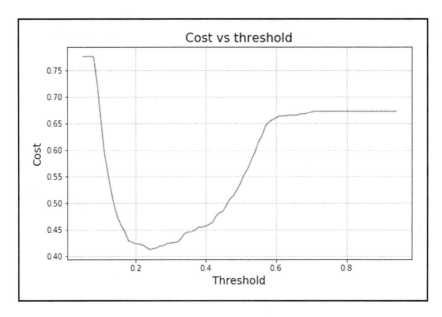

If this were the case (a false positive costing 3 and a false negative costing 1), then we see that the threshold that minimizes the cost is 0.24:

```
min_cost_th = thresholds[costs.argmin()]
```

Finally, the corresponding confusion matrix, precision, and recall with this threshold will be the following:

```
y_pred = (y_pred_prob > min_cost_th).astype(int)
precision = precision_score(y_test, y_pred)
recall = recall_score(y_test, y_pred)
print("Precision: {:0.1f}%, Recall: {:.1f}%".format(100*precision,
100*recall))
CM(y_test, y_pred)
```

This will give us the following output:

	Pred Paid	Pred Default
Obs Paid	2996	883
Obs Default	394	727

Precision: 45.2%, Recall: 64.9%

This type of evaluation is more likely to make sense to the business stakeholders.

The k-fold cross-validation

So far, we have been evaluating our models in the test set. By now, it is clear why we do it; however, there is one point we have not discussed yet. Let's go back to the diamond prices problem. In this chapter, we have built a simple multiple linear regression model and we have calculated some metrics on the test set. Let's say that we will use the MAE for evaluating the model. When we calculated this metric, we got 733.67. Now let's repeat the same steps for model building:

- Train-test split
- Standardize the numeric features
- Model training
- Get predictions
- Evaluate the model using the same metric

Here we have the code again:

```
## Train-test split
X_train, X_test, y_train, y_test = train_test_split(X, y, test_size=0.1,
random_state=2)

## Standardize the numeric features
scaler = StandardScaler()
scaler.fit(X_train[numerical_features])
X_train.loc[:, numerical_features] =
scaler.fit_transform(X_train[numerical_features])
X_test.loc[:, numerical_features] =
scaler.transform(X_test[numerical_features])

## Model training
ml_reg = LinearRegression()
ml_reg.fit(X_train, y_train)

## Get predictions
y_pred = ml_reg.predict(X_test)

## Evaluate the model using the same metric
mae = mean_absolute_error(y_true=y_test, y_pred=y_pred)
print("MAE: {:,.2f}".format(mae))
```

We have repeated the same steps as before, but the MAE is now 726.87, so which is it? 726.87 or the one we got before, 733.67? Did the model just improve by running it again? What happened?

This is exactly the same code as before, with only one modification: in the `train_test_split` function, we changed the `random_state` parameter from 1 to 2, which means we now have different test and training sets (although in both cases they have the same size). So which one is the real MAE? The first or the second one? The answer is neither. Both are just estimations of the real expected MAE of the model. Since the observations are randomly assigned to training and testing sets, what we are getting is a MAE estimation that is a random variable.

The drawback of using the train/test strategy is that we only get one estimation of the metric we are using for evaluating the model. This is not recommended if we are interested in giving a good assessment of the real value of metric we are using.

Since we know that the metric we are using for model evaluation can change, it would be better to get more than one of these estimations and average them to get a better sense of the true expected value of the metric. There are many techniques for doing this, mainly divided on resampling techniques and cross-validation approaches. In this section, we will talk about the most popular approach for getting many estimations of the evaluation metrics – k-fold cross-validation.

The idea of cross-validation is simple—divide the dataset into k equal parts (folds), in the first iteration use the first part as testing and the rest k—one part for training, after training the model, calculate the metrics in the first part to get the first estimation. In the second iteration, use the second part for testing and the rest for training. Get the second estimation of the metrics from the second part and continue until you have used all the parts for testing; in this way, we will get k estimations of the metrics. The following diagram illustrates this process ($k=4$):

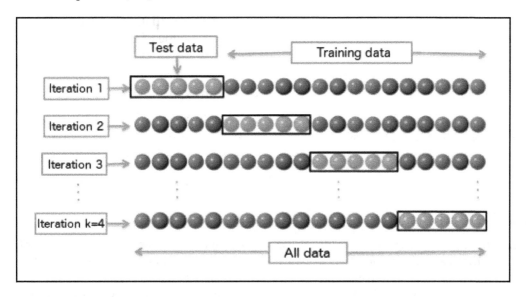

By Fabian Flöck – own work, CC BY-SA 3.0, https://commons.wikimedia.org/w/index.php?curid=51562781

The most common values for k are 5 or 10. Let's implement 10-fold cross-validation to make a more accurate assessment of the MAE metric for our regression model. The `cross_validate` function uses an estimator and a scoring metric for calculating the k-fold cross-validation:

```
from sklearn.model_selection import cross_validate

## Scaling the whole dataset
scaler = StandardScaler()
```

```
scaler.fit(X[numerical_features])
X.loc[:, numerical_features] = scaler.fit_transform(X[numerical_features])

## 10-fold cv
ml_reg = LinearRegression()
cv_results = cross_validate(ml_reg, X, y,
scoring='neg_mean_absolute_error', cv=10)
scores = -1*cv_results['test_score']
```

For technical reasons, scikit-learn uses the negative values of the metrics (neg_mean_absolute_error), which is why we are multiplying by -1 when getting the scores:

```
array([ 720.83563282,  663.1562278 ,  695.18142822,  950.88984768,
       2043.71156001,  890.10617501,  539.98283615,  624.44948736,
        584.63334965,  604.29011263])
```

As you can see, there is some variation on these scores. By calculating the mean of the scores, we can get a better estimation of the true expected value of the MAE:

```
scores.mean()
```

This gives 831.72, a better estimation of the MAE we can expect if we use this model.

The k-fold cross-validation is very useful, not only for getting a more accurate estimation of the metrics of our model but for hyperparameter tuning, which is the subject of the next chapter.

Summary

In this chapter, we delved deeper into the model evaluation, which is a very important task in the predictive analytics process. We studied various techniques for model evaluation. The k-fold cross-validation (or another resampling method) is also discussed. Don't forget to always connect your evaluation strategy with the business problem you are trying to solve.
In the next chapter, we will learn about the techniques to improve the quality of our predictions.

Further reading

- *Domingos, P. (2012).* A few useful things to know about machine learning. Communications of the ACM, 55(10), 78-87.
- *Provost, F., & Fawcett, T. (2013).* Data Science for Business: What you need to know about data mining and data-analytic thinking. O'Reilly Media.

8
Model Tuning and Improving Performance

This chapter is about some of the things you can do in order to improve the quality of the predictions our models make.

This chapter is divided into two main sections. In the first, we discuss hyperparameter tuning, which is the way to choose those values that define our model that are not directly learned from data. We start by discussing the simplest case, which is how to tune one parameter, and then we move on and show one of the most popular methods for optimizing more than one hyperparameter at the same time—we use the concept of cross-validation and k-fold cross-validation in this section, so it is important that you have learned these concepts from the previous chapters.

In the second section, we show how sometimes trying a different model can improve the quality of our predictions. Then, we use some of the information we got from the **Exploratory Data Analysis (EDA)** process to perform a transformation to our target feature (of the diamond prices dataset) to see whether that improves our results. We end this section and the chapter by analyzing the predictive power of our model through different perspectives and then talk about the necessity of matching the performance of the model to the business problem we are trying to solve.

These are the topics we cover in this chapter:

- Hyperparameter tuning
- Improving model performance with EDA
- The importance of the business perspective when performing evaluation

Technical requirements

- Python 3.6 or higher
- Jupyter Notebook
- Recent versions of the following Python libraries: NumPy, pandas, matplotlib, Seaborn, and scikit-learn

Hyperparameter tuning

So far, we have worked with some parametric models—those that learn some parameters from the data, for example, multiple linear regression, logistic regression, and multilayer perceptrons. However, in most models there are some parameters that are not directly learned from data. We need to choose their values, which are called **hyperparameters**. I have been choosing those hyperparameters for different models in the examples using the libraries' defaults or what I think might be good values based on my experience and best practices in the field of predictive analytics. However, if we want our model to perform better, we need to do some **hyperparameter tuning**—the activity of finding good values for the hyperparameters of our models.

In the first example of the section, we will use our diamond prices dataset:

1. Let's do the necessary imports:

```
import numpy as np
import pandas as pd
import matplotlib.pyplot as plt
import seaborn as sns
import os

%matplotlib inline
```

2. Second, load the dataset:

```
DATA_DIR = '../data'
FILE_NAME = 'diamonds.csv'
data_path = os.path.join(DATA_DIR, FILE_NAME)
diamonds = pd.read_csv(data_path)
```

3. Now prepare the dataset:

```
## Preparation done from Chapter 2
diamonds = diamonds.loc[(diamonds['x']>0) | (diamonds['y']>0)]
diamonds.loc[11182, 'x'] = diamonds['x'].median()
diamonds.loc[11182, 'z'] = diamonds['z'].median()
diamonds = diamonds.loc[~((diamonds['y'] > 30) | (diamonds['z']
> 30))]
diamonds = pd.concat([diamonds, pd.get_dummies(diamonds['cut'],
prefix='cut', drop_first=True)], axis=1)
diamonds = pd.concat([diamonds,
pd.get_dummies(diamonds['color'], prefix='color',
drop_first=True)], axis=1)
diamonds = pd.concat([diamonds,
pd.get_dummies(diamonds['clarity'], prefix='clarity',
drop_first=True)], axis=1)

## Dimensionality reduction
from sklearn.decomposition import PCA
pca = PCA(n_components=1, random_state=123)
diamonds['dim_index'] =
pca.fit_transform(diamonds[['x','y','z']])
diamonds.drop(['x','y','z'], axis=1, inplace=True)
```

4. Now let's apply the training-test split:

```
X = diamonds.drop(['cut','color','clarity','price'], axis=1)
y = diamonds['price']

from sklearn.model_selection import train_test_split
X_train, X_test, y_train, y_test = train_test_split(X, y,
test_size=0.1, random_state=7)
```

5. Finally, let's standardize the dataset:

```
numerical_features = ['carat', 'depth', 'table', 'dim_index']
from sklearn.preprocessing import StandardScaler
scaler = StandardScaler()
scaler.fit(X_train[numerical_features])
X_train.loc[:, numerical_features] =
scaler.fit_transform(X_train[numerical_features])
X_test.loc[:, numerical_features] =
scaler.transform(X_test[numerical_features])
```

6. Now we are ready for hyperparameter tuning. First, let's do the simplest case—tuning a single parameter.

Optimizing a single hyperparameter

k-nearest neighbors (**KNN**) is an example of a non-parametric model, meaning it has no parameters to be learned from data; however, it has one very important hyperparameter—the number of neighbors. Back in `Chapter 4`, *Predicting Numerical Values with Machine Learning*, we used a KNN model with 12 neighbors in our diamond prices dataset, and that model gave us the best result when compared with multiple linear regression and lasso. We used 12 because I thought it was a good value, however, there is no guarantee it is the *best value*; why not nine or 15 neighbors? Maybe 10 works best. That is what the activity of hyperparameter optimization is all about—finding the set of best hyperparameters, or, more often, a set of good hyperparameters so our model performs better.

For optimizing a single hyperparameter, the first thing we need to define is how are we going to evaluate our model. The simplest thing is to choose one main metric of interest. Let's say that we are going to use **Mean Absolute Error** (**MAE**) to measure the performance of our diamond prices model. Now, we need to know what the possible candidate values are for the hyperparameter that we are going to optimize. Then, what we have to do is simply to find what is the value of the metric associated with each of the candidate values.

Now, to obtain the pairs (`candidate_value`, `metric_value`) we need to introduce the concept of **validation set**, which is a subset of the dataset that will be used to measure the performance of the model under different candidate values for the hyperparameter. Why not do this evaluation in the test set? Because then we would be implicitly using the data in the test set to adjust some aspect of the model. If we do this, then the hyperparameter will be adjusted to the data in the test set and the whole point of having a test set is to simulate how the model will perform with data it has not seen previously. This is the reason the test set must remain untouched during the whole the model-building process, including hyperparameter tuning, which is why we need a validation set.

Here is the code to assign 10% of the training samples for validation:

```
X_train, X_val, y_train, y_val = train_test_split(X_train, y_train,
test_size=0.1, random_state=13)
```

Now a simple `for` loop will do the trick of obtaining the pairs (`candidate_value`, `metric_value`):

```
from sklearn.neighbors import KNeighborsRegressor
from sklearn.metrics import mean_absolute_error

candidates = np.arange(4,16)
mae_metrics = []
for k in candidates:
```

```
    model = KNeighborsRegressor(n_neighbors=k, weights='distance',
metric='minkowski', leaf_size=50, n_jobs=4)
    model.fit(X_train, y_train)
    y_pred = model.predict(X_val)
    metric = mean_absolute_error(y_true=y_val, y_pred=y_pred)
    mae_metrics.append(metric)
```

Let's visualize the MAE associated with each value of K:

```
fig, ax = plt.subplots(figsize=(8,5))
ax.plot(candidates, mae_metrics)
ax.set_xlabel('Hyper-parameter K', fontsize=14)
ax.set_ylabel('MAE', fontsize=14)
ax.grid();
```

This will give the following output:

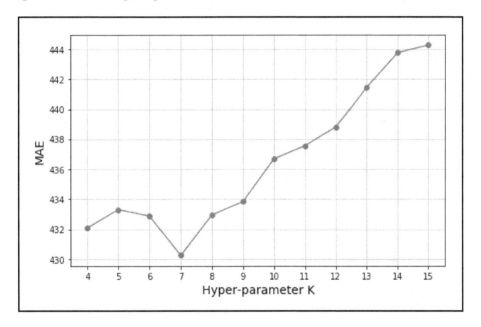

Since we know that lower MAE is better, according to this graph the best value for K is 7. Can we now declare that 7 is the best value for the K hyperparameter? According to this analysis, yes. But we can do better. Remember that the MAE on the test set is just one estimation of the real MAE—it can fluctuate due to the randomness associated with creating the training and validation sets. As we learned back in the previous chapter, we can make a better estimation of an evaluation metric by using k-fold cross-validation.

So, now, let's perform the same calculation but now instead of getting a single estimation of the MAE, let's get the cross-validation value, since we will be doing k-fold cross-validation. We don't need a validation set anymore (under this procedure, each of the k-folds will play the role of the validation set). Since we modified the training set by creating the validation set, let's recalculate the train-test split (including the standardization):

```
X_train, X_test, y_train, y_test = train_test_split(X, y, test_size=0.1,
random_state=7)
scaler = StandardScaler()
scaler.fit(X_train[numerical_features])
X_train.loc[:, numerical_features] =
scaler.fit_transform(X_train[numerical_features])
X_test.loc[:, numerical_features] =
scaler.transform(X_test[numerical_features])
```

Now let's run exactly the same loop, except this time, using 10-fold cross-validation to get the metrics; of course, it will take more time to run:

```
from sklearn.model_selection import cross_val_score
candidates = np.arange(4,16)
mean_mae = []
std_mae = []
for k in candidates:
    model = KNeighborsRegressor(n_neighbors=k, weights='distance',
metric='minkowski', leaf_size=50, n_jobs=4)
    cv_results = cross_val_score(model, X_train, y_train,
scoring='neg_mean_absolute_error', cv=10)
    mean_score, std_score = -1*cv_results.mean(), cv_results.std()
    mean_mae.append(mean_score)
    std_mae.append(std_score)
```

Let's see the graph of cross-validated MAE score against K once again:

```
fig, ax = plt.subplots(figsize=(8,5))
ax.plot(candidates, mean_mae, "o-")
ax.set_xlabel('Hyper-parameter K', fontsize=14)
ax.set_ylabel('Mean MAE', fontsize=14)
ax.set_xticks(candidates)
ax.grid();
```

The output will be as follows:

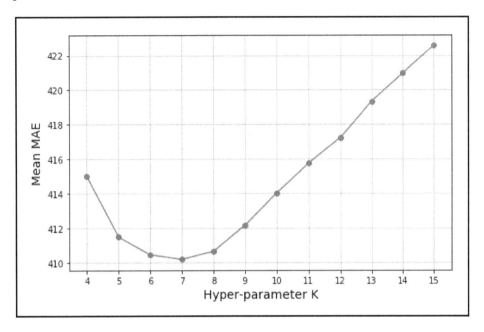

Now we see again that the best value is K=7, although the mean MAE is not very different from the result with K=8 or K=6. Given that the mean MAE values are very close, in practice either values 6, 7, or 8 will work very similarly. Another important statistic that we have collected from the cross-validation procedure is the standard deviation of each of the 10 MAE estimations (we got 10 estimations for each candidate value). Here we have the graph:

```
fig, ax = plt.subplots(figsize=(8,5))
ax.plot(candidates, std_mae, "o-")
ax.set_xlabel('Hyper-parameter K', fontsize=14)
ax.set_ylabel('Standard deviation of MAE', fontsize=14)
ax.set_xticks(candidates)
ax.grid();
```

This will give the following output:

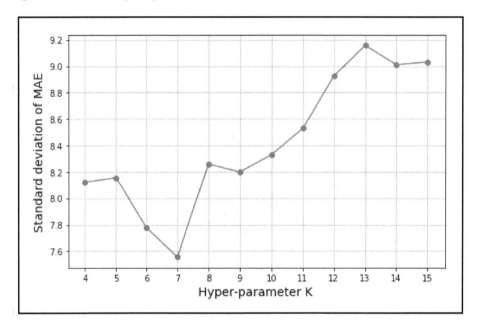

The values we see in this plot are estimations of what is known as the **variance** of the model – the sensitivity of the model to small fluctuations in the dataset. Intuitively, it measures how big the change is in the results of the model when the training samples change; the high variance is generally not desirable, as it would mean the model is not stable. We see that our models show a relatively low variance and that the model with the lowest variance is the one with K=7. From this, we conclude that the optimal parameter for our KNN model is K=7. Congratulations! You have done your first parameter optimization.

I used quotes in optimal because K=7 is optimal only under the evaluation we made: we used MAE to decide which model was better. If you use another evaluation metric, the optimal value for K may be different. Another reason to use quotes is that K=7 is the optimal only among those values we tried. In principle, it could be possible that another K will produce a better result, however, given the tendency we see in the plot of candidates versus mean MAE, it seems that as K increases, the model gets worse, so it is reasonable to assume that this trend will continue with larger values of K. However, keep in mind that although we are not sure about K=7 being the best value, it would be impractical to try every single possible value for K, so it is reasonable to call K=7 the optimal value for K.

Now that we know what we mean by hyperparameter tuning, let's see how we can optimize more than one hyperparameter at the same time.

Optimizing more than one parameter

For this example, we will go back to our credit card default example. As always, let's run all the code we need to get our dataset ready:

```
import numpy as np
import pandas as pd
import matplotlib.pyplot as plt
import seaborn as sns
import os

%matplotlib inline
```

This is how we prepare the dataset:

```
# Loading the dataset
DATA_DIR = '../data'
FILE_NAME = 'credit_card_default.csv'
data_path = os.path.join(DATA_DIR, FILE_NAME)
ccd = pd.read_csv(data_path, index_col="ID")
ccd.rename(columns=lambda x: x.lower(), inplace=True)
ccd.rename(columns={'default payment next month':'default'}, inplace=True)

# getting the groups of features
bill_amt_features = ['bill_amt'+ str(i) for i in range(1,7)]
pay_amt_features = ['pay_amt'+ str(i) for i in range(1,7)]
numerical_features = ['limit_bal','age'] + bill_amt_features +
pay_amt_features

# Creating creating binary features
ccd['male'] = (ccd['sex'] == 1).astype('int')
ccd['grad_school'] = (ccd['education'] == 1).astype('int')
ccd['university'] = (ccd['education'] == 2).astype('int')
ccd['married'] = (ccd['marriage'] == 1).astype('int')

# simplifying pay features
pay_features= ['pay_' + str(i) for i in range(1,7)]
for x in pay_features:
    ccd.loc[ccd[x] <= 0, x] = 0

# simplifying delayed features
delayed_features = ['delayed_' + str(i) for i in range(1,7)]
for pay, delayed in zip(pay_features, delayed_features):
```

```
    ccd[delayed] = (ccd[pay] > 0).astype(int)
# creating a new feature: months delayed
ccd['months_delayed'] = ccd[delayed_features].sum(axis=1)
```

Finally, this is how we split and standardize our dataset:

```
numerical_features = numerical_features + ['months_delayed']
binary_features = ['male','married','grad_school','university']
X = ccd[numerical_features + binary_features]
y = ccd['default'].astype(int)

## Split
from sklearn.model_selection import train_test_split
X_train, X_test, y_train, y_test = train_test_split(X, y, test_size=5/30,
random_state=25)

## Standarize
from sklearn.preprocessing import StandardScaler
scaler = StandardScaler()
scaler.fit(X[numerical_features])
X_train.loc[:, numerical_features] =
scaler.transform(X_train[numerical_features])
X_test.loc[:, numerical_features] =
scaler.transform(X_test[numerical_features])
```

Now we are ready for model building. In the previous chapter, we used a random forest to make our predictions. For reference, let's calculate the cross-validated score for the metric we will use in this example—the **area under curve (AUC)**:

```
from sklearn.model_selection import cross_val_score
from sklearn.ensemble import RandomForestClassifier
ref_rf = RandomForestClassifier(n_estimators=25,
                                max_features=6,
                                max_depth=4,
                                random_state=61)

ref_rf_scores = cross_val_score(ref_rf, X, y, scoring='roc_auc', cv=10)
```

This gives us a mean AUC value of 0.7591. These are the results of using some hyperparameter values that were chosen somewhat arbitrarily. Now, let's take a look at the documentation of this estimator to see what these hyperparameters mean:

- n_estimators: The number of trees in the forest
- max_depth: The maximum depth of the tree
- max_features: The number of features to consider when looking for the best split

Of course, there are other hyperparameters we could try to optimize; however, for the purpose of this example, these three will be enough.

The method we are going to use is called **exhaustive grid search**; it is a way to try all possible combinations of the different values of the hyperparameters that we would like to try. For instance, if you try two values for `n_estimators` and three values for `max_depth`, then we have in total 2 x 3 = 6 different pairs of values we can try.

Keep in mind that if you want to try many different values for each hyperparameter and you have many hyperparameters for tuning, then you will have a lot of different combinations and exhaustive grid search will try them all; besides, since it is always recommended to use cross-validation, this method will fit k models for every combination when using k-fold cross-validation, so as you may guess this is of course, computationally, very costly. We will use `GridSearchCV` to perform exhaustive grid search. The simplest way of using `GridSearchCV` is to first define a **parameter grid**, which is a dictionary containing a list of possible values that we would like to try for every hyperparameter:

```
from sklearn.model_selection import GridSearchCV
param_grid = {"n_estimators":[25,100,200,400],
              "max_features":[4,10,19],
              "max_depth":[4,8,16,20]}
```

You can also pass a list of dictionaries as a parameter grid to define even better which combinations of parameters you would like to try. For instance, if you would like to try deeper trees only with a low number of estimators, and small trees with a large number of estimators, then you could define a parameter grid such as this:
```
param_grid = [ {'n_estimators': [25, 100],
"max_depth":[16,20], "max_features":[4,10,19]},
{'n_estimators': [200, 400], "max_depth":[4,8],
"max_features":[4,10,19]}, ]
```

In this case, some undesired combinations won't be tried, thereby improving the time in searching for the best parameters.

OK, so in this example, we have four values for `n_estimators`, three values for `max_features`, and four values for `max_depth`, making a total of 48 = 4 x 3 x 4 different hyperparameter combinations.

Once we have defined our parameter grid, we create an instance of the `GridSearchCV` class:

```
rf = RandomForestClassifier(random_state=17)
grid_search = GridSearchCV(estimator=rf,
                           param_grid=param_grid,
                           scoring='roc_auc',
                           cv=5,
                           verbose=1)
```

We have passed the base estimator we would like to tune (`RandomForestClassifier`), the parameter grid, the metric we will use for measuring performance (AUC, in this case), and the number of the fold for the k-fold cross-validation, 5 in this case. Once created, we can use the fit method for the process to start:

```
grid_search.fit(X_train, y_train)
```

We'll see the following message:

```
Fitting 5 folds for each of 48 candidates, totalling 240 fits
```

Once the process is completed, we can access the `grid_search.cv_results_` dictionary, which contains statistics about model fitting and the cross-validation results. We are interested in `mean_test_score`. To see the results and the associated combination of parameters, let's create the following pandas series:

```
gs_results = pd.Series(grid_search.cv_results_['mean_test_score'],
index=grid_search.cv_results_['params'])
gs_results.sort_values(ascending=False)
```

This is what we will get:

```
{'max_depth': 8, 'max_features': 10, 'n_estimators': 400}    0.771326
{'max_depth': 8, 'max_features': 10, 'n_estimators': 200}    0.771129
{'max_depth': 8, 'max_features': 10, 'n_estimators': 100}    0.770636
{'max_depth': 8, 'max_features': 19, 'n_estimators': 200}    0.770251
{'max_depth': 8, 'max_features': 19, 'n_estimators': 400}    0.770065
{'max_depth': 8, 'max_features': 19, 'n_estimators': 100}    0.769861
{'max_depth': 8, 'max_features': 10, 'n_estimators': 25}     0.768982
{'max_depth': 8, 'max_features': 4, 'n_estimators': 400}     0.768858
{'max_depth': 8, 'max_features': 4, 'n_estimators': 200}     0.768732
{'max_depth': 8, 'max_features': 4, 'n_estimators': 100}     0.768362
{'max_depth': 8, 'max_features': 19, 'n_estimators': 25}     0.767242
{'max_depth': 8, 'max_features': 4, 'n_estimators': 25}      0.765414
{'max_depth': 16, 'max_features': 4, 'n_estimators': 400}    0.765067
{'max_depth': 4, 'max_features': 19, 'n_estimators': 200}    0.764648
{'max_depth': 4, 'max_features': 19, 'n_estimators': 400}    0.764607
{'max_depth': 16, 'max_features': 4, 'n_estimators': 200}    0.764532
{'max_depth': 4, 'max_features': 10, 'n_estimators': 200}    0.764499
{'max_depth': 4, 'max_features': 10, 'n_estimators': 400}    0.764350
{'max_depth': 4, 'max_features': 19, 'n_estimators': 100}    0.764184
{'max_depth': 4, 'max_features': 10, 'n_estimators': 100}    0.763871
{'max_depth': 16, 'max_features': 10, 'n_estimators': 400}   0.762903
{'max_depth': 16, 'max_features': 10, 'n_estimators': 200}   0.762595
```

From the results we can see that the best set of parameters is `max_depth: 8`, `max_features: 10`, and `n_estimators: 400`. However, note that the AUC values for the following combinations of parameters are also extremely close to the best value. Notice also that all the top combination of parameters have `max_depth: 8`; this is a good indication that this is a good value for this hyperparameter.

> When performing hyperparameter tuning, it is important to leave a test set outside of the tuning process so we can confirm our estimation for the metric we will obtain when using the model on data the model has never seen.

Our results indicate that by using the values we arbitrarily picked. So by using the values we arbitrarily picked (`max_depth: 4, max_features:4, n_estimators: 25`) we will get a lower AUC metric than if we use, say, any of the top three combinations from the 48 we explored. To compare and analyze more accurately how much we have gained by tuning the parameters, let's compare the precision-recall curves from both models:

```
from sklearn.metrics import precision_recall_curve
## Fitting the initial (not tuned) model:
ref_rf.fit(X_train, y_train)

## Getting the probabilites
y_prob_tunned = grid_search.predict_proba(X_test)[:,1]
y_prob_not_tunned = ref_rf.predict_proba(X_test)[:,1]

## Values for plotting the curves
prec_tuned, recall_tuned, _ = precision_recall_curve(y_test, y_prob_tunned)
prec_not_tuned, recall_not_tuned, _ = precision_recall_curve(y_test,
y_prob_not_tunned)
```

Here we have both curves in a single plot:

```
fig, ax = plt.subplots(figsize=(8,5))
ax.plot(prec_tuned, recall_tuned, label='Tuned Model')
ax.plot(prec_not_tuned, recall_not_tuned, label='Not Tuned Model')
#ax.set_title('Precision and recall for different thresholds', fontsize=16)
ax.set_xlabel('Precision', fontsize=14)
ax.set_ylabel('Recall', fontsize=14)
ax.set_xlim(0.3,0.7); ax.set_ylim(0.1,0.9)
ax.legend(); ax.grid();
```

The output will be as follows:

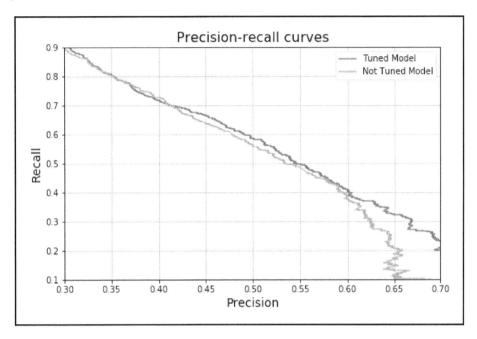

We observe that, although very close, the curve corresponding to the tuned model is a bit to the left of the other one, meaning that, for a given value of recall, it gives more precision. Although in this case the difference is not very large, in many real-world settings, such as credit scoring, a difference in precision of 1 or 2% could mean thousands or millions of dollars.

Finally, it is important to mention that exhaustive grid search is not the only method for tuning many hyperparameters at the same time and not even the only one that is included in scikit-learn. Please take a look at the documentation on hyperparameter tuning (`https:/ /scikit-learn.org/stable/modules/grid_search.html`) to find out more about other methods such as randomized parameter optimization.

Improving performance

In this section, we will try a couple of things to see whether we can improve the performance of our models. As we have said previously, there are cases where a small improvement in performance could translate to a large impact in the domain of application of the predictive analytics model.

Improving our diamond price predictions

Although we have found the best value of K for a KNN regression model, a neural network still seems a more promising model. To improve the accuracy of our diamond prices predictions, we will do two things:

- Fit a neural network
- Transform the target

Fitting a neural network

We have used a neural network previously for this problem and we got very good results. Let's fit a similar model to the one we fitted back in Chapter 6, *Introducing Neural Nets for Predictive Analytics*:

```
from keras.models import Sequential
from keras.layers import Dense

n_input = X_train.shape[1]
n_hidden1 = 32
n_hidden2 = 16
n_hidden3 = 8

nn_reg = Sequential()
nn_reg.add(Dense(units=n_hidden1, activation='relu',
input_shape=(n_input,)))
nn_reg.add(Dense(units=n_hidden2, activation='relu'))
nn_reg.add(Dense(units=n_hidden3, activation='relu'))
# output layer
nn_reg.add(Dense(units=1, activation=None))
```

Now let's compile and train our network:

```
batch_size = 32
n_epochs = 50
nn_reg.compile(loss='mean_absolute_error', optimizer='adam')
nn_reg.fit(X_train, y_train, epochs=n_epochs, batch_size=batch_size,
validation_split=0.05)
```

After the neural network has been trained, we can get the value for the test MAE:

```
y_pred = nn_reg.predict(X_test)
mae_neural_net = mean_absolute_error(y_test, y_pred)
print("MAE Neural Network: {:0.2f}".format(mae_neural_net))
```

We are getting a test MAE of 344.84 (much better than the optimal KNN model).

Great! We have made the quality of our predictions considerably better by using a more sophisticated model. Can we do even better? Let's try our second idea.

Transforming the target

Back in `Chapter 3`, *Dataset Understanding – Exploratory Data Analysis*, we did EDA on this dataset and we observed a fact about the distribution of the diamond prices: they are very skewed, we haven't in our process. Let's take a look again at the distribution of the diamond prices:

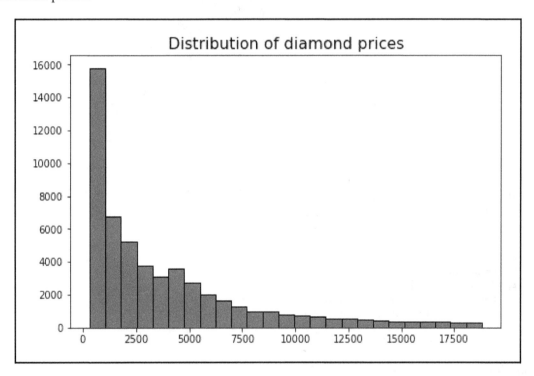

Sometimes, regression models work best when the target has a more symmetric distribution. There are many transformations we can apply to our target to make its distribution more symmetric. Since we have only positive values, one of the most common transformations for skewed features is the logarithmic transformation. Let's apply this transformation to the training set and take a look at the distribution of the transformed target:

```
y_train = np.log(y_train)
```

```
pd.Series(y_train).hist(bins=25, ec='k', figsize=(8,5))
plt.title("Distribution of log diamond prices", fontsize=16)
plt.grid(False);
```

This will give us the following graph:

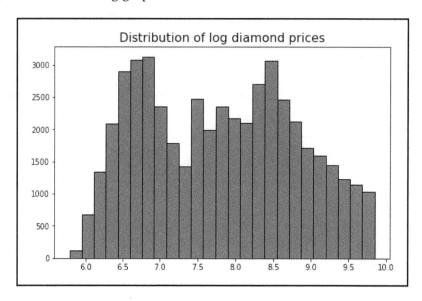

The distribution is not exactly symmetrical, but at least we have addressed the highly skewed distribution of our original target. Let's fit the same neural network with only the transformed target and see what we get:

```
nn_reg = Sequential()
nn_reg.add(Dense(units=n_hidden1, activation='relu',
input_shape=(n_input,)))
nn_reg.add(Dense(units=n_hidden2, activation='relu'))
nn_reg.add(Dense(units=n_hidden3, activation='relu'))
# output layer
nn_reg.add(Dense(units=1, activation=None))
```

Compiling and fitting is shown in the following:

```
batch_size = 32
n_epochs = 40
nn_reg.compile(loss='mean_absolute_error', optimizer='adam')
nn_reg.fit(X_train, y_train, epochs=n_epochs, batch_size=batch_size,
validation_split=0.05)
```

Finally, let's calculate the predicted prices and the MAE; keep in mind that, for our results to be comparable, we should change the predictions to prices (this neural network is predicting log prices):

```
y_pred = nn_reg.predict(X_test).flatten()
# transformation from log prices to prices
y_pred = np.exp(y_pred)
mae_neural_net2 = mean_absolute_error(y_test, y_pred)
print("MAE Neural Network (modified target):
{:0.2f}".format(mae_neural_net2))
```

We get a value of 320.2, an improvement of 7.7% in our metric. It might be small but it is an important improvement, considering that we only had to perform a little transformation to our target variable.

Analyzing the results

Besides evaluating the model using a metric (MAE in this case), as we suggested in the previous chapter, it is always a good idea to evaluate the model using some graphical methods. Let's take a look at the residuals plot:

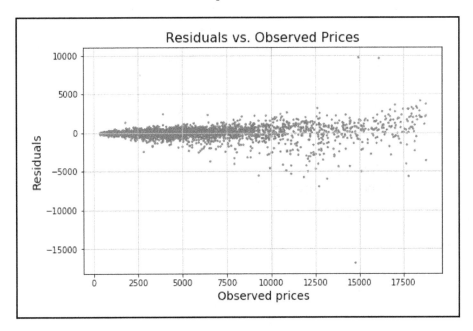

We can notice two things from this plot: first, the largest residuals (the biggest model mistakes) are associated with high diamond prices. On the other hand, with a couple of exceptions, all of the residuals for diamonds of a price of 5,000 or less are below 2,000. From these observations, can we conclude that the model has more predictive power with lower prices than with higher prices? Well, that depends on what we called **predictive power**. If we judge the model by the (absolute) size of the mistakes it is making, then yes, the size of the residuals is likely to increase with price. In fact, if we calculate the MAE using the values of the diamonds below 7,500 dollars, we get a much smaller number:

```
mask_7500 = y_test <=7500
mae_neural_less_7500 = mean_absolute_error(y_test[mask_7500],
y_pred[mask_7500])
print("MAE considering price <= 7500:
{:0.2f}".format(mae_neural_less_7500))
```

We get 192.6. Wow! That is a big improvement.

But wait, predictive power could mean a different thing. Yes, the size of the residuals is bigger for higher prices, but how big is this residual as a proportion of the real price? For instance, consider the following two cases:

- **Case 1**: A prediction of 400 and a real price of 500 dollars. Here the residual is 100, but 100 dollars is 20% of the actual price.
- **Case 2**: A prediction of 4,800 and a real price of 5,000 dollars. Here the residual is 200 (twice as much as in *Case 1*), but those 200 dollars are just 4% of the actual price.

Which prediction is better, *Case 1* or *Case 2*? To answer this question, you have to answer what you mean by predictive power, and how you answer this question must depend on the business problem you are trying to solve.

Let's take a look at the plot of the residuals as a percentage of the actual price; the red lines are reference for those points whose percentage error is within ±15%:

```
fig, ax = plt.subplots(figsize=(8,5))
percent_residuals = (y_test - y_pred)/y_test
ax.scatter(y_test, percent_residuals, s=3)
ax.set_title('Pecent residuals vs. Observed Prices', fontsize=16)
ax.set_xlabel('Observed prices', fontsize=14)
ax.set_ylabel('Pecent residuals', fontsize=14)
ax.axhline(y=0.15, color='r'); ax.axhline(y=-0.15, color='r');
ax.grid();
```

The output will be as follows:

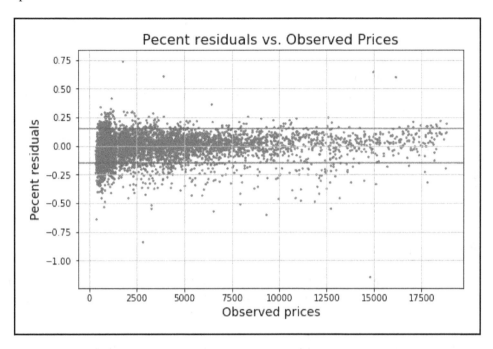

Not only a technical problem but a business problem

For me, when doing predictive analytics, improving performance is not only about better models, transformations, and hyperparameter tuning; you must also really understand the business problem and use that information to provide the best solution or a list of options that will help stakeholders decide what they consider best.

For instance, if the business model of **IDR** (short for **Intelligent Diamond Reseller**) depends on the absolute size of the residuals being low, then I would recommend that they use the model only for diamonds whose prices are below, say, 7,500 (if the model predicts something like 13,000, then that diamond should be given another evaluation procedure). That is a limitation of the model, but this limitation also improves performance in its new domain of applicability: diamonds in the low-price range. On the other hand, if the business model of IDR depends on the relative error of the prediction, then they must be careful when they use the model with diamonds that are likely to be valued under, say, 1,000 dollars.

As we said back in `Chapter 2`, *Problem Understanding and Data Preparation*, predictive analytics is not a linear process: your evaluation of the model can lead to different insights and you may need to change some of the decisions you have already made in light of new findings. You may have decided that the best way to evaluate your model was with MAE, but when you analyze your results and discuss them with others, you may realize that you need to change your evaluation metric, which will get you back to model building, and consider different models again. This is what we mean when we say that predictive analytics is not a linear process.

Changing your mind about your decisions and conclusions is not a bad thing, it's the opposite – admitting ignorance and changing perspectives will open the door for new and potentially better approaches. I have found this advice useful not only in predictive analytics, but in life.

Summary

In this chapter, we discussed some of the things we can do to improve the quality of our models, such as hyperparameter tuning to find the value or the combination of values among a set of candidate values that will give the best performance in our model. We also looked at how good defaults are important to starting experimentation with other candidate values. We discussed cross-validation when performing hyperparameter tuning and how it is important to leave a test set untouched so you can properly evaluate the results of the optimized model. Failing to do this can actually lead to adjusting the hyperparameters to the test set so that, depending on the applications, small improvements in performance could have great business impacts.

We also learned how some transformations to the target feature could improve the model. We used a logarithmic transformation to address the severe skewness we observed in diamond prices. With classification problems, you could try to fuse some of the categories or to redefine which observations belong to a certain category. And then, finally, we learned that improving prediction quality is not only about machine learning: it is always important to connect the analysis of the performance, metrics, residuals, and so on with the business problem you are trying to solve, as this can suggest new approaches or a different way to improve the performance of the model, not necessarily through better models or better parameters.

When doing predictive analytics in practice, you will find yourself trying different ideas. Some will be bad and lead nowhere, some will be good, and some may reveal new information about the problem that you did not know previously. Here is when creativity comes into play: there is no recipe you can follow to improve the results of a model.

9
Implementing a Model with Dash

This is the penultimate chapter of the book. It is about the last phase of the predictive analytics process—model communication and deployment. The point of building a model is using it in some way to solve a problem, so we always need to implement the model; despite this necessity, this stage is often forgotten and overlooked in many courses and resources on machine learning and predictive modeling. This chapter aims to fill this gap.

First, we will talk about the model communication and deployment phase—we will explain the main ways in which we implement a predictive analytics solution—a technical report, a feature of an existing application, or an analytic application. In this section, we talk about some important tips and considerations when communicating the results of a predictive modeling project.

In the following sections, we introduce the Dash library, which we will use to build a web application that will serve a model's predictions. First, we will build a couple of simple applications to understand the basics of Dash, and then, in the following section, we will implement the neural network model from the diamond prices problem as a web application that will receive inputs from the user and will return the respective prediction.

The following topics will be covered in this chapter:

- The model communication/deployment phase
- Introducing Dash
- Implementing a predictive model as a web application

Technical requirements

- Python 3.6 or higher
- Jupyter Notebook
- Recent versions of the following Python libraries: NumPy, pandas, matplotlib, Seaborn, scikit-learn, and Keras
- Basic libraries for Dash (see the next section for installation instructions)

Model communication and/or deployment phase

The goal of building a predictive model is to put it to use to solve a business problem. This is the step that many books and courses on the subject of predictive analytics and machine learning don't talk about. In the end, we don't analyze data and build predictive models just for the sake of building them; when applying these techniques in the real world, we always have a goal in mind.

There are three main ways in which a predictive analytics project can be implemented:

- A technical report
- A feature of an existing product
- An analytic application

Let's briefly discuss these three common cases.

Using a technical report

Often, you will be asked to produce a technical report explaining the results, main conclusions, and recommendations. This is often accompanied with a presentation where you give a talk in front of key stakeholders and you will explain things such as methodology and the most important findings. This is why data scientists and people working in analytics are often asked to have good communication skills; your solution might have been impressive from the technical point of view, but if you really want the people to recognize the job you did, you need to communicate in an effective and engaging way.

One of the most useful pieces of advice to keep in mind when preparing your report and/or presentation is to understand your audience. Always remember that the output you are producing is for them, so it is about them, and not about you. Having your audience in mind will let you decide the style of presentation—formal or informal, the amount of jargon you will use, the technical level, the main points you would want to communicate, and so on.

Every project is different, but here we have some of the sections or topics you will often cover in a report or presentation:

- Context
- Business problem
- Analytical approach to the problem
- Methodology
- Issues with the data
- Main findings
- Implications of predictions
- Model limitations
- Recommendations

You will use data visualizations heavily when reporting your findings, so mastering how to use visualization to communicate properly is necessary. A very useful resource I recommend you to read is *Knaflic* (2015). In this book, the author explains how to "tell stories" with data. She goes through the process of using visualizations as a way to communicate in six lessons:

1. **Understand the context**: Who is your audience? What do you need that audience to know or do?
2. **Choose an appropriate visual display**: What is the most appropriate type of visualization communicating our point?
3. **Eliminate clutter**: In every visualization, use only the elements that are absolutely necessary, avoiding redundant or non-informative things.
4. **Focus attention on where you want it**: Use different techniques to focus the audience's attention on the main points you want to communicate.
5. **Think like a designer**: It means that form follows function. Think about the message and the function we want the visualization to serve, and then create a visualization (form) that will allow the message to be presented to the audience.
6. **Tell a story**: Stories resonate and stick with us in ways that data alone cannot. Humans are storytellers. So try to frame the business problem and your solution as a cohesive story, not only as a list of facts.

Finally, try to articulate your report or presentation in a way that is engaging both emotionally and logically.

A feature of an existing product

Often, the results of the model will become an additional feature of a larger application. We are familiar with customer applications such as the Amazon store or the YouTube website, or an app that includes some features such as recommendations that are part of the result of predictive analytics.

On the other hand, software systems used internally by companies in all industries and organizations of all types include some features that result from the use of predictive analytics. *Siegel* (2013) shows many of the applications of predictive analytics in different fields. Some examples include the following:

- **Marketing**: Predicting the results of a direct-marketing campaign.
- **Finance**: Predictive analytics solutions are the core of black-box trading; in fact, most of the transactions in the largest financial markets in the world are being made by algorithms, and not by humans.
- **Retail**: For example, predict which customers are pregnant, so the company can target them with special offers.
- **Human resources**: Predict which employees are likely to quit.
- **Health care**: Different types of medical devices have predictive capability features.
- **Aviation**: Predict the delay of the flights.

If you have a software engineering background, it will be easy for you to become part of the development team that includes these predictive features into a piece of software. If you don't have that background (like me), then it is very likely that you still need to collaborate with software development teams to ensure that these features work as intended, so you need to be able to understand the fundamentals of their language—you will find yourself in the realm of concepts such as integration, testing, packaging, version control, deployment, and so on.

This type of activity is commonly done by teams, so my advice is this: try not to become the unicorn who knows about everything—predictive analytics, cluster configuration, cloud computing, parallel computing, data pipelines, software engineering, DevOps, design, and so on. Just try learning the fundamentals of some of the fields that are related to software development so you will be able to communicate effectively with the rest of the team.

Using an analytic application

Sometimes, it will be required to deliver the applications of the model through an application—desktop, web, or mobile. This is very similar to the previous case; however, in this case, the output of the predictive model is the star of the show, and other features of the application are just there to support the main goal of the application, which is serving predictions.

There are some common approaches for choosing a model and developing an application; the following are the common ones used:

- **Re-implementation**: Most enterprise-level applications must be developed using industry standards, and that includes the use of fast, secure, and low-level programming languages, such as Java, C, or C++. After finishing a model with Python, for taking the solution to production, you may re-implement the solution using one of these low-level languages; the main advantage of this approach is that you get all the benefits of developing in such robust languages, especially in terms of performance. The main drawback of this approach is that it is time-consuming, and that is a problem if the model needs to be revised frequently.
- **Using a serialized object**: In my opinion, this is an easier way. In this case, we produce a model and then save it on disk in a serialized object. Then, this object can be used to serve an application written in Python and compatible technologies. In this chapter, we will build an analytic application following this approach.

There are other such as using **Predictive Model Markup Language** (**PMML**), which is an XML-based predictive model interchange format. It provides a way for analytic applications to describe and exchange predictive models. This language supports the most commonly used predictive analytics models (including the ones we have been using in the book). Although this language can be used in different operating systems and platforms, it is not widely used by the Predictive Analytics community; however, it is an option you can explore, so take a look at `http://dmg.org/`.

Keep in mind that, usually, it takes a team of engineers at least several weeks to deploy an enterprise-level analytic application in production. So, what we are going to build in this chapter should be considered only a prototype, but, despite its simplicity, we will learn how we can deploy a web application that will serve the predictions of a trained model.

Introducing Dash

In this section, we will provide a brief, hands-on introduction to the Dash library by building a couple of simple applications. This will, of course, be an incomplete introduction, as we will be learning just enough to be able to show how we can produce a prototype of an application that can serve the predictions of one of the models we have created.

What is Dash?

This is the last library we will talk about in this book. **Dash** is a Python framework for building web applications quickly and easily, without knowing JavaScript, CSS, HTML, server-side programming, or related technologies that belong to the web development world. Let's look at some of its features:

- Framework for building data visualization apps in pure Python with extensively customized user interfaces.
- Dash abstracts technologies and protocols that are required for building interactive web applications using a couple of simple patterns.
- They are cross-platform, as all apps created in Dash are rendered in web browsers. These can be deployed on servers and shared using URLs.

Plotly

Plotly is a visualization library produced by the same company that developed Dash. These two technologies are meant to be used together. It is one of the libraries that have been gaining popularity recently.

Since the goal of the library is to produce interactive visualization in the web browser, the company offers a service to host visualizations online. You can also use the library in the offline mode, which is what we will do here. Besides a couple of basic concepts, we won't be covering Plotly in this chapter, but if you are interested in producing interactive visualizations, I encourage you to take a look at the library's documentation (`https://plot.ly/python/getting-started/`).

Installation

We will follow the instructions from the documentation and install the library using `pip` (if you are using virtual environments from Anaconda, remember to activate your environment for every installation); we will install the most up-to-date versions at the time of writing:

```
pip install dash==0.28.5 # The core dash backend
pip install dash-html-components==0.13.2 # HTML components
pip install dash-core-components==0.35.0 # Supercharged components
```

The application layout

The application layout describes how the app looks. The layout is a hierarchical tree of components—meaning the components are made of other components that are made of other components, and so on. The components that belong to another component are called its **children**, and one component can have zero or many children. For building the layout and its components, we will use basically two libraries:

- `dash_html_components`: This library provides classes for all of the HTML tags, and the keyword arguments describe the HTML attributes such as `style`, `className`, and `id`. If you are familiar with HTML, here is where you will find the standard HTML tags for `headers`, `divs`, `body`, `title`, and so on. If you are not familiar with HTML, it is a very easy subject, and there are many online tutorials, but don't worry about it, since in our examples we will be using only a few elements.
- `dash_core_components`: This library generates higher-level components, such as controls and graphs.

In the layout, you will place all the components of your application. Conceptually, I like thinking that every component of an interactive application belongs to one of these categories:

- **Static components**: Headers, texts, images, and so on. You can use these elements to provide a description of the application. You will mostly use the `dash_html_components` library to create these components.
- **Input components**: These are the ones capturing the inputs from the user—dropdowns, date pickers, input boxes, and so on. You will mostly sue the `dash_core_components` library to create these components.

- **Outputs components**: These are the elements of the application that will change as a result of user interaction—text, graphs, tables, and so on. Depending on the output type, you will use both the `dash_html_components` and the `dash_core_components` libraries to create these components.

Let's build a basic app with no interactivity.

Building a basic static app

We will get started with Dash by building our first app; this is a very simple static application. You can find the whole script in the book's repository, in the `dash-example-no-user-inputs.py` file. We will simply visualize the histogram of diamond prices, although the visualization will be interactive (it is done with Plotly); we are calling this a static app because the user can't give inputs.

The steps we will follow to create this small app will be the following:

1. Make the necessary imports
2. Import the dataset
3. Create the app instance
4. Create the Plotly figure
5. Create the layout
6. Run the server

Here, we have the necessary imports:

```
import dash
import dash_core_components as dcc
import dash_html_components as html
import plotly.graph_objs as go
import pandas as pd
import os
```

Because we will use the diamond prices dataset, let's import it:

```
DATA_DIR = '../data'
FILE_NAME = 'diamonds.csv'
data_path = os.path.join(DATA_DIR, FILE_NAME)
diamonds = pd.read_csv(data_path)
```

The following line will create the app instance:

```
app = dash.Dash(__name__)
```

Now we will create the two main elements of the Plotly histogram:

1. The first is the `trace`; a single plot can have many traces. If you are familiar with plotting in Excel, you can think of traces as the *Series* from Excel graphs. Since this is a histogram, we will create it using the graphics object `Histogram`, and as input, we will only give data for the *x*-axis, which will be the price column of our diamonds DataFrame:

```
trace = go.Histogram(
        x = diamonds['price']
        )
```

2. The second basic element that we almost always create in a Plotly graph is the `Layout`, where we define elements such as axis labels, titles, legends, and so on. Here, we are just setting the `title` and the `axis` labels:

```
layout = go.Layout(
        title = 'Diamond Prices',
        xaxis = dict(title='Price'),
        yaxis = dict(title='Count')
        )
```

The two main elements of our Plotly graph have been created, and now we can create the figure object; the `data` argument should be a list of traces, and in this case, we only have one:

```
figure = go.Figure(
        data = [trace],
        layout = layout
        )
```

Now let's create the layout of our Dash app. It will be very simple—it consists of only two HTML headers, one paragraph, and the graph object that will contain the figure we just created. Note that the highest component on the hierarchy, an HTML div (https://developer.mozilla.org/en-US/docs/Web/HTML/Element/div) (content division element), has four children, the four components in the list. Each of these children has only one child, which is its respective content:

```
app.layout = html.Div(children = [
        html.H1('My first Dash App'),
        html.H2('Histogram of diamond prices'),
        html.P('This is some normal text, we can use it to describe
something about the application.'),
        dcc.Graph(id='my-histogram', figure=figure)
        ])
```

Finally, we need a couple of final lines of code that will start the local server that will serve the application:

```
if __name__ == '__main__':
    app.run_server(debug=False)
```

We are ready to run our small app. When running it on the command line (in Windows), you will see something like this:

```
C:\Windows\system32\cmd.exe
 * Serving Flask app "dash-example-no-user-inputs" (lazy loading)
 * Environment: production
   WARNING: Do not use the development server in a production environment.
   Use a production WSGI server instead.
 * Debug mode: on
 * Restarting with stat
 * Debugger is active!
 * Debugger PIN: 962-614-663
 * Running on http://127.0.0.1:8050/ (Press CTRL+C to quit)
```

In your favorite browser, go to the indicated URL, and you will see the application:

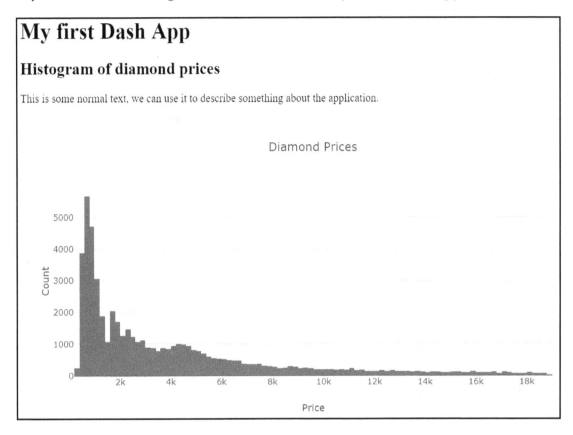

My first Dash App

Histogram of diamond prices

This is some normal text, we can use it to describe something about the application.

You will notice that you can interact with the histogram by zooming, panning, and so on—great! Now, we are ready for the next step—building an app with some user interactivity.

Building a basic interactive app

Now let's create another simple app, but this one will accept inputs from the user, making it interactive. For this example, we will again use the diamond prices dataset. These are the steps we will follow:

1. Make the necessary imports
2. Import the dataset
3. Create the app instance

4. Import an external CSS file
5. Create the inputs for interactivity
6. Create the layout
7. Create the callback function for interactivity
8. Run the server

You can find the whole code in the script in the repository for the book; it is named `dash-example-user-inputs.py`. As always, let's begin with the imports:

```
import dash
import dash_core_components as dcc
import dash_html_components as html
from dash.dependencies import Input, Output
import plotly.graph_objs as go
import pandas as pd
import os
```

We will now load the dataset; since we will be doing a simple visualization, we will take a sample of 2,000 observations:

```
DATA_DIR = '../data'
FILE_NAME = 'diamonds.csv'
data_path = os.path.join(DATA_DIR, FILE_NAME)
diamonds = pd.read_csv(data_path)
diamonds = diamonds.sample(n=2000)
```

We are now ready to create the app instance:

```
app = dash.Dash(__name__)
```

Now we will import an external CSS file (`https://en.wikipedia.org/wiki/Cascading_Style_Sheets`); this is just for our app to look a bit nicer:

```
app.css.append_css({
    'external_url': 'https://codepen.io/chriddyp/pen/bWLwgP.css'
})
```

This app will consist of a scatter plot made from two of the numerical features from the dataset. We need to create two controls for the user to choose which variable goes along the *x*-axis and which goes along the *y*-axis. From the many components available for us in the `dash_core_components` library, we will use the `Dropdown`—an interactive drop-down element for selecting one or more items. We need one of these for each of the two variables on our scatter plot. This object usually receives at least three inputs:

- `id`: This is the identifier that will be used to refer to the object in the application
- `options`: This is a list of dictionaries of the form {`'label'`: `label_for_user`, `'value':value`}
- `value`: This is the default value selected

The possible options for our dropdowns are the numerical variables in our dataset; using them, we can create the list of options:

```
numerical_features = ['price','carat','depth','table','x','y','z']
options_dropdown = [{'label':x.upper(), 'value':x} for x in
numerical_features]
```

Now let's create the dropdown for the variable along the *x*-axis; we will use this dropdown as a child of a div element:

```
dd_x_var = dcc.Dropdown(
        id='x-var',
        options = options_dropdown,
        value = 'carat'
        )

div_x_var = html.Div(
        children=[html.H4('Variable for x axis: '), dd_x_var],
        className="six columns"
        )
```

Here is the other dropdown, for the variable along the *y*-axis:

```
dd_y_var = dcc.Dropdown(
        id='y-var',
        options = options_dropdown,
        value = 'price'
        )

div_y_var = html.Div(
        children=[html.H4('Variable for y axis: '), dd_y_var],
        className="six columns"
        )
```

We gave the divs containing the dropdowns a `className="six columns"` for them to occupy only six columns in the browser; in this way, they will appear next to one another.

Now let's create the layout of the application. This is, again, very simple—a couple of headers, a div containing the dropdowns, and the graph object:

```
app.layout = html.Div(children=[
        html.H1('Adding interactive controls'),
        html.H2('Interactive scatter plot example'),
        html.Div(
                children=[div_x_var, div_y_var],
                className="row"
                ),
        dcc.Graph(id='scatter')
        ])
```

Now we will add the interactivity. In Dash, we do this through functions with decorators. The decorator uses the **output** that will be modified—using the ID of the object and the property to be modified. It also uses a list of **inputs** that will be monitored to update that output; we need to provide the id of the input and the property that will be used to provide the update. This will be more clear with the following example:

```
@app.callback(
        Output(component_id='scatter', component_property='figure'),
        [Input(component_id='x-var', component_property='value'),
Input(id='y-var', component_property='value')])
def scatter_plot(x_col, y_col):
    trace = go.Scatter(
            x = diamonds[x_col],
            y = diamonds[y_col],
            mode = 'markers'
            )
    layout = go.Layout(
            title = 'Scatter plot',
            xaxis = dict(title = x_col.upper()),
            yaxis = dict(title = y_col.upper())
            )
    output_plot = go.Figure(
            data = [trace],
            layout = layout
            )
    return output_plot
```

As you can see, both inputs and outputs identify the corresponding objects in the application, using the `component_id`. The `component_property` is the property that will be changed in the output and the property that will be read from the inputs. The output from the function is the one that will be assigned to the `component_property` of the output; in our example, it is a Plotly `Figure` object.

Finally, let's write the line that will start the server:

```
if __name__ == '__main__':
    app.run_server(debug=True)
```

When you run the script and go to the indicated URL, you will see something like this:

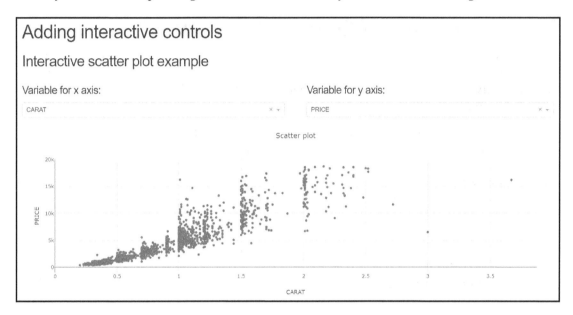

As you can tell by using the application yourself, it works as intended.

Now that we know how to add interactivity, let's build the application that will serve the diamond prices predictions. For more on Dash interactivity, take a look at the official tutorial (`https://dash.plot.ly/getting-started-part-2`).

Implementing a predictive model as a web application

Now we know the basics of building an interactive web application with Dash, we are ready to build an application to deploy our model so it can be used to make predictions. This will be a very simple and basic prototype, but, as we said before, building an enterprise-level application will take a team of engineers many weeks.

Even though this application will be very simple, I have delivered similar minimal applications to my clients in my consulting practice (doing it with either Python's Dash or R's Shiny), and they have found it very useful, so these applications can actually be used in real-world projects.

Producing the predictive model objects

Let's say that we have presented our model results to the management of IDR, and they are very happy with the results of our neural network model; they approve it and tell us that they are ready to start using the model in their business. That is fantastic! Now it's time for us to deliver the model through a web application.

First, we need to run a script that will train the model and will produce a trained model plus a couple of other objects necessary to make the predictions.

You will find the code in the script named `diamonds-model-training.py`. We have seen the code in this file before; in fact, we have built and explained most of the following lines throughout the book. Here, we have the following steps:

1. Imports
2. Data loading
3. Data transformation:

```
## Imports
import numpy as np
import pandas as pd
import os
from keras.models import Sequential
from keras.layers import Dense
from sklearn.externals import joblib

## Loading the dataset
DATA_DIR = '../data'
FILE_NAME = 'diamonds.csv'
data_path = os.path.join(DATA_DIR, FILE_NAME)
diamonds = pd.read_csv(data_path)

## Preparing the dataset
diamonds = diamonds.loc[(diamonds['x']>0) | (diamonds['y']>0)]
diamonds.loc[11182, 'x'] = diamonds['x'].median()
diamonds.loc[11182, 'z'] = diamonds['z'].median()
diamonds = diamonds.loc[~((diamonds['y'] > 30) | (diamonds['z']
> 30))]
```

```
diamonds = pd.concat([diamonds, pd.get_dummies(diamonds['cut'],
prefix='cut', drop_first=True)], axis=1)
diamonds = pd.concat([diamonds,
pd.get_dummies(diamonds['color'], prefix='color',
drop_first=True)], axis=1)
diamonds = pd.concat([diamonds,
pd.get_dummies(diamonds['clarity'], prefix='clarity',
drop_first=True)], axis=1)

## Dimensionality reduction
from sklearn.decomposition import PCA
pca = PCA(n_components=1, random_state=123)
diamonds['dim_index'] =
pca.fit_transform(diamonds[['x','y','z']])
diamonds.drop(['x','y','z'], axis=1, inplace=True)
```

4. Next, we will produce the objects to train the model. Now that we have decided the model we will use, we can use the whole dataset for training:

```
## Creating X and y
X = diamonds.drop(['cut','color','clarity','price'], axis=1)
y = np.log(diamonds['price'])

## Standardization: centering and scaling
numerical_features = ['carat', 'depth', 'table', 'dim_index']
from sklearn.preprocessing import StandardScaler
scaler = StandardScaler()
X.loc[:, numerical_features] =
scaler.fit_transform(X[numerical_features])
```

5. Now let's create the neural network:

```
## Building the neural network
n_input = X.shape[1]
n_hidden1 = 32
n_hidden2 = 16
n_hidden3 = 8

nn_reg = Sequential()
nn_reg.add(Dense(units=n_hidden1, activation='relu',
input_shape=(n_input,)))
nn_reg.add(Dense(units=n_hidden2, activation='relu'))
nn_reg.add(Dense(units=n_hidden3, activation='relu'))
# output layer
nn_reg.add(Dense(units=1, activation=None))
```

6. We are ready for training our model:

```
## Training the neural network
batch_size = 32
n_epochs = 40
nn_reg.compile(loss='mean_absolute_error', optimizer='adam')
nn_reg.fit(X, y, epochs=n_epochs, batch_size=batch_size)
```

Finally, the whole point of this script is to produce the objects that we will use to make the predictions. Here, we have three objects:

- The PCA object that will transform the x, y, and z dimensions into a new feature: dimension index
- The feature scaler
- The trained model

We will serialize these objects so we can use them in other programs without the need to produce them every time we need to use them:

```
## Serializing:
# PCA
joblib.dump(pca, './Model/pca.joblib')

# Scaler
joblib.dump(scaler, './Model/scaler.joblib')

# Trained model
nn_reg.save("./Model/diamond-prices-model.h5")
```

These objects are now on disk. We can use them to build our application.

Building the web application

Finally! It is time for us to build the application that will serve our model's predictions. You can find the full script named `predict-diamond-prices.py`. Here are the steps we will follow:

1. Make the necessary imports
2. Create the app instance
3. Import an external CSS file
4. Load the trained objects
5. Build the input components and their respective divs
6. Build the prediction function

As always, in *Step 1*, we begin with the imports:

```
import dash
import dash_core_components as dcc
import dash_html_components as html
from dash.dependencies import Input, Output

from keras.models import load_model
from sklearn.externals import joblib

import numpy as np
import pandas as pd
```

Now follow *Step 2* and *Step 3*; create the app instance and import the CSS file:

```
app = dash.Dash(__name__)
app.css.append_css({
    'external_url': 'https://codepen.io/chriddyp/pen/bWLwgP.css'
})
```

Next, *Step 4*, load the objects we have prepared and trained from the former script:

```
model = load_model('./Model/diamond-prices-model.h5')
pca = joblib.load('./Model/pca.joblib')
scaler = joblib.load('./Model/scaler.joblib')
## We have to do this due to some Keras' issue
model._make_predict_function()
```

OK, *Step 5* is to build the objects that will receive the user's inputs. Remember that we have numerical and categorical features, and we will use input boxes to input the values of numerical features and drop-down menus for the categorical ones. We have nine inputs, and we will place each input in its own four-column `div` (this CSS file we are using divides the browser window in 12 columns). Here, we have the six inputs for the numerical values:

```
## Div for carat
input_carat = dcc.Input(
    id='carat',
    type='numeric',
    value=0.7)

div_carat = html.Div(
        children=[html.H3('Carat:'), input_carat],
        className="four columns"
        )

## Div for depth
input_depth = dcc.Input(
    id='depth',
```

```
        placeholder='',
        type='numeric',
        value=60)

div_depth = html.Div(
        children=[html.H3('Depth:'), input_depth],
        className="four columns"
        )

## Div for table
input_table = dcc.Input(
    id='table',
    placeholder='',
    type='numeric',
    value=60)

div_table = html.Div(
        children=[html.H3('Table:'), input_table],
        className="four columns"
        )

## Div for x
input_x = dcc.Input(
    id='x',
    placeholder='',
    type='numeric',
    value=5)

div_x = html.Div(
        children=[html.H3('x value:'), input_x],
        className="four columns"
        )

## Div for y
input_y = dcc.Input(
    id='y',
    placeholder='',
    type='numeric',
    value=5)

div_y = html.Div(
        children=[html.H3('y value:'), input_y],
        className="four columns"
        )

## Div for z
input_z = dcc.Input(
    id='z',
```

```
        placeholder='',
        type='numeric',
        value=3)

div_z = html.Div(
        children=[html.H3('z value: '), input_z],
        className="four columns"
        )
```

Here, we have the three inputs for the categorical values:

```
## Div for cut
cut_values = ['Fair', 'Good', 'Ideal', 'Premium', 'Very Good']
cut_options = [{'label': x, 'value': x} for x in cut_values]
input_cut = dcc.Dropdown(
    id='cut',
    options = cut_options,
    value = 'Ideal'
    )

div_cut = html.Div(
        children=[html.H3('Cut:'), input_cut],
        className="four columns"
        )

## Div for color
color_values = ['D', 'E', 'F', 'G', 'H', 'I', 'J']
color_options = [{'label': x, 'value': x} for x in color_values]
input_color = dcc.Dropdown(
    id='color',
    options = color_options,
    value = 'G'
    )

div_color = html.Div(
        children=[html.H3('Color:'), input_color],
        className="four columns"
        )

## Div for clarity
clarity_values = ['I1', 'IF', 'SI1', 'SI2', 'VS1', 'VS2', 'VVS1', 'VVS2']
clarity_options = [{'label': x, 'value': x} for x in clarity_values]
input_clarity = dcc.Dropdown(
    id='clarity',
    options = clarity_options,
    value = 'SI1'
    )
```

```
div_clarity = html.Div(
        children=[html.H3('Clarity:'), input_clarity],
        className="four columns"
        )
```

Now it makes sense to group these nine inputs into three groups:

- **Numerical characteristics**: carat, depth, and table
- **Dimensions**: x, y, and z
- **Categorical features**: cut, color, and clarity

We will use a div for each group; note that the children of these grouping divs are the corresponding divs we have created previously:

```
## Div for numerical characteristics
div_numerical = html.Div(
        children = [div_carat, div_depth, div_table],
        className="row"
        )

## Div for dimensions
div_dimensions = html.Div(
        children = [div_x, div_y, div_z],
        className="row"
        )

## Div for categorical features
div_categorical = html.Div(
        children = [div_cut, div_color, div_clarity],
        className="row"
        )
```

Now it's time for the soul of the application—the function that will take the values from the user and will produce the price prediction:

```
def get_prediction(carat, depth, table, x, y, z, cut, color, clarity):
    '''takes the inputs from the user and produces the price prediction'''
    cols = ['carat', 'depth', 'table',
            'cut_Good', 'cut_Ideal', 'cut_Premium', 'cut_Very Good',
            'color_E', 'color_F', 'color_G', 'color_H', 'color_I',
'color_J',
            'clarity_IF','clarity_SI1', 'clarity_SI2', 'clarity_VS1',
'clarity_VS2','clarity_VVS1', 'clarity_VVS2',
            'dim_index']

    cut_dict = {x: 'cut_' + x for x in cut_values[1:]}
    color_dict = {x: 'color_' + x for x in color_values[1:]}
```

```
    clarity_dict = {x: 'clarity_' + x for x in clarity_values[1:]}
    ## produce a dataframe with a single row of zeros
    df = pd.DataFrame(data = np.zeros((1,len(cols))), columns = cols)
    ## get the numeric characteristics
    df.loc[0,'carat'] = carat
    df.loc[0,'depth'] = depth
    df.loc[0,'table'] = table
    ## transform dimensions into a single dim_index using PCA
    dims_df = pd.DataFrame(data=[[x, y, z]], columns=['x','y','z'])
    df.loc[0,'dim_index'] = pca.transform(dims_df).flatten()[0]
    ## Use the one-hot encoding for the categorical features
    if cut!='Fair':
        df.loc[0, cut_dict[cut]] = 1
    if color!='D':
        df.loc[0, color_dict[color]] = 1
    if clarity != 'I1':
        df.loc[0, clarity_dict[clarity]] = 1
    ## Scale the numerical features using the trained scaler
    numerical_features = ['carat', 'depth', 'table', 'dim_index']
    df.loc[:,numerical_features] =
scaler.transform(df.loc[:,numerical_features])
    ## Get the predictions using our trained neural network
    prediction = model.predict(df.values).flatten()[0]
    ## Transform the log-prices to prices
    prediction = np.exp(prediction)
    return int(prediction)
```

Great! We have almost finished. Now let's build the application's layout. The component of the application that will show the output (prediction) is the H1 component with id='output':

```
## App layout
app.layout = html.Div([
        html.H1('IDR Predict diamond prices'),
        html.H2('Enter the diamond characteristics to get the predicted
price'),
        html.Div(
                children=[div_numerical, div_dimensions, div_categorical]
                ),
        html.H1(id='output',
                style={'margin-top': '50px', 'text-align': 'center'})
        ])
```

The last thing is to build the decorator (callback) that will update the output using the nine inputs, and we will use the *pythonic* list comprehension to build the callback's list of inputs:

```
predictors = ['carat', 'depth', 'table', 'x', 'y', 'z', 'cut', 'color',
'clarity']
@app.callback(
        Output('output', 'children'),
        [Input(x, 'value') for x in predictors])
def show_prediction(carat, depth, table, x, y, z, cut, color, clarity):
    pred = get_prediction(carat, depth, table, x, y, z, cut, color,
clarity)
        return str("Predicted Price: {:,}".format(pred))
```

Finally, write the code that will run the server:

```
if __name__ == '__main__':
    app.run_server(debug=True)
```

And now we have finished!

When you run the application, you should see something like this:

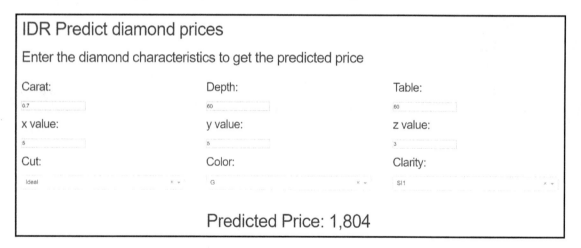

Congratulations! *You have built an interactive web application that can serve a neural network's output!* Even if your mom can't understand the last sentence, she will be proud of you—mine is. :)

Summary

In this chapter, we learned the basics of Dash and showed how to deploy a model with a hands-on example. Some key points that we discussed were the model implementation phase, three main ways in which a predictive analytics report can be implemented, use of predictive analytics models, and how to use trained models to build an application.

We also learned how to use the Dash framework and Plotly library to build an application. And we learned how to provide interactivity in Dash by writing decorators in functions that take inputs and modify outputs for the application.

Finally, always keep in mind that the point of predictive analytics is to solve problems. When deploying a predictive model, think about the users of your solution first and how to build the solution that works best for them.

Further reading

- *Knaflic, C N (2015). Storytelling with data: A data visualization guide for business professionals* by John Wiley & Sons, Inc.
- *Provost, F, & Fawcett, T (2013). Data Science for Business: What you need to know about data mining and data-analytic thinking* by O'Reilly Media.
- *Siegel, E. (2013). Predictive analytics: The power to predict who will click, buy, lie, or die,* by John Wiley and Sons, Inc.

Other Books You May Enjoy

If you enjoyed this book, you may be interested in these other books by Packt:

TensorFlow: Powerful Predictive Analytics with TensorFlow
Md. Rezaul Karim

ISBN: 978-1-78913-691-3

- Learn TensorFlow features in a real-life problem, followed by detailed TensorFlow installation and configuration
- Explore computation graphs, data, and programming models also get an insight into an example of implementing linear regression model for predictive analytics
- Solve the Titanic survival problem using logistic regression, random forests, and SVMs for predictive analytics
- Dig deeper into predictive analytics and find out how to take advantage of it to cluster records belonging to the certain group or class for a dataset of unsupervised observations
- Learn several examples of how to apply reinforcement learning algorithms for developing predictive models on real-life datasets

Building Machine Learning Systems with Python - Third Edition
Luis Pedro Coelho, Willi Richert, Matthieu Brucher

ISBN: 978-1-78862-322-3

- Build a classification system that can be applied to text, images, and sound
- Employ Amazon Web Services (AWS) to run analysis on the cloud
- Solve problems related to regression using scikit-learn and TensorFlow
- Recommend products to users based on their past purchases
- Understand different ways to apply deep neural networks on structured data
- Address recent developments in the field of computer vision and reinforcement learning

Leave a review - let other readers know what you think

Please share your thoughts on this book with others by leaving a review on the site that you bought it from. If you purchased the book from Amazon, please leave us an honest review on this book's Amazon page. This is vital so that other potential readers can see and use your unbiased opinion to make purchasing decisions, we can understand what our customers think about our products, and our authors can see your feedback on the title that they have worked with Packt to create. It will only take a few minutes of your time, but is valuable to other potential customers, our authors, and Packt. Thank you!

Index